THE COST
OF THESE
DREAMS

For Wallace, Sonia, and Mama

Contents

Preface

My wife and I went to dinner last night at a supper club on Moon Lake. It was early summer, the cotton small and fragile in its rows. With the car windows rolled down, the air smelled like the river. The ruins of the casino Tennessee Williams wrote about still hovered in the shadows if you knew where and when to look. We'd come home to the Mississippi Delta to bring our new baby to visit her grandmama and to unwind for a few days. My hometown is an agricultural community named Clarksdale, at the intersection of Highways 61 and 49. If you know it at all, it's as the home of the Delta blues, the droning, driving 12 bars of pain and joy that sprang from the surrounding plantations. Whenever I hear that music, it takes me home. I love driving through the Delta, which is as flat as Montana is tall, especially in the last hour of daylight. The sun hangs big and low and makes the fields and collapsed shacks and faded mansions glow a brilliant gold. All of it seems anointed or ready to be burned.

We rode through the glow on the way to Moon Lake, out Friars Point Road toward U.S. Highway 1, which traces the Mississippi River. We drove past the once mighty King & Anderson plantation, broken up by inheritance and time and greed and cotton prices and estate taxes. About the only thing left of that world is the music. Every time anyone listens to the Delta blues, they hear the dreams and the cost.

We'd come to Clarksdale because when I'm really tired or beaten down, there's nothing like home to put me back together again. I'd been on a long run: our first baby born, trips to Japan, to Italy and

India then Italy again, to Paris, London, and Manchester, plus criss-crossing the continental United States. I'd been on the road for months straight if I thought about it one way or for the past 20 years if I thought about it another. My wife, Sonia, is firmly in Camp Latter. When I first left my hometown, I was determined to see the world, all of it, and that's what I've been lucky enough to do in my job, from dark pool halls in Argentina to a forward operationing base in Iraq to a civil war in Kenya. That was my dream, and it came true: I've been nearly everywhere people play and watch games, everywhere they look for freedom with a ball in their hands or at their feet, everywhere people invest complicated, tribal ideas of home and family in sporting events played by strangers. Sometimes the individual dispatches feel like exhaust fumes from an ongoing, overarching search. A hunger has long kept me out looking for the next thing, and the thing after that. But what was that hunger about? I figured that if there was anything this preface called for, it was some sort of self-examination of how this collection came to be and what there is to be learned from reading about sports.

I wondered how to sum up stories that mean more to me than I can reasonably explain without embarrassment. As I talked about it with Sonia, she told me something I'd never heard her say before. She said she had often viewed herself as a corner man in a boxing ring. Her job in between my reporting trips was to calm me down and squirt water in my mouth and fix my cuts and bruises and get me in reasonably good enough shape to go back out and fight another round. To me, the title of this book—which comes from a Drive-By Truckers song—was a piece of connective tissue between the people and places I've written about. So often I crawl around in the lives of men and women who yearn for a different kind of self and future and pay a price for that yearning. But to Sonia, the title was about me.

I remember the first time I read Gary Smith's letter from the Pine Ridge Reservation, a parable about the power and limits of sports to provide an escape; and when I discovered Frank Deford's profile of Bobby Knight, which was true when it ran and only got truer with the passing years; and what I understood about the importance of cutting through myths to find something real when I read Charles P. Pierce's story on Tiger Woods. I learned about ambition, including my own, when I read Richard Ben Cramer's masterpiece on Ted Williams, and in Gay Talese's profile of Joe DiMaggio I found a reflection on the fleeting nature of fame and greatness—what relief it brings those who burned themselves chasing it, and what pain it can't begin to touch. Those of us who write these kinds of sports stories, which feels like an ever-shrinking pool, are not after the symphony of a novel, or the jazz improv of a poem, but the hard, rough gut-punch of a blues riff.

If this book has an organizing principle, then, it is this: The literary magazine sports story is a minor but vital form of uniquely American art. I get angry when people don't learn the canon or hold the line on matters of ethics, ambition, and work. That's what I owe those who came before and what I owe the version of myself who wanted so badly to be good at this. I never want to shortchange them, or me, or the form. Maybe that's what Sonia meant when she described the cost of my obsession and her hope that I might learn something about myself from all the myopic, driven people I've written about for the past two decades.

From Pat Riley we learn how far and fast a man will run to escape something in his past, and from Tiger Woods we learn the dangers of living both a private and public life at the same time, as one almost inevitably consumes the other. Over and over we learn the value of a selfless father and the dangers of a selfish one. From Michael Jordan we learn the benefits and toll of a man constructing himself into the perfect machine to manage the first 40 years of his life while creating a version of himself completely unsuited for the next 40. That's a universal truth: The tools required to gain greatness often prevent someone from enjoying it. From Ted Williams and his family we see the multigenerational inheritance of pain and how Richard Ben Cramer's profile documented the rock but not the lake or the ripples. We see Dan Gable use his pain as fuel, later finding it so hard-wired into his daily life that he struggled to put it down once its usefulness has expired. We see all these people, and maybe we steal a glimpse of ourselves.

My love of this craft began at the University of Missouri, where a group of us debated and dreamed and wondered how the stories we loved came to exist. But the ideas that drove me to need a craft began much earlier, on the streets just outside the plateglass window where I found myself sitting the morning after Moon Lake, in the corner of a coffee shop on Yazoo Avenue in Clarksdale, four blocks from the house where I grew up.

So many of these stories are about understanding a real world hidden behind a facade. Some of them are about deciphering the codes and meaning of home. Some are about people who carry the place of their birth and its gravitational pull with them even as they run themselves out trying to escape. Some are about people who get the things they wanted and must make an accounting of what they exchanged for them. These deep lifelong interests of mine began in Clarksdale, Mississippi.

The themes I've returned to again and again were first explored when I was a young man, trying to come to terms with the beauty and inequality of the place I called home. In Clarksdale, powerful ideas often relegated to philosophy classes or history books played out in real time day after day. As you grew up, you were taught either to ignore the dichotomy or to train yourself to always see it—to hunt for it—no matter what obstacles are erected to keep it hidden. Becoming a journalist was born from this desire to see things as they truly were and not as so many interested actors wanted them to appear. I understood that people protected themselves with the stories they told about themselves. That urge fascinated me. It still does. The most interesting place exists between how people see themselves and how other people do. That knowledge was born in Clarksdale. It's funny when I look at the past two decades through that prism, sitting in a coffee shop across from the old offices of *The Clarksdale Press Register*, where I worked a long time ago.

Four blocks toward Desoto Avenue is the building where my father's law office was located; I spent hours there, using his office supplies to send off *Sports Illustrated*s to be signed by the famous athletes on the covers. His illness and death, and the hole that left inside me, has provided much of my ambition and fuel. You'll find a lot of stories about fathers and sons in my work, much of which is no doubt a selfish attempt to use my job to help ask myself the same questions as the people I got paid to interview and profile. For years, I wanted to be successful enough for both of us, to raise up myself and him at the same time. Only since the birth of my daughter, Wallace, have I understood that I have taken exactly the wrong lesson from his death. All his life, I heard him talk about what he and my mother would do together, about the life they'd share, once his own personal race had been run. He died before those dreams were realized, and now I know that success means reaching your goals and enjoying them and that one without the other is empty and meaningless. Not long ago, I went to the funeral of the legendary sportswriter William Nack, and as his kids talked about how much they loved vacations with him, and how much he loved his family and enjoyed cooking big meals for all of them, I realized that his work was a means to an end and not the supreme and total end.

I have made a career by exploring all the things that fascinated me as a boy. College students often ask me how to succeed in this business, and I've given a lot of different answers, some about craft and some about work ethic, but the real answer is that you must be curious and then stay that way. You must remain amazed at people and places and then forever push yourself to transmit that wonder in more and more powerful and accurate ways. My mom always thought this collection should be called *Dispatches from a Worldview*, which is super pompous but strikes me now as prescient. I grew up in a place unlike other places, with its own music and food and history, where grown-ups saw up and called it down, where people were capable of great kindness and great cruelty, sometimes the same person capable of both. I learned as many lessons working in the cotton fields for Cliff Heaton and Freddie Gordon as I did in classrooms. Everything good that's happened to me in my work life springs from Mississippi, from the little town that still feels like home.

Recently I got an email from Delta Airlines telling me that I'd passed a million miles flown on their airline. They meant it to be congratulatory, I'm sure. But it carried a warning, too, hints of the costs that Sonia articulated that night at Moon Lake. I've been reading a lot of Thomas Merton lately. It seems to me that the point of studying other people, whether through a sports story or a novel or a song or a movie, is to organize our thoughts and construct a framework that might help us better understand ourselves. At Moon Lake I made Sonia a promise that I would protect the curiosity and drive that created these stories, while trying to let slip the angst and insecurity and fierce ambition that so fueled me as a younger man.

I'm hoping this preface serves not just as an introduction for a book but as a public vow that I will learn from the people I've written about. I promised that I would still follow the dreams that I'd dreamed since I was a boy but that I'd be vigilant about slipping off the path. My whole life is in this book—and yet none of it is. My little girl is 20 weeks old. My wife has put up with my travels and searching and loves me still. My friends understand what pulls me out on the road and what more and more pulls me home. There are stories to tell, and worlds to discover, and sunset roads to drive. My life will start tomorrow and then the tomorrow after that. Maybe some college student is reading this right now, hungry and ambitious and willing to pay whatever cost for his or her dreams. The sun is golden and hanging low. The fields stretch out on either side of the blacktop. Everywhere around me I see furrows and river bends and oxbows and lakes and marshes and swamps and white clapboard churches and beer joints and a hot mean sun, all timeless, weightless, airless—universal and infinite. I see a road that leads to the world and also back home again.

Wright Thompson
July 2018

THE COST
OF THESE
DREAMS

Michael Jordan Has Not Left the Building

As he turns 50, MJ is wondering where there are any more asses to kick.

CHARLOTTE, N.C.—Five weeks before his 50th birthday, Michael Jordan sits behind his desk, overlooking a parking garage in downtown Charlotte. The cell phone in front of him buzzes with potential trades and league proposals about placing ads on jerseys. A rival wants his best players and wants to give him nothing in return. Jordan bristles. He holds a Cuban cigar in his hand. Smoking is allowed.

"Well, shit, being as I own the building," he says, laughing.

Back in the office after his vacation on a 154-foot rented yacht named *Mister Terrible*, he feels that relaxation slipping away. He feels pulled inward, toward his own most valuable and destructive traits. Slights roll through his mind, eating at him: *worst record ever, can't build a team, absentee landlord.* Jordan reads the things written about him, the fuel arriving in a packet of clips his staff prepares. He knows what people say. He needs to know. There's a palpable simmering whenever you're around Jordan, as if Air Jordan is still in there, churning, trying to escape. It must be strange to be locked in combat with the ghost of your former self.

Smoke curls off the cigar. He wears slacks and a plain white dress shirt, monogrammed on the sleeve in white, understated. An ID badge hangs from one of those zip line cords on his belt, with his name on the bottom: Michael Jordan, just in case anyone didn't recognize the owner of a struggling franchise who in another life was the touchstone for a generation. There's a shudder in every child of the '80s and '90s who does the math and realizes that Michael Jordan is turning 50. Where did the years go? Jordan has trouble believing it, difficulty admitting it to himself. But he's in the mood for admissions today, and there's a look on his face, a half-smile, as he considers how far to go.

"I . . . I always thought I would die young," he says, leaning up to rap his knuckles on the rich, dark wood of his desk.

He has kept this fact a secret from most people. A fatalist obsession didn't go with his public image and, well, it's sort of strange. His mother would get angry with him when he'd talk to her about it. He just could never imagine being old. He seemed too powerful, too young, and death was more likely than a slow decline. The universe might take him, but it would not permit him to suffer the graceless loss and failure of aging. A tragic flaw could undo him but never anything as common as bad knees or failing eyesight.

Later that night, standing in his kitchen, he squints across his loft at the television. His friend Quinn Buckner catches him.

"You gonna need to get some glasses," Buckner says.

"I can see," Jordan says.

"Don't be bullshitting me," Buckner says. "I can see you struggling."

"I can see," Jordan insists.

The television is built into the modern stone fireplace in his sprawling downtown condo, the windows around them overlooking South Tryon Street. An open bottle of Pahlmeyer merlot sits on an end table. Buckner, a former NBA guard from near Chicago and a Pacers broadcaster, is in town for an upcoming game. They've been talking, about Jordan's birthday and about the changes in his life, all seeming to happen at once. Jordan feels in transition. He moved out of his house in Chicago and is moving into a new one in Florida in three weeks. He's engaged. Inside he's dealing, finally, with the cost of his own competitive urges, asking himself difficult questions. To what must he say goodbye? What is there to look forward to?

Catching an introspective Jordan is like finding a spotted owl, but here he is, considering himself. His fiancée, Yvette Prieto, and her friend Laura laugh over near the kitchen island. Jordan relights his cigar. It keeps going out.

"Listen," Buckner says, "Father Time ain't lost yet."

The idea hangs in the air.

"Damn," Buckner continues. "Fifty."

He shakes his head.

"Can you believe it?" Jordan says quietly, and it sounds like he's talking to himself.

A day before, Jordan had flown to Charlotte from Chicago, a trip he's made many times. This flight was different from all the others. When his Gulfstream IV, which is painted to look like a sneaker, took off and turned south, he no longer lived in the city where he had moved in 1984. The past months had been consumed with a final flurry of packing, putting the first half of his life in boxes. He has felt many emotions in his 50 years: hope and anger, disappointment, joy and despair. But lately there's been a feeling that would have disgusted the 30-year-old version of himself: nostalgia.

The packing and cataloging started several years ago, after his divorce. One night at his suburban Chicago mansion, he sat on the floor of his closet with Estee Portnoy. She manages his business enterprises and, since the divorce, much of his personal life—his consigliere. It was 1 in the morning. They were flummoxed by a safe. Jordan hadn't opened it in years, and he couldn't remember the combination. Everything else stopped as this consumed him. After 10 failed attempts, the safe would go into a security shutdown and need to be blown open. None of the usual numbers worked. Nine different combinations failed; they had one try left. Jordan focused. He decided it had to be a combination of his birthday, February 17, and old basketball numbers. He typed in six digits: 9, 2, 1, 7, 4, 5. *Click.* The door swung open, and he reached in, rediscovering his gold medal

from the 1984 Olympics. It wasn't really gold anymore. It looked tar-
nished, changed—a duller version of itself.

The memories came to him, how he felt then. "It was very pure,
if I can say it right," he'd explain later. "It was pure in 1984 . . . I was
still dreaming." During the Olympics, he was deep in negotiations
with Nike for his first shoe contract. He traded pins with other athletes. Eight years later, when he was the most famous person in the
world and the Dream Team was forced to stay outside the Olympic
Village, he'd be disappointed when that separation kept him from
swapping pins again.

Jordan saw an old pair of shorts that didn't fit anymore. He found
first-edition Air Jordans. In his cavernous Nike closet, he counted
nearly 5,000 boxes of shoes, some of which he marked to keep, others to give to friends. There was his uniform for the Dream Team.
An employee found letters he'd written his parents as a college student at North Carolina, and what struck her as she flipped through
the pages was how *normal* he seemed. Despite all the things that
had been gained in the years since, that person had been lost. The
kid in the letters hadn't yet been hardened by wealth and fame and
pressure. He told his parents about grades, and practice, and the
food in the dining hall. He always needed money. One letter ended:
P.S. Please send stamps.

For a rage-filled day and a half, he thought he'd lost two of his
Bulls championship rings, No. 3 and No. 5. He tore the house apart
screaming, "Who stole my rings? Who stole No. 5?"

"You talk about a mad fucking panic," he says.

Following the final title, the Bulls presented him a case with
room for all six rings, but Jordan had never put them together. Now
as he found them spread around the house, he slipped each one into
its slot. He began plotting amendments to his will that if the missing rings emerged for sale after his death, they should be returned
immediately to his estate. Buying a duplicate wouldn't be worth it,
because even if he didn't tell anyone, *he'd* know. Finally the missing

rings were found in a memorabilia room, and the set of six was complete. He could exhale and continue packing.

He discovered old home movies, seeing his young kids. They're all in or out of college now. Warmups had collected dust alongside his baseball cleats and a collection of bats and gloves. The astonishing thing to him was how much he enjoyed this. "At 30 I was moving so fast," he says. "I never had time to think about all the things I was encountering, all the things I was touching. Now when I go back and find these things, it triggers so many different thoughts: *God, I forgot about that.* That's how fast we were moving. Now I can slow it down and hopefully remember what that meant. That's when I know I'm getting old."

He laughs, knowing how this sounds, like a man in a midlife crisis, looking fondly at something that's never coming back.

"I value that," he says. "I like reminiscing. I do it more now watching basketball than anything. Man, I wish I was playing right now. I would give up everything now to go back and play the game of basketball."

"How do you replace it?" he's asked.

"You don't. You learn to live with it."

"How?"

"It's a process," he says.

The remembering continues in Charlotte, with Jordan and his best friend, George Koehler, crowding around an iPad map, trying to find Jordan's first house in Chicago.

There's circular poetry about George being here. When Jordan first landed in Chicago in 1984, he stepped out of O'Hare and found that the Bulls had neglected to send anyone to get him. Still a country boy, Jordan was nervous and uncertain. A young limo driver saw him and gave him a ride. That was George, and he's been with Jordan ever since. They're together much of the time. Jordan trusts

Koehler completely. Koehler might have more famous athletes pro-grammed into his phone than anyone on the planet, since one of the best ways to find Jordan is to call George.

"Where you looking at?" George asks, pointing.

"Essex Drive," Jordan says, finding his old street. "I remember going up to that McDonald's and getting my damn McRib. When I first got there."

There was a finished basement in that place. Charles Oakley lived behind him. So did another Bulls forward, Rod Higgins, who runs the Bobcats' basketball operations. The basement had a hot tub and a pool table that could be converted for pingpong. They'd play for hours, listening over and over to the first Whitney Houston album. Last year Jordan was sitting on the Bobcats' bench with Curtis Polk, his lawyer and a team executive, when Polk received a text saying Houston had died. Her death really affected Jordan, not be-cause he and Houston were close friends but because it made him aware of his own mortality. It made him measure the distance be-tween 50 and pingpong on Essex Drive.

"They had some battles down there," George says, laughing.

"Me and Oak," Jordan says.

Higgins is standing with them and is looking at the map too.

"I used to kill him in pool," Jordan says, nodding toward Rod.

"I got a different version," Higgins cracks.

"Kill or be killed," Jordan woofs. "Losing is killing."

There's an unspoken shadow over the stories about that town house on Essex Drive. James Jordan remodeled the basement for his son. Did all the work himself, because he'd never let Michael pay for something he could do on his own. The first winter, while Michael was out of town for the All-Star Game, his pipes froze. His dad ripped out the walls, replacing the pipes himself, patching and repainting when he finished. He spent two weeks fixing his son's home. James and Mike—that's where all this nostalgia has been headed, from the moment it began.

Dear Mama and Pops . . . Please send stamps.

George Koehler looks down at the ring on his finger. It's from the Bulls' first championship. Jordan gave replicas to family and close friends.

"I don't know if I ever told you the story why I wear this ring," George says.

"Nope," Jordan says.

"I made a promise to your dad," George says.

George was always scared he'd get robbed, so he kept the ring at home. James, known to everyone as Pops, busted him: "Where's your ring? My son didn't spend his money to have you put that shit in a drawer."

"I can hear him saying it," Jordan says, smiling.

Pops told George that if someone stole his ring, "we'll get you another one."

Jordan roars over the word "we."

"I like that," he says, his shoulders heaving. "That sounds like him too."

"After what happened to him," George says, "I wear the ring."

Memories come back. The day Pops was killed, he was scheduled to fly to Chicago. He'd called George the night before to ask for a ride. George waited at O'Hare, but Pops never came out. A half hour passed, and George called Mama J, his name for Deloris Jordan. Just wait, she said. Pops probably missed his plane. Two or three hours later, the next flight from Charlotte landed. Pops didn't get off the plane. George dialed Mama J again, and she said that something must have come up and that Pops would call. Pops never called.

"Fucker," George finally says, clearing his throat, "made me cry."

George tries to change the subject. He is attuned to Jordan's moods and knows that when Michael gets sad, he becomes quiet, withdrawn, turning inward.

"You know how many jump shots I took to get this thing?" George jokes.

"Played your ass off, George," Jordan shoots back.

But the ghost of Pops is in the room now. "He never met my fian-cée," Jordan says. "He never got to see my kids grow up. He died in '93. Jasmine was a year old. Marcus was 3 years old. Jeffrey was 5 years old."

"Where do you most feel your dad's presence?" he's asked.

Five seconds pass, then 10. Silence. He leans back into his chair, limp, his paunch noticeable for the first time. The sky outside is gray. He scrunches his mouth, rubs his neck. Suddenly he looks older, his eyes glassy, and even 20 years after his father was murdered—robbed of a Lexus and two championship rings given to him by his son—it's clear that Jordan still needs his dad. He finally answers.

"Probably with him," Jordan says, nodding toward George.

On the floor, leaning against the wall, waiting to be hung, is a framed print Jordan moved here from Chicago. It's of an empty arena, dark and quiet, with a bright white light coming out of the open tunnel doors, beckoning. Really, it's about dealing with losses: with aging, with retirement, with death. In it, Jordan is walking toward the light and there's a ghost walking next to him, with a hand on his shoulder. It's his dad.

"The thing we'd do," he says, "we'd stay up all night and watch cowboy movies. Westerns."

Jordan still watches them obsessively, and it's easy to imagine he does it to feel the presence of his father. One of his employees joked that she'd rather fly commercial than on Jordan's Gulfstream be-cause a passenger on his plane is subjected to hours of shootouts and showdowns.

"Name a Western," George says. "He'll tell you the beginning, middle, and end."

"I watch 'em all the time," Jordan says. "I watch Marshal Dillon. I watch all of 'em."

"I think his favorite Western is my favorite Western," George says.

"You and I have three we really like," Jordan says.

"*Outlaw Josey Wales*," George says.

"That's my favorite," Jordan says.

"*Two Mules . . .*," George begins.

". . . *for Sister Sara*," Jordan finishes.

"The other one I like is *Unforgiven*," George says.

"My father loved that," Jordan says.

The opposite of this creeping nostalgia is the way Jordan has always collected slights, inventing them—nurturing them. He can be a breathtaking asshole: self-centered, bullying, and cruel. That's the ugly side of greatness. He's a killer, in the Darwinian sense of the word, immediately sensing and attacking someone's weakest spot. He'd moo like a cow when the overweight general manager of the Bulls, Jerry Krause, would get onto the team bus. When the Bulls traded for the injury-prone Bill Cartwright, Jordan teased him as Medical Bill, and he once punched Will Perdue during practice. He punched Steve Kerr, too, and who knows how many other people.

This started at an early age. Jordan genuinely believed his father liked his older brother, Larry, more than he liked him, and he used that insecurity as motivation. He burned, and thought if he succeeded, he would demand an equal share of affection. His whole life has been about proving things, to the people around him, to strangers, to himself. This has been successful and spectacularly unhealthy. If the boy in those letters from Chapel Hill is gone, it is this appetite to prove—to attack and to dominate and to win—that killed him. In the many biographies written about Jordan, most notably in David Halberstam's *Playing for Keeps*, a common word used to describe Jordan is "rage." Jordan might have stopped playing basketball, but the rage is still there. The fire remains, which is why he searches for release, on the golf course or at a blackjack table, why he spends so much time and energy on his basketball team and why he dreams of returning to play.

He's in his suite at the Bobcats' arena, just before tip-off of another loss, annoyed that one of his players is talking to the opponents. Tonight he's going to sit on the bench, to send a message that the boss is watching. He used to sit there a lot, but he got a few phone calls from NBA commissioner David Stern telling him to chill with the screaming at officials. Mostly he watches in private, for good reason. Once, when he was an executive with the Washington Wizards, mad at how the team was playing, he hurled a beer can at his office television, then launched whatever he could find after it, a fusillade of workplace missiles. Now, 10 years later, he mostly just yells.

"I'm going downstairs," he says.

"Be nice," someone in the suite says.

"I'll try," he says, and is out the door.

The inner circle stays behind, gathered in Suite 27, just across the concourse from the executive offices. They've all been around for years, some from the very beginning. Estee Portnoy is here, and George. Rod Higgins and Bobcats president Fred Whitfield, an old friend from North Carolina, come and go. They're waiting on Jordan to return after the game, killing time, handling work stuff, telling stories.

Back when Jordan used to shoot a lot of commercials, his security team would wait for him in his trailer while he was on set. A woman named Linda cooked Michael's meals, and he loved cinnamon rolls. She'd bake a tray and bring it to him. When it came time to film, he'd see the guards eyeing the cinnamon rolls and he'd walk over and spit on each one, to make sure nobody took his food.

In the late '80s, Jordan looked in Whitfield's closet and saw that half of it was filled with Nike and the other half filled with Puma. Jordan bundled the Puma gear in his arms, tossing it onto the living room floor. He took a knife from the kitchen and cut it to shreds. Call Howard White, his contact at Nike, he told Fred, and tell him to replace it all. Same thing happened with George. He bought a pair of New Balance shoes he loved, and Jordan saw them one day and insisted he hand them over. *Call Howard White at Nike.*

"He demands that loyalty," Whitfield says.

"Anywhere we go," Portnoy says, "he looks at people's feet."

"First thing he looks at," Whitfield says. "He looks down all the time."

"You know what's funny?" Portnoy says. "I do the same thing now."

"I do too!" Whitfield says, laughing.

A group from Nike comes into the suite, along with a team from the ad agency Wieden+Kennedy. Around these people, you see most clearly that Jordan is at the center of several overlapping universes, at the top of the billion-dollar Jordan Brand at Nike, of the Bobcats, of his own company, with dozens of employees and contractors on the payroll. In case anyone in the inner circle forgets who's in charge, they only have to recall the code names given to them by the private security team assigned to overseas trips. Estee is Venom. George is Butler. Yvette is Harmony. Jordan is called Yahweh—a Hebrew word for God.

Jordan is used to being the most important person in every room he enters and, going a step further, in the lives of everyone he meets. The Gulfstream takes off when he steps onboard. He has left a friend in Las Vegas who was late, and recently left two security guards behind. He's been trying to leave George for years but can never beat him to the plane. He does what he wants, when he wants. On a long trip to China in the Nike plane, he woke up just as everyone else was taking an Ambien and settling in to sleep. Didn't matter. He turned on the lights and jammed the plane's stereo. If Michael is up, the unwritten rule goes, everybody is up. People cater to his every whim, making sure a car is waiting when he lands, smoothing out any inconvenience. In Chicago there was someone who kept gas in his cars. Not long ago he called his office from Florida, fuming, stuck at a gas station, unable to fill up.

"What's my billing zip code?" he asked.

It was down in Florida, where he was spending time with Yvette's

Cuban family, that he got a taste of the life he'd traded for the jet-set circus of modern celebrity. They weren't fawning—her grandparents, who speak little English, aren't basketball fans—and he sat at a dinner table, with people laughing and eating home-cooked food. That's what it was like growing up in Wilmington. "It's gone," he says. "I can't get it back. My ego is so big now that I expect certain things. Back then, you didn't."

The people in the suite know about his ego, and his moods, and his anger. They know better than most. George jokes a lot about the bite marks on his ass. But they also know Jordan, and if they're being honest, they love him. They know how kind he can be, having roses sent on Mother's Day to every mom who works for him. They see him gutted after meeting with another Make-a-Wish child. They see him swell with pride over any success of his children. They've been inside the machine, seeing firsthand the siege of fame, the hardness and cynicism it demands. So they think all the stories of Michael being Michael are funny, even endearing, while someone from the outside can hear the same story and be horrified, seeing a permanent adolescent spitting on food or cutting up clothes.

His friends, for instance, watched the Hall of Fame speech and laughed.

In the three and a half years since Jordan built his induction remarks around all the slights that pushed him toward greatness, the speech has become Exhibit A for those who believe Jordan is, as one basketball writer put it, "strangely bitter" and "lost, wandering." They're not wrong, not exactly, but something was obscured when the speech became a metaphor for swollen ego and lack of self-awareness.

The speech itself, if you watch it again, is an open window into what Jordan is like in private: funny, caustic, confident, sarcastic, competitive. He sees himself not as a gifted athlete but as someone who refused to lose. So standing at the podium—after he composed himself, wiping away tears nine times before he even began, sniffling well into the first section—he said that he had a fire inside and that "people added wood to that fire." Then he listed every doubter, cataloging all their actions, small and large. He started with his brothers and worked through high school to college to the NBA. He took a shot at longtime nemesis Jerry Krause: "I don't know who invited him . . . I didn't." It was petty but also startlingly honest.

The unspoken thread that runs through the criticism is that Jordan didn't understand what was required of a retired athlete, a mixture of nostalgia and reflection. The five-year wait is supposed to give those emotions time to sprout and grow. People wanted the Jordan on the floor of his closet, not the one who did whatever it took to win. That's the allure of a Hall of Fame speech. It reveals that these icons were sort of like us all along. Jordan didn't give that speech, and the reason is both simple and obvious. He didn't see himself as part of the past or as someone who'd found perspective. He wasn't nostalgic that night. The anger that drove his career hadn't gone away, and he didn't know what to do with it. So at the end of the speech, he said perhaps the most telling and important thing in it, which has been mostly forgotten.

He described what the game meant to him. He called it his "refuge" and the "place where I've gone when I needed to find comfort and peace." Basketball made him feel complete, and it was gone.

"One day," he said, "you might look up and see me playing the game at 50."

Chuckles rippled through the room. His head jerked to the side, and he cut his eyes the way he does when challenged, and he said, "Oh, don't laugh."

Everyone laughed harder.

"Never say never," he said.

He's trying to change, taking small steps. For the past few years, he's gone on sailing trips because Yvette loves them, even though he hates the water. The first time, he went stir-crazy on the boat. This most recent trip, he felt his rage dissolve. It was a victory. He didn't watch basketball. Every morning he'd wake with the sun and plant himself in the fishing chair, popping his first Corona by 8 with his friends, reeling in big yellowfin tuna. They make great sushi. Jordan was happy. "Drinking and eating and drinking and eating and drinking and eating" is how he described the vacation to a friend, going through cases of his favorite tequila, fully unplugged, which lasted until he flew home. Then he was around the game again, and the old urges began to eat at him.

In Charlotte, he starts thinking about 218.

Every morning since returning from the islands, he's been in the gym. At mealtime he texts his nutritionist to find out what he can and can't eat. Ostensibly, the reason is that he stepped on a scale after leaving the excess palace of *Mister Terrible* and saw this number staring back: 261. Nine days later, sitting in his office and surrounded by basketball, he's down to 248. He'll claim it's about health, or looking good for his 50th birthday party. But in his mind, there's a target: 218, a familiar and dangerous number in Jordan's world.

That's his playing weight.

When he mentions that Yvette never saw him play basketball, he says, "She never saw me at 218." On the wall of his office there's a framed photograph of him as a young man, rising toward the rim, legs pulled up near his chest, seeming to fly. He smiles at it wistfully.

"I was 218," he says.

The chasm between what his mind wants and what his body can give grows every year. If Jordan watches old video of Bulls games and then hits the gym, he says he'll go "berserk" on the exercise machines. It's frightening. A while back, his brother Larry, who works for the team, noticed a commotion on the practice court. He looked out the window of his office and saw his brother dominating one of the best players on the Bobcats in one-on-one. The next morning, Larry says with a smile, Jordan never made it into his office. He got as far as the team's training room, where he received treatment.

"You paying the price, aren't you?" Larry asked.

"I couldn't hardly move," Jordan said.

There's no way to measure these things, but there's a strong case to be made that Jordan is the most intense competitor on the planet. He's in the conversation, at the very least, and now he has been reduced to grasping for outlets for this competitive rage. He's in the middle of an epic game of Bejeweled on his iPad, and he's moved past level 100, where he won the title Bejeweled Demigod. He mastered sudoku and won $500 beating Portnoy at it. In the Bahamas, he sent someone down to the Atlantis hotel's gift shop to buy a book of word-search puzzles. In the hotel room, he raced Portnoy and Polk, his lawyer, beating them both. He can see all the words at once, as he used to see a basketball court. "I can't help myself," he says. "It's an addiction. You ask for this special power to achieve these heights, and now you got it and you want to give it back, but you can't. If I could, then I could breathe."

Once, the whole world watched him compete and win—Game 6, the Delta Center—and now it's a small group of friends in a hotel room playing a silly kid's game. The desire remains the same, but the venues, and the stakes, keep shrinking. For years he was beloved for his urges when they manifested on the basketball court, and now he's ridiculed when they show up in a speech.

His self-esteem has always been, as he says, "tied directly to the game." Without it, he feels adrift. Who am I? What am I doing? For the past 10 years, since retiring for the third time, he has been running, moving as fast as he could, creating distractions, distance. When the schedule clears, he'll call his office and tell them not to bother him for a month, to let him relax and play golf. Three days later they'll get another call, asking if the plane can pick him up and take him someplace. He's restless. So he owns the Bobcats, does his endorsements, plays hours of golf, hoping to block out thoughts of 218. But then he gets off a boat, comes home to a struggling team. He feels his competitiveness kick in, almost a chemical thing, and he starts working out, and he wonders: Could he play at 50? What would he do against LeBron?

What if?

"It's consumed me so much," he says. "I'm my own worst enemy. I drove myself so much that I'm still living with some of those drives. I'm living with that. I don't know how to get rid of it. I don't know if I could. And here I am, still connected to the game."

He thinks about the things Phil Jackson taught him. Jackson always understood him and wasn't afraid to poke around inside Jordan's psyche. Once during his ritual of handing out books for his players to read, he gave Jordan a book about gambling. It's a Zen koan Jordan needs now, in this new challenge: To find himself, he must lose himself. Whenever he obsesses about returning to play, he tries to sleep, knowing that when he wakes up, things will be better. He knows he won't get to 218. He knows he won't ever play pro basketball again. He knows he's got to quiet these drives, to find a way to live the life he worked so hard to create, *to be still.*

"How can I enjoy the next 20 years without so much of this consuming me?" he asks, sitting behind his desk as his cell phone buzzes with trade offers. "How can I find peace away from the game of basketball?"

He's home.

Jordan steps into his loft, which is dark and modern, with exposed ductwork and a sparkling backsplash in the kitchen. The design feels masculine, vaguely Asian. A pool table with tan felt is to the left, cigar ashtrays scattered around the place. There's an hour until the Bobcats-Celtics tip-off in Boston, which he'll watch from his favorite chair, a rich brown, low-slung lounger.

"Where you at?" he calls toward the rear of the condo.

Yvette's voice sounds bright and cheerful.

"Hey, honey," she says. "I'm back here."

She's 34 years old, has worked in a hospital and in real estate, and is happiest with the domestic life that Jordan lost long ago. This past year, Portnoy got a birthday present from her boss, as usual, but for the first time in 16 years, she also got a card. It was from the store Papyrus. She recognized it, and inside, Jordan had signed his name. Estee laughed, mostly at her own surprise over such ordinary behavior. Yvette had done what any person would do when a birthday approached. She'd bought a card on her own. She didn't staff it out.

Whatever changes he's made are because of her, and she offers him the best hope to rediscover pieces of the boy who wrote those letters from college. Two Easters ago, Yvette went with him to North Carolina to visit family, which is spread around the state. She'd been bugging him about taking her to Wilmington, to show her where he grew up. Like most people, she sometimes struggled to imagine him before. She wanted to meet the Mike Jordan who needed his mom and dad to send stamps. This required about seven hours of driving, which he didn't want to do. Finally, he gave in. "It's amazing what women can talk you into doing," he says. "Make you change. Ten years ago, we'd have been arguing all fucking day. I would've won. This time, this stage where I am, you win. That's progress."

Tonight, the guys are ordering Ruth's Chris to go, and Yvette and Laura are making salads. Friends gather around the kitchen island, and the place is filled with laughter. They're washing lettuce. It's easy and loose. Jordan is killing Buckner about drinking all his wine, everyone erupting at the volleyed barbs, and later, when George hands Quinn an expensive bottle of merlot with a bendy straw in it, Yvette falls into hysterics. It was a joint George-Yvette operation, from the sound of her giddy cackling.

She pushes Jordan, making him try new things. The home in Florida is almost finished, and it will be theirs together. In conversation among his staff, the golf club estate has been called a "retirement home," and Jordan's friends like to imagine him in the huge outdoor living area, lounging on a big couch, relaxing. Their wish for him is peace.

He seems to have it tonight, at least for a moment.

"Baby," Yvette says, "can you get us some wine?"

Jordan ducks into the climate-controlled wine room and comes out with one of his favorites. The cork pops softly. Glasses line the counter, and he pours wine into each one, handing them off as he finishes.

"Here ya go, ladies," he says.

Over the next seven hours, all of it spent watching one basketball game after another, he's again pulled inward, on a Tilt-a-Whirl of emotion, mostly shades of anger, from active screaming to a slow, silent burn. He transforms from a businessman returning from the office—*Honey, I'm home!*—to a man on fire. The first sparks come from a *SportsCenter* debate, one of those impossible, vaguely ridiculous arguments that can, of course, never be won: Who's a better quarterback, Joe Montana or Tom Brady?

"I can't wait to hear this conversation," he says.

He stretches his legs out on the ottoman, wearing sweats and socks, and as one of the guys on television argues for Brady, Jordan laughs.

"They're gonna say Brady because they don't remember Montana," he says. "Isn't that amazing?"

Aging means losing things, and not just eyesight and flexibility. It means watching the accomplishments of your youth be diminished, maybe in your own eyes through perspective, maybe in the eyes of others through cultural amnesia. Most people live anonymous lives, and when they grow old and die, any record of their existence is blown away. They're forgotten, some more slowly than others, but eventually it happens to virtually everyone. Yet for the few people in each generation who reach the pinnacle of fame and achievement, a mirage flickers: immortality. They come to believe in it. Even after

Jordan is gone, he knows people will remember him. *Here lies the greatest basketball player of all time.* That's his epitaph. When he walked off the court for the last time, he must have believed that nothing could ever diminish what he'd done. That knowledge would be his shield against aging.

There's a fable about returning Roman generals who rode in victory parades through the streets of the capital; a slave stood behind them, whispering in their ears, "All glory is fleeting." Nobody does that for professional athletes. Jordan couldn't have known that the closest he'd get to immortality was during that final walk off the court, the one symbolically preserved in the print in his office. All that can happen in the days and years that follow is for the shining monument he built to be chipped away, eroded. Maybe he realizes that now. Maybe he doesn't. But when he sees Joe Montana joined on the mountaintop by the next generation, he has to realize that someday his picture will be on a screen next to LeBron James as people argue about who was better.

The debaters announce the results of an Internet poll, and 925,000 people voted. There was a tie: 50 percent said Montana and 50 percent said Brady. It doesn't matter that Montana never lost a Super Bowl or that, unlike Brady, he never faded on the biggest stage. Questions of legacy, of greatness, are weighted in favor of youth. Time itself is on Brady's side, for now.

Jordan shakes his head.

"That doesn't make any sense," he says.

Jordan plays his new favorite trivia game, asking which current players could be nearly as successful in his era. "Our era," he says over and over again, calling modern players soft, coddled, and ill-prepared for the highest level of the game. This is personal to him, since he'll be compared to this generation, and since he has to build a franchise with this generation's players.

"I'll give you a hint," he says. "I can only come up with four."

He lists them: *LeBron, Kobe, Tim Duncan, Dirk Nowitzki.* As he's making his point, Yvette walks into the living room area and, in a tone of voice familiar to every husband who argues sports with his buddies, asks, "You guys need anything?"

When someone on TV compares LeBron to Oscar Robertson, Jordan fumes. He rolls his eyes, stretches his neck, frustrated. "It's absolutely . . . ," he says, catching himself. "The point is, no one is critiquing the personnel that he's playing against. Their knowledge of how to play the game . . . that's not a fair comparison. That's not right . . . Could LeBron be successful in our era? Yes. Would he be as successful? No."

The Bobcats game starts and the Celtics jump all over them. The officials aren't helping, and Jordan sits up, livid, certain that the Celtics are getting all the calls because they have the stars.

"COME ON, MAN!" he screams.

"You ain't getting that one," Buckner says. "But you used to get away with shit other people couldn't get away with."

There's a hard silence in the room. Jordan's voice lowers.

"I don't believe that," he growls.

"Bull. Shit," Buckner says. "Let's not get carried away now. You and Larry."

Jordan ignores him; he's locked in.

"That's a foul!" he yells. "See what I mean? THAT'S A FOUL!"

It's a nice night, and Jordan moves out to his balcony, on the seventh floor, looking down the barrel of South Tryon Street. The TV is up in the right corner. He smokes a cigar. The Bobcats tie the game, then fall behind again.

"Getbackgetbackgetback," Jordan yells at the TV. "Matchup, MATCHUP. Where you GOING? DIVE FOR THE BALL!"

They're going to lose—he's going to lose—and he is quiet on the couch. It's over. He doesn't talk for a minute, then mutters something, then is silent for another half a minute.

He changes the channel to the Heat-Jazz game. During the broadcast, he is the answer to a trivia question. This is the court where he made his most famous shot, and he points to the place where he took it. He remembers how tired he felt at the end of that game. A cell phone rests on Jordan's chest. His legs stretch out on a tree-trunk coffee table.

"What's Bird up to?" Jordan asks.

"Down in Naples," Buckner says.

"Playing golf every day?" Jordan asks.

"Bored," Buckner says.

"Think he'll ever get back in?" Jordan asks.

"He'll damn sure get back in it," Buckner says. "He didn't say it, but I just know him."

The announcers gush about LeBron, mentioning him in the same sentence with Jordan, who hears every word. Those words have an effect on him. He stares at the TV and points out a flaw in LeBron's game.

"I study him," he says.

When LeBron goes right, he usually drives; when he goes left, he usually shoots a jumper. It has to do with his mechanics and how he loads the ball for release. "So if I have to guard him," Jordan says, "I'm gonna push him left so nine times out of 10, he's gonna shoot a jump shot. If he goes right, he's going to the hole and I can't stop him. So I ain't letting him go right."

For the rest of the game, when LeBron gets the ball and starts his move, Jordan will call out some variation of "drive" or "shoot." It's not just LeBron. He sees fouls the officials miss, and the replays prove him right. When someone shoots, he knows immediately whether it's going in. He calls out what guys are going to do before they do it, more plugged in to the flow of the game than some of the players on the court. He's answering texts, buried in his phone, when the play-by-play guy announces a LeBron jump shot. Without looking up, Jordan says, "Left?"

The outdoor heater makes the porch warm. Hours pass, creating distance from the Bobcats loss. Nobody says much. George plays Bejeweled on an iPad. The air is filled with the sounds of basketball:

horns, squeaking sneakers, the metallic clang of the rim. These are the sounds of Jordan's youth.

He holds a cigar and relights it every now and then, the whoosh of the butane torch breaking the silence. The heater's flame is reflected on three different windows, shadows flickering on Jordan's face. He never says it, but it seems as though he's playing the game in his head, using his rage for its intended purpose. He still knows how to play. He could shut down LeBron, if his body wouldn't betray him, if he could hold off time, if he could get to 218.

George goes to bed. An hour later, the last game of the night ends. Buckner says goodbye and rides the elevator down. Yvette and her friend Laura headed toward the back of the condo long ago.

Jordan is alone.

He hates being alone, because that means it's quiet, and he doesn't like silence. He can't sleep without noise. Sleep has always been a struggle for him. All the late-night card games, the trips to the casino during the playoffs, they've been misunderstood. They weren't the disease; they were the cure. They provided noise, distraction, a line of defense. He didn't even start drinking until he was 27 and complained of insomnia to a doctor. Have a few beers after the game, he was advised. That would knock off the edge.

The house is dark. It's almost 1 a.m., and he opens the iPad app that controls the loft's audio-visual system. Every night he does the same thing, and he does it now: Turn the bedroom television to the Western channel. The cowboy movies will break the darkness, break the silence, allow him to rest. It's just like the old days, him and Pops. Jordan climbs into bed. The film on the screen is *Unforgiven*. He knows every scene, and sometime before the shootout in the saloon, he falls asleep.

The Last Days of Tony Harris

What drove the former college basketball star
to his death in the Brazilian jungle?

FRIDAY, NOVEMBER 2, 2007, BRASÍLIA, BRAZIL

The city outside the window of Room 1507 at the Carlton Hotel is an unlikely place to go insane. Designed as living modern art, Brasília is defined by its order. But Tony Harris doesn't see order. He sees danger. He knows how this must sound, to the locals he's confiding in, to the friends and family he's emailing and calling back in Seattle. He knows he sounds out of his mind. But something is after him. An idea is forming in his subconscious: *Run.*

While the city outside is light, the hallway is darker than the bottom of a river. The halogens only come alive when a motion sensor detects life. The room itself is worn, a step or two down from the place he stayed the last time he played basketball here, more than two years ago. But then again, at 36, he's worn, too. He'd never planned on playing again. There are two narrow beds and tan bedspreads and brown carpet. The bedside table is cracked, the original wood grain visible beneath the varnish. A single page in the thick phonebook is creased: the page for funeral homes.

Wireless Internet is his best friend, the connection making him feel safe. He needs it. The emails coming to the United States from Tony Harris are scary. Just the other day, he wrote his mother-in-law:

I know that I can be paranoid at times but I know when I hear things. And when people stop talking when I come into the area, I just pray

that I am wrong Connie I want to see my family again and I LOVE MY
WIFE SO MUCH I WANT TO SEE OUR CHILD THAT LORI AND I ARE
HAVING. I DIDN'T COME BACK HERE FOR THEM TO SET ME UP
AND KILL ME.

The phone next to the bed is his other lifeline. Dial 8-2 for a wake-up
call. Dial 2 for room service, like he did yesterday, to have a little
piece of home sent up: a steak and a Coca-Cola. Dial 0 for an outside
line. Zero takes him home. Yesterday, he talked with his wife, Lori.
He told her of the closing darkness, of the whispers in the locker
room: *He had slept with someone's wife the last time he played here,
or that he'd fled because he had AIDS.* That's why he brought proof
of his negative AIDS test—to show the players and stop the whispers. They didn't seem interested. He didn't understand. So last
night, on the phone with Lori, confused and scared, he began settling his accounts. *Tell my mama I love her. Tell my son I love him
and to finish school and make something of himself and that I'm
proud of him.*

"You're scaring me," she said.

"I need to tell you this in case something happens to me," he said.

Last night, he thought he was dead for sure. This morning, a plan
begins to form. He asks Brent Merritt, a friend from Seattle who
played here, to call the team. He follows up with an email, asking
Brent to call back if he doesn't hear from him. Ask to speak to me, he
instructs. But then a thought enters his head: What if the team has
someone pretend to be him? What would Brent do? He needs a test.
Yes, a test. That's it. So he gives Brent a password of sorts. Ask the
person claiming to be me what the name of my dog is. If he doesn't
say Enya, then it ain't me.

Then he goes to play for his new team, Universo. Once, not that
long ago, Tony was one of the best players in the Brazilian league.
Tonight, he doesn't take a single shot. When the game is finally over,

he rushes back to his hotel room, away from the tailing cars and lobby whispers.

The sun has gone down. If he could see this from above, like a god or an omniscient narrator, he'd see this city as an island of lights in a vast darkness. Out the window to the left is the famous television tower, the highest man-made point in Brazil, the raised fist of those who came out here into the bush five decades ago to hack out civilization. To the right, over the top of the Hotel das Américas, is a highway climbing out toward a tiny village named Bezerra, toward the wilderness. He'll go in both directions before his running is finished.

He sends an email to his wife:

To: Lori J Harris
From: T bone
Date: 11/02/2007

I am home now. I just feel like crying all night. Babe I am really paranoid I still think that they are going to try and do me harm. Why do I feel this way I am not sure. Forgive me please babe I am sorry. Tell me why when I got home into my apartment the TV was way up loud and when I left it was really low and the maids cleaned my room earlier.

Soon, Tony Harris falls asleep. It will be the last night of his old life.

REAL DANGER OR PARANOIA?

Our man in Brasília orders a caipirinha. Gauchos around him carry skewers of meat. He wears a green shirt, and his head is crowned with a full crop of hair. His name is Simon Henshaw, a diplomat's name. His title is consul general, a diplomat's title. He has been around the world, to the banana republics of Latin America, the Pacific, and Africa. He is a man who has heard truth and lies, who has seen light and dark, and who has learned there is but a thin line separating the two. He lives in the city but understands the wilderness. It surrounds him. A half hour out of town in any direction, he says, there is desolation. For the past month, he has been investigating the strange case of Tony Harris: Seattle basketball prep star to Washington State Cougar to international professional to . . . gone. He, too, wants to know what happened *out there*. It's so hard to make sense of it all.

He wants to know what you will be writing. Well, you tell him, there's a lot of Joseph Conrad in this tale. A man travels down his own personal Congo, a descent, until the jungle consumes him at journey's end. He learns there is danger and evil in the world and is unable to escape its fated pull.

Henshaw mulls this over. "Who's Kurtz?" he asks.

The darkness chasing Tony Harris, is it out in the world? Or is it inside his mind?

SATURDAY, NOVEMBER 3, FLEEING BRASÍLIA

Another game ends. Tony shows a flicker of the man who led the Cougars to the NCAA Tournament in 1994, helping to jump-start Kelvin Sampson's coaching career. He scores eight points and doesn't dribble the ball off his foot, as he did a few days ago. But the panic that started in his mind has now reached his legs: *Run! Run! Run!*

He nervously changes into a gray tracksuit, ties his blue-and-white, size 13 Nikes, and asks a teammate he trusts, Estevam Ferreira, to give him a ride to the Carlton. Estevam says sure, and they climb into his Renault. Back at the Carlton, Tony invites his friend upstairs. On the 15th floor, Tony begins packing. This isn't the first time he has done this.

"Tony, what's happening?" Estevam asks.

"I miss my wife" is all Tony has by way of explanation. "I want to get away from here."

Tony is in a hurry but not rushing. Methodically, as if following a well-practiced escape plan, he takes about 15 minutes to get a backpack ready: laptop, a change of clothes, a few other essentials. The rest of his belongings he leaves behind. Tony and Estevam walk into the hall, the movement clicking on the light, down the elevator, toward the bar, left past the front desk. When Tony steps out of the hotel, there is no turning back.

The airport sits about 10 miles south of the main urban corridor, on the road winding down toward the lake, past the zoo. Tony begins to lose control. He has fought so hard for the past four days, trying to talk these feelings away or stuff them deep down inside and get through just one more season. But he can fight no longer. Now he must *Run!* There is a cost for crossing the thin line between imaginary and real, between light and dark.

"I'm afraid," he sobs.

"What are you afraid of?" Estevam asks.

"There is someone trying to get me."

"Who?"

Tony doesn't answer. He weeps. He is silent. He weeps again. An elaborate drama is playing out in his head, behind a thick stage curtain, the tears muffled noises that let his audience of one know something is happening, something powerful and awful, even if Estavam cannot catch a glimpse of the action.

Finally, they arrive at the airport. Tony asks Estevam to wait, then goes inside alone. Only he does not buy a plane ticket home. Who knows why? Instead, he purchases a ticket to Natal, a beach town in the northeast of Brazil. He is planning to fly there, where his friend Erika lives, then figure out what to do next. Erika worked at the hotel where he stayed when he played here before. At security, though, he hits a wall: He doesn't have his passport. The team has it. With a game each day and the need to provide documents for each player before each game, it's easier if the team keeps them. It's standard practice, but Tony's sure the team is in on this plot to kill him. Can't ask the team. Now he doesn't know what to do.

Estevam, sitting in his car, watches his friend coming out of the airport. Tony looks scared. His plan has fallen apart. Without structure, the night becomes even more frightening.

"So tell me what you wanna do now," Estevam says.

"I don't know," Tony says. "Please help me."

To Estevam, who is also nervous now, this feels like a spy movie. He has known Tony for years, and if someone is trying to kill Tony, might they also try to kill him? He thinks. Thinks. Thinks. He and Tony call Lori, and a new plan is hatched. The bus station. Goiânia is a city close to Brasília. Buses leave every hour. Tony likes this. He has a friend in Goiânia, an ex-girlfriend, Daniela. They drive back toward Brasília, to the bus station, a half-hour trip.

Estevam still doesn't understand. "Let's go to the police," he says. Tony says no. No cops. No U.S. embassy. Only escape.

The bus station finally appears in front of them, and the two men go inside. Tony purchases a ticket, and Estevam walks him to the correct bus. Something is coming to an end. Both men sense it. Tony hugs his teammate and says, "You live in my heart."

Estevam searches for the words. "Go with God," he says.

The tears are gone, replaced by a lost look in Tony's eyes. What is going on behind those eyes? What do they see? Estevam searches his friend's face for clues, for some sort of road map of the journey to come. He sees sadness but also relief. Tony climbs the bus steps and finds his seat. The bus pulls away. Before it leaves the comforting glow of the station, Estevam sees Tony sitting by the window. The men lock eyes a final time. Tony gives him a thumbs-up. In the last breath of the vanishing light, he takes his right hand and beats on his chest.

You live in my heart.

WHAT CHANGES WHEN A MAN HAS SEEN THE EVIL OF THE WORLD?

In Seattle, as word spreads of Tony's disappearance, his friends and family try to make sense of it. They know Tony is running. Some know Tony has a history of paranoid behavior. Some know it isn't the first time he has been scared.

The first time, eight years ago, he was in South Korea playing basketball. He was out with a teammate, Derrick Johnson, and two girls in the VIP section of a Seoul club. A group of Korean men, speaking Russian, attacked the woman with Tony, striking her in the face with a bottle. Later, after she had jumped in their cab to escape, a van chased them down, cut them off on a bridge, and the woman was yanked from the car by the same men. Johnson laughed it off. Tony didn't. He started seeing danger in every shadow. He stopped going out. Something inside of him changed. "From there I saw the paranoia," Johnson says. "Tony made it through the rest of the season. It was toward the end of the season. The paranoia didn't happen to the point where he left." Tony eventually got home and everything was fine. He'd left the fear in Korea.

The second time was three years ago, in Brazil. That time, he could not control it. He'd been there for five seasons, a popular star, leading his team to titles. Kids rushed to him after games for hugs and autographs. Girls waited at every exit of the gym. Everybody loved Tony Harris. But on February 11, 2005, soon after returning to the country after being in America for a few months, he said he had food poisoning and refused to play or go to the hospital or even leave the locker room until the game was over. Bad shrimp, he said. The next day, at 6 a.m., he called the team's general manager and asked for a ride to the airport. He had to get home immediately. Tony paid for his own ticket.

This time, different people got different stories. Tony told the team his son from a prior relationship had been in a horrific car accident. He described the accident, and the hospital procedures, in great detail and would continue the elaborate lie when he returned in 2007. The general manager was very worried about his friend, not knowing there had been no car accident. Tony told two basketball friends he just didn't have it anymore. But the story he told his pastor was more frightening: After a dispute with the team over money, some men took him way out into the wilderness and left him, wanting to send a message. Message received. Only this time, he brought the fear home with him. "When Tony came back from Brazil last time, something was not right with him," family friend Glynis Harps says. "Something heavy was on his mind, and he was preoccupied. I don't know what happened. Tony was scared."

He believed people were following him. Once, he yelled "duck" to a friend. There was no one there. Once, he saw a man he'd fought with as a preteen walk into a gym. He ran from the gym, leaving his gear behind, explaining later that the guy was going to hurt him. A friend says the long-lost "enemy" never knew Tony was in the gym. He stopped going to gyms entirely, giving up basketball for the first time in his life.

SUNDAY, NOVEMBER 4, GOIÂNIA TO BEZERRA

Tony Harris stands outside the green gate, next door to the motorcycle repair shop, waiting on a cabdriver to let him in. Jose Lindomar Jesus, called Baiano by his friends, steps into the light, eyeing the tall man before him. He's carrying a backpack and seems scared, looking around as if he's expecting someone. It's Sunday morning, and there is no one else on the street.

Baiano shows Tony a place against the turquoise walls of the house where he can sit. Baiano goes into the house. Tony slumps down. It had been a long night. He arrived at the bus station in Goiânia at around 2 a.m. He called Erika and tried to get Daniela's number; they were all friends in Uberlândia. Erika didn't have it. The plan was not working. He asked how to get to Natal from Goiânia.

She told him to take a bus. No, he explained, that bus went through Brasilia, and he could not have that. Finally, they came up with a solution—a cab to Salvador, where he'd get a friend of Erika's to meet him and accompany him to Natal. OK. Good. Tony walked a few blocks to find a cab parked in front of a local hospital. That guy wouldn't do it, but he thought his friend might. Now it is 8:30 a.m., and Tony is still here.

Soon, Baiano comes outside, dressed and cleaned up. Sliding across the black leather seats, Tony gets into the front of the white Chevy cab. Baiano takes a right out of his driveway, past the motor-cycle repair shop, winds through the gears as they climb the hill toward the center of town. Tony wants to go to the Bank of Brazil, which accepts American ATM cards. The machine is in the far back-right corner, and Tony slides his card, enters his PIN, and . . . is declined. The cabdriver tries to read the screen over his shoulder. Tony is at his daily withdrawal limit. He'd taken out money already at the bus station. What to do? Harris gives the cabdriver about $340, most of the money he has on him, and promises to pay the remaining $1,100 in Salvador. This means altering the plan yet again. Tony finds an Internet café, a dark, narrow shotgun building with low ceil-ings and green walls, buys a half hour of Web time and a phone card, sits down at Terminal 3, a stark white cubicle, and sends an email. Back home in Seattle, Lori's computer is set to ding when she gets mail. It's before dawn in Seattle, which doesn't matter to Tony.

He sends the first email at 9:34 a.m.

Babe what are you doing this it tony i need to talk to you cause i have to put some money in some ones account so that i can get to erikas city please respond

Less than a minute later, he writes again, virtually the same mes-sage. Ding! This time, Lori hears and answers. Tony gives her Baia-no's cell phone number and license number, tells her the plan, and then logs off. Soon, Baiano's phone rings. It's Lori. She and Tony talk. It's a short call, just a few details. This is the last time they will ever hear each other's voices.

"Love you," Tony says.

"Love you too," Lori says.

The errands finished, Tony and Baiano leave Goiânia. Tony chain smokes, getting through three cigarettes until the rain comes and Baiano rolls up the window. After an hour and a half, they cross the border between the state of Goiás and the Federal District. A big sign above the road marks the boundary. It also reads: BRASÍLIA 54 KM.

Without a word, Tony dives over the passenger seat, legs in the air, clawing for the back seat until he's lying down, curled up, and all that's visible from the window is the rainy-season sky overhead, clouds so big and nasty they seem to swallow you whole. When it's clear, the sky above Brazil looks like the front porch of heaven, all impossible blues and pillowy clouds. But when rainy season comes, and the storms roll in, the sky seems angry.

Baiano asks Tony what he's doing.

"I have a headache," Tony says.

They drive through Brasília, past the television tower and the Carlton Hotel. Tony cowers, out of sight. Finally, Tony is coaxed back up front and the journey continues toward Salvador, until about 2 p.m., when Baiano gets hungry.

A town appears on the horizon, a badlands outpost named Bezerra. The car rolls past a barren savanna, the road lined with concrete poles and barbed wire protecting a military artillery range. There is an opening in the wire just before the village, near a small shantytown hugging the road. The centerpiece of Bezerra is a Texaco station, with a little diner attached called Sabor Gaucho. Long-haul truckers fill the sprawling parking lot, fueling up on the run to the coast. Baiano parks. Tony refuses to go inside for lunch, so he waits in the car. After lunch, they pull up to the pump a few yards away. Tony hands Baiano his debit card and agrees to wait some more.

Something changes his mind. Tony gets out of the car, leaving his backpack inside. He walks into the small convenience store, which is in between the diner and the office where you pay for gas. A young man named Warley Dyone is behind the register. Everything seems normal. Tony asks the price of a bottle of orange juice and a small package of cookies. Warley tells him.

Out of nowhere, a troubled expression crosses Tony's face.

"Where's the taxi driver?" he asks.

"He's in the office paying for the gas," Warley says.

Tony does not reply. Is the neon sign in his head flashing again? *RUN! RUN! RUN!* He wheels around, out the glass doors, past the pumps, running, making a hard left at the highway, past the restaurant next door, out of sight. Warley chases after him. So does Baiano, who was going to ask for the PIN. Without it, the charge will be declined, later showing up on Tony's credit card statement as a failed attempt.

When Warley and Baiano reach the street, they see nothing. Tony has left behind a past, a future, a city of fans, a 14-year-old son, a pregnant wife, a change of clothes, a backpack, and the laptop computer that has kept him tethered these past few days.

He has disappeared into the woods.

WHY DID HE RETURN TO BRAZIL?

Two weeks after the shocking details finally became public, Estevam Ferreira walks off the basketball court following a Universo practice. He knows how afraid Tony had been the last time he was here. Like everyone else, he has a question: "Why did he come back?"

You tell him the story. Life was hard for Tony after Brazil. He tried to do the right thing—whatever scared him also made him grow up. He married Lori, joined a church, volunteered at a local homeless shelter. For a while, he worked with children at a juvenile detention center named Echo Glen. His past followed him, though. When his job was about to become full-time, a background check found a report about child abuse. Years before, a teacher found Tony had spanked his son, leaving a mark, just before dropping him off for school. Never mind that the report absolved Tony of abuse. Almost two years to the day since he had left Brazil, he lost his job. That was nine months ago. Then Lori got pregnant, and he felt emasculated by his inability to support his family. Tony tried, applying for work at more than 50 places. But without a bachelor's degree, his fleeting fame did him no good. No one seemed to remember, or care, that he'd taken Washington State to the NCAA Tournament. He withdrew into himself, fighting with Lori, even briefly moving out. But he kept trying, moving back in the house, taking correspondence courses, applying for more jobs, even one at a grocery store, anything to feed his family. Then the phone rang. It was his old general manager from Brazil, desperately in need of a replacement player for an upcoming tournament. Tony was desperate too. For his family, he would try to keep it together.

You look Estevam in the eyes. "He needed the money," you say.

This lays Estevam low. He turns away, crosses his arms, sighs, cannot speak. He thinks of his friend, a man terrified of this place but willing to risk it all to provide for his wife and child. The courage that must have taken. He thinks about his friend, and when the words don't come, he touches his chest with his fist.

You live in my heart.

NOVEMBER 4–7, BEZERRA

Tony Harris is hiding. What must he be thinking, crouching in the woods, counting the minutes and hours until it's safe to come out? Baiano drives up and down the street for a while, but after an hour and a half heads home, with Tony's backpack in his car. Sometime Sunday evening, Tony comes out of the wilderness. He begs for food. Migrant workers and hobos frequent this road, stopping for work when they can find it, so people don't think this is strange.

No one sees Tony on Monday. There are no reports of him walking the road. But Monday afternoon, about 4:30, he finds a phone, according to team trainer Mario Saraiva. He dials a familiar number: Mario's. He was once a friend, but is now someone who Tony thinks might be part of the plot to kill him.

Tony says hello.

"Where are you?" Mario says. "I'm gonna pick you up."

Tony must make a decision. There is a struggle inside of him, these competing urges. Is Mario a friend? Is he an enemy? Tony shakes off the doubt. The sign is telling him to *Run!*

"No," Tony says. "I won't tell you. You'll tell the others, and they'll come to kill me."

Tony hangs up. He disappears again, and no one sees him Monday or Tuesday. Police will later assume he was hiding in the bush, burning up during the day, freezing at night. The U.S. embassy will say it had no more confirmed sightings, but the Brazilian police, along with a resident in the town, say he made one more walk into the light.

On Wednesday morning, according to police records, a man looking like Tony knocked on a woman's door, begging for coffee and bread. On Wednesday afternoon, a few wandering hobos talked to him briefly. He was covered in dirt and grime and asked them for a clean shirt. They would say later they gave him one, but it was never found.

That night, around 7 o'clock, Harris stumbled toward the gas station, where this all began, past the pumps, back through the glass doors. Maria Paula Gonçalves, wearing her red uniform, stood behind the counter. The man was nervous, she would say later, barely looking at her, looking over his shoulders instead. He asked for a pack of Derby cigarettes and paid in the Brazilian equivalent of dimes.

Three and a half hours later, he returned. Maria had finished giving her husband his nightly medicine and making a plate of leftovers for a beggar when Tony appeared in the diner. For a moment, she thought he was the same person she just fed.

"I'm hungry," he said.

"I already gave you food," she said.

Then she looked down. The other man wore flip-flops. This man was wearing gigantic basketball shoes. It was the same guy who bought cigarettes. A few days later, after seeing his picture on television, she would say it was Tony Harris. Right now, he was just a man who needed food. She fixed him a plate, some leftover meat, rice, and beans, wrapped it up to go. This time he was calm, not looking over his shoulder. He took the food and headed back out into the night. It's about four miles to where he would complete this final walk. Maybe he went down the highway a quarter of a mile, left through the gap in the barbed wire near the mini shantytown. Poor people often fish at a lake through there, which is why the fence was down. Was that where he went? No one knows for sure.

No known person would ever again see Tony Harris alive.

WHAT REALLY HAPPENED OUT THERE?

Pedromar Augusto de Souza is the chief of police in the nearest city. The Formosa station house has six bullet holes in the door; police work is serious business here in Brazil, where cops and gangsters have running gun battles. Eye for an eye, tooth for a tooth, and, as if to prove it, Pedromar pulls a big hog-leg .45 automatic from his waistband, ejects the magazine from the butt, jacks the chambered round, which bounces three times and settles. He hands over the shiny gun for inspection. The bullet? A hollow point. Goes in little, comes out big.

He has been working hard investigating the bizarre death of Tony Lee Harris, American citizen. It's the only case assigned directly to him. From afar, he has heard the conspiracy theories from the folks back in the States: that Universo lured Tony down to Brazil to kill him; that the police are covering up a crime, or worse; or even that the Brazilian army killed him. Most of the theories are rooted in misinformation: Some media reports in Seattle included errors, which aroused suspicion; the cremation of the body was viewed as suspicious, though family members back home didn't know there was really nothing left but skin, bones, and worms. He knows people think he's not being thorough. "It would be easy to say it's a suicide and close the case," he says. "I want to make really sure it was not homicide. To be 100 percent sure."

There are a few questions left. The decomposition of the body prohibited an accurate toxicology report. The cause of death is still officially undetermined, and lab officials cannot say with complete certainty that it was a death by hanging. They are virtually certain, but the state of the corpse has hindered the detective work. And there are other stray facts: Two cigarette butts were found near the body. Lab technicians are working to determine whether these were smoked by Tony, though no lighter was found near his body. Tony's wedding ring was missing. His wallet was missing. His sweatpants were missing. There was likely money missing, though how much is unknown.

And then there's the biggest mystery of all: the curious extra shoelace.

De Souza needs answers before closing the case. Right now, there is a sliver of doubt. A heartbreaking possibility exists: Could Tony Harris have been losing his mind, running from people who were not chasing him, only to end up surrounded by actual danger? "The most likely [cause] is suicide," de Souza says. "But some people walking around the street asking for money, maybe they saw him and thought this guy has money and they killed him. That's another question."

Will it ever be possible to conclusively prove what happened?

De Souza considers the question. The body had no bullet holes or stab wounds, no broken bones or tissue under the fingernails. But the rain and the wilderness erased any other forensic clues.

"No," he says.

THE FINAL DAYS, OUTSIDE BEZERRA

The walk to the monkey pepper tree is long and difficult, no matter the route. Tony Harris leaves the gas station and disappears into the *cerrado*, a sprawling Brazilian savanna that surrounds the town. *Cerrado* means "inaccessible" in Portuguese.

The land is frightening and foreign, quilts of open field dotted with termite mounds and tall, tropical trees. There are long runs of covered forest. The greens are psychedelic. Jaguars roam the forests and grasslands, their roar like a loud cough. Water flows, maybe a stream, maybe runoff from a recent shower. Large birds circle the tops of the trees, their shrieks breaking the peaceful gurgle of the water. Songbirds sing a sweet melody in the background. During the day, the sun bakes down, steaming all living things with alternating flurries of sun, rain, then more sun. At night, the chill comes and with it a darkness unlike anything a man from a civilized world has ever seen. At night, it's like God himself forgot the *cerrado*.

How long was Tony lost out here? A day? Two? Three? The soldiers say you could live for a month, if you knew what you were doing. The place is covered with edible fruit and fresh water. No one knows where Tony Harris walked or what he thought or felt as he wove deeper and deeper into the mazelike wilderness. Was he scared? Did he stop running? Did someone stop him from running? Somehow he ended up at the monkey pepper tree. It's clearly visible, atop the crown of a small mound, in a clearing, a few smaller trees setting a perimeter. Though there is deeper forest around it, from the tree, a man can look up and see heaven.

No one knows exactly what happened to Tony Harris in his last minutes, but they do know where he was found. Police estimate he died on or about Friday, November 9. An anonymous call came in on Sunday, November 18, his birthday. About 20 feet from the monkey pepper tree is a fishing hole, though you can't see it without crawling through dense vegetation. A walking path to it, if you know where to dip into the forest, goes past the tree. Police believe the tipster is an illegal fisherman without permission to be on military property. That's yet another heartbreaking detail: Tony Harris loved to fish, and some investigators believe he might have been out of his mind from dehydration. But if he had walked more or less straight here from town, he ended up only 20 yards shy of life-saving water and more fish than he could have eaten in a month.

Police and soldiers arrive on the scene. They smell it before they see it, a grotesque, barely human form, bleached white in spots and warped by the sun and rain, skin losing to gravity in big folds, those big basketball shoes just a foot off the ground. Bugs swarm, and body fluids stain the trunk of the tree black. The corpse, no longer Tony Harris, hangs from a sturdy branch by a black shoelace. They notice that both of the shoelaces are in place. So he brought an extra shoelace with him from Brasília, managed to keep it despite losing his computer, pants, wallet, and ring? Could have happened.

The location of the pepper tree leads everyone who sees it to think suicide. This place seems too remote for anyone to have carried a body so far, and forensic evidence suggests Tony's life ended in this clearing, hanging from a monkey pepper tree, four miles from Bezerra, 6,000 miles from Seattle, totally and utterly alone.

It's the perfect tree. A short step up onto a low branch, an easy reach to tie the shoelace around a higher branch, then a quick step off. Death would have begun quickly, air cut off, the pressure on the spinal column beginning a domino effect, motor ability lessened or lost. Did his life flash before his eyes? Did he see a lost job and rejected applications? Did he see people chasing him and shadows and whispers? Or did he see other, happier things? Maybe a boy in Seattle pointing so many years ago and telling his mom: That's Tony Harris. He plays for Garfield. Maybe a bear hug with Kelvin Sampson after making it to the NCAA Tournament. Or did he see his 14-year-old son, who looks just like him, or his wife, or his mother, or his friends? Did he see his future?

No one knows. But the police do believe this: The very last act of

Tony Harris was to fight for his life. As he hung from that shoelace, his time now down to seconds, unable to use his arms and legs, he bit down on the tree, sinking his teeth into the trunk, as if to buy one inch of life-saving air. He failed, and he died there, hanging from the monkey pepper tree.

The day after cutting his body down, police found a hole burrowed deep into the bark of the tree. Laying on the ground below was a tooth, the last will and testament of a man struggling for light in a place consumed by darkness.

EPILOGUE

The two letters addressed to Tony Harris made it real. The first was from the state of Washington, absolving him of any further child support. There was a space for "reason" and one box had been checked: deceased. The next letter hurt even more. It was from a grocery store. Sorry, it began, we cannot extend you an offer. His application had been denied. Lori wept, for the man Tony wanted to be and for the man she'd lost. "He was always well intentioned," she says. "He really had a heart of gold. It just broke my heart, because I could see the potential and the goodness in him, and nobody would give him a break."

She replays the last months. She's a mental health worker, and yet she never saw signs of a serious problem. Sure, he was really down, refusing to talk about his pain, finding solace alone on a lake, fishing. But the contract in Brazil seemed to make him whole again. Why kill himself now, with a child on the way, with so much to live for? She doesn't believe it. It doesn't make sense. "Tony was a pretty boy," she says. "It's very hard to even imagine how awful his last days must have been in order for him to end up like that. All I have is the image of how he was found and his body was decomposed and that last phone conversation. It just makes it almost impossible to feel like you can move on. It's so hard."

On the day of the funeral, a butterfly lands at the foot of the monkey pepper tree, flapping its wings slowly, refusing to fly away. Soon, another joins it. A continent away, his family spreads Tony's ashes on the Green River in Washington, where he had so often found peace, the water slowly taking him away forever. At the service, they mourn the end of Tony Harris's life and begin the rest of their own lives without him. His son, D'Nique, goes to a gymnasium. He's on the JV team, and his first high school game is that night.

In the locker room, D'Nique quietly asks if he can switch jerseys with a teammate for the game. He wants to take that court with No. 4 on his back, the number Tony wore during happier times, when he was a star in Brazil. D'Nique doesn't talk about that, though he also writes a "4" on his own sneakers. He will offer tribute to his father in the only way he knows how: with a game. He walks onto the court, already 6-foot-3 and growing, looking so much like his father, wearing his father's number. He can't miss that night from 3-point range, and in the stands, next to his mom, sits a man who'd seen Tony play. The hairs on the back of the man's neck stand up. It is as if he has seen a ghost.

JANUARY 2008

Ghosts of Mississippi

In 1962, the Ole Miss campus erupted in
violence over integration and swelled with pride over a
powerful football team. Mississippi native Wright Thompson
explores how that tumultuous fall still grips the state.

When I was 5 or 6, because of my dad's political activism in the Mississippi Delta, local white supremacists burned a cross in our front yard. My parents had a decision to make: Wake me up, or let me sleep. They chose sleep. On that night, hate and fear would not be passed to another generation.

In the years that followed, my parents raised my brother and me to leave old prejudices behind. They enforced strict rules that made our home something of an oasis. Respect all people. Understand other points of view. And, of course, no N-word, ever, under any circumstance. That certainly made our house different from many in town. My dad ran the local Democratic Party, so I grew up around whites and blacks, which also made me different from many of my friends. Still, there were things never discussed. We never really talked much about the civil rights era, about things my parents had seen. The South during the '60s was like that cross in our front yard: something they experienced but wanted to shield their children from.

Once I grew up and moved away, I began to study the history of the South. The 1962 Ole Miss football team fascinated me. That year, perhaps because of the school's near self-destruction over integration, or perhaps in spite of it, the team managed the most remarkable season seen in Oxford before or since. The star quarterback, Glynn Griffing, was born near my family's farm, which his uncle managed, and my dad idolized him growing up, wearing No. 15 as a high school quarterback to be just like Glynn. It was the team that made my dad love football. It was also a team not discussed much, just a quick story here and there. They seemed forgotten, their legend small despite big accomplishments, and I wanted to find out why.

A few months back, I dove into the Ole Miss library's special collection, containing records and artifacts from the 1962 riots. Each page changed the way I looked at the place around me, the way I looked at the places inside myself where I love my state and its traditions. Why hadn't I been taught any of this in school? I'd had an entire Mississippi history class in junior high. We talked mostly about Indians. More recently, my aggravation had been stoked by ignorant election emails from my great-uncle in Jackson, ones that seemed to be from a time long past.

I came upon a box containing two small notebooks used by the soldier tasked with guarding James Meredith, the first African American student at Ole Miss. They were Nifty brand, cost a dime, and were filled with descriptions of suspicious characters, of license plate numbers and names. I flipped through the pages . . . until a familiar name stopped me cold.

My great-uncle, the emailer's brother. Last name: Wright.

Two questions went through my mind:

What is the cost of knowing our past? . . .

And what is the cost of not?

I. THE BATTLE

1. SEPTEMBER 25, 1962

Attorney General Robert F. Kennedy places a phone call to Ross Barnett, the segregationist governor of Mississippi. They've been talking for weeks now. Every day, it's a different story. Mississippi politicos joke that whoever gets to Barnett last wins the argument. Kennedy is finding this out firsthand. Federal courts have ordered Ole Miss to admit Meredith. Barnett is resisting. A bumbling and unpopular politician—he'd been booed at Ole Miss games—he is now soaking in some newfound adulation for standing down the Kennedy brothers. It is a drug, and Barnett's hooked.

"We have been part of the United States," he tells Kennedy, "but I don't know whether we are or not."

There is silence on the phone. Kennedy doesn't know what to say, really. It's 1962. And Mississippi is threatening to secede?

"Are you getting out of the union?" he finally asks.

2. SEPTEMBER 29, 1962

The players can hear the noise. They cannot see anything but the locker room walls inside Mississippi Memorial Stadium in Jackson, but they can hear the noise.

It's halftime, and Ole Miss is beating overmatched Kentucky, though just barely, 7–0. What's worse, the Rebels have been uncharacteristically sloppy. Early in the game, bruising fullback Buck Randall, considered by many the baddest SOB on campus, has a touchdown called back because of a penalty. This is not like a team coached by John Vaught, who runs his squad like a corporation. All business, no rah-rah speeches. The critics love to pick on Vaught for his soft schedules, his inability to win a big game, the fact that his team couldn't tackle LSU's Billy Cannon three years earlier with a national title on the line, but nobody ever faults his discipline.

The scene in the stands above the locker room is alive with color, a circus of motion, most of the 41,000 spectators furiously waving Confederate battle flags. The band marches onto the field in Confederate battle flag uniforms, carrying the world's largest Confederate battle flag. The band plays "Dixie." The crowd sings along, waves those flags, cheers. There are no black fans in the stadium, and on nights like these, it's easy to forget the South lost the war. In some ways, that's precisely the point.

A young politician named William Winter looks around and feels like a stranger. How can this be happening? The crowd shakes with indignation, the air filling with Rebel yells, from the mouths of doctors and bankers and lawyers and priests, and Winter thinks: *So this must be what a Nazi rally felt like.*

The crowd screams for Barnett to speak. Unbeknownst to them, hours earlier, he'd made a secret deal with the Kennedys to have Meredith enrolled. But, once again, he's on the verge of changing his mind. He has been so hated and now is so loved. He can't help himself; the enthusiasm of the crowd is taking him out to sea.

A microphone appears at midfield. A single spotlight swings across the field until it illuminates the governor. Barnett walks to the microphone. The crowd falls silent. He raises his right fist. "I loooooove Mississippi!" he yells.

The crowd roars. Even the moderates in the crowd feel chills. The flag waving grows frantic. One hundred and one years earlier, all but four students at Ole Miss dropped out of school to form Company A of the 11th Mississippi Infantry. The University Greys. On July 3, 1863, at Gettysburg, the unit rose from safety and made a futile rush from Seminary Ridge. Everyone was killed or injured, and history named their suicide mission Pickett's Charge. The school's sports teams would be called Rebels to honor their sacrifice. The young men and women in the stands today are just three generations removed from those soldiers. One of them, senior Curtis Wilkie, received a letter from his mother before the game. She anticipated what the young man might be feeling: *Son, Your great-grandfather Gilmer set out to fight the federals from Ole Miss with the University Greys, called the Lamar Rifles, nearly a hundred years ago. He didn't accomplish a thing! See that you don't get involved!!!*

William Winter grew up listening to his grandfather tell about riding with the Confederate army. The male students especially, who've grown up with similar stories, feel something move deep inside themselves. Later, most will deny it. But tonight, the emotions are real, and in case anyone misses the connection, the next morning's paper will devote two pages to Robert E. Lee's march north.

Barnett looks out at them and feels the emotions too.

"I looooooove her people!"

The roar gets louder.

"I looooooove her customs!"

The yelling and screaming drowns him out, and Barnett doesn't say another word. He doesn't have to. He stands at midfield, soaking up the love and adulation, a wide grin spread across his face.

3. THE PRIDE BEFORE THE FALL

Mississippi in the fall of 1962 is a doomed civilization at its apogee. Enrollment at Ole Miss stands at an all-time high. The football team has been to five consecutive bowl games, won three SEC championships in the past decade, and gone 27-2-1 in the past three years. In 1959 and 1960, Ole Miss coeds won back-to-back Miss America crowns. Pageant moms around the country send their daughters to Oxford, an invasion of leggy blondes whose influence can still be seen in the state's gene pool.

Of course, that's just half of the story. To be an African American in this world isn't much different than it was in 1861, and the Mississippi of 1962 has been forming in earnest for 14 years, with segregation becoming more and more formalized. In 1948, President Harry Truman signed the first civil rights legislation. That year, something new popped up at Ole Miss football games: Confederate battle flags. The band started playing "Dixie." Someone commissioned the largest Rebel flag ever for the band to carry onto the field. Vaught, in his second season as coach, gave fans something to cheer about. The football team might not have intended it, but to people in the state, the squad became the last Confederate soldiers. "You see them moving away from this larger national narrative," says D. Gorton, an Ole Miss student who witnessed the Meredith riots and later became a photographer for *The New York Times*. "They're no longer part of the United States. They really saw themselves as an archipelago. That led to their great football. What else would explain it?"

By 1962, the atmosphere is intoxicating for half the population, toxic for the other. A young African American boy named LeRoy Wadlington, who'd grow up to be an influential preacher, lives off the highway leading out of town and learns to dread home football games. Fans, many drunk on illegal booze, yell racial slurs at his family as they inch back home. The black community feels under siege.

On the day of the Kentucky game, radio stations around the state play "Dixie" over and over again. Myrlie Evers, whose husband, Medgar, is head of the Mississippi NAACP, is working in her kitchen, with two radios playing for surround sound, and as the hours go by, she catches herself singing along with the radio: *I wish I was in the land of cotton; old times there are not forgotten . . .* She is horrified. She despises "Dixie," but even she is being sucked in.

By halftime, when Barnett has finished his speech, the state is in a frenzy. Leaflets circulate through the stadium with lyrics to a new song, which also had been printed in that morning's paper. A few people leave in disgust, but many stay and sing:

> *Never, never, never, never*
> *No, never, never, never*
> *We will not yield an inch of any field.*
> *Fix us another toddy, ain't yielding to nobody.*
> *Ross is standing like Gibraltar; he shall never falter.*
> *Ask us what we say, it's to hell with Bobby K.*
> *Never shall our emblems go*
> *From Colonel Reb to Old Black Joe.*

That's all Barnett needs to hear. The deal is off. James Meredith will not be enrolled.

Never.

4. SEPTEMBER 29, 1962

Vaught brings his team out for the second half. He knows the whole
state is being pulled into something, and it's his job to keep it from
destroying his squad. This group has worked so hard the past few
years, and these players seem capable of finally getting it right.
Seven times in the past 14 years, he has come within one loss or one
tie of a perfect record. It eats at him.

The Rebels go on to beat Kentucky, though they manage just one
more touchdown. As the players are pulling on their street clothes,
Barnett heads back to the governor's mansion, where he will call
Washington to reveal what he'd decided earlier, amid the halftime
adulation: no deal.

In Washington, the wheels are turning. Staff members take papers to President John F. Kennedy that, when signed, will federalize
the Mississippi National Guard and begin the process of sending
U.S. Army regulars to the South, something he'd desperately hoped
to avoid.

Kennedy sits down in the Treaty Room to sign and date the document. "Is it past midnight?" he asks.

"It's 20 seconds past 12," a staffer says.

Kennedy nods, signs the order, then writes the date: September
30, 1962. The genie is out of the bottle, and no force on earth, least
of all Ross Barnett, will be able to push it back in.

5. SEPTEMBER 30, 1962

James Meredith waits. He has been waiting his entire life. When he
was just a kid, his daddy told him stories about their family, about
how his great-grandfather had been the last legitimate chief of the
Choctaw Nation. The indignity of that fall from grace cast a shadow
on Meredith's early life, and it shaped him, convinced him to leave
segregated Mississippi and join the Air Force, sent him to Asia,
brought him back home a 29-year-old who wanted to destroy white

supremacy. On the day of Kennedy's inauguration, he applied to Ole Miss.

In other words, he has been preparing for this moment for decades, mostly getting his mind ready, reading, trying to find out the secret to ordinary men doing extraordinary things. One thing he read sticks with him. Back in the day, he says, the reigning pope and his army conquered Rome, and after the battle, the pope walked alone into the city, stone cold, to show people that he had no fear of troops or weapons or death. He knew his calm in the face of such danger would intimidate those who wished him harm. For years, Meredith has practiced making the face he imagines the pope's face must have looked like on his lonely stroll into Rome.

Meredith fought in the courts, eventually winning the right to matriculate. For most of September, federal agents were trying to enroll him but were turned back by politicians. Meredith and the feds thought a deal had been arranged, that the waiting was finally over, but Barnett's call fixed that.

That's OK. Meredith knows how to wait. In his hometown of Kosciusko, Mississippi, a field of pine trees grows slowly. His father gave them to him when Meredith got out of the military; one day, his dad told him, these trees would be worth something. They grow, inch by inch. As long as something lives, it can reach the sky. Meredith, just a small man—5-foot-6, 135 pounds—with the biggest dreams, finds comfort in that. Sitting at a Naval Air Station outside Memphis, Meredith watches a pro football game on television as the politicians work on yet another deal. Finally, fed up, Robert Kennedy threatens Barnett. The president is going on live television to tell the nation, and Mississippians in particular, that the governor has been promising them one thing while dealing with the hated Kennedys behind their backs.

"You mean the president is going to say that tonight?"

"Of course he is; you broke your word. Now you suggest we send in troops, fighting their way through a barricade."

"Why don't you fly in this afternoon? Please let us treat what we say as confidential."

That's what it takes. Segregation is about to end at Ole Miss. Meredith and head marshal Jim McShane climb into a green, twin-engine Border Patrol Cessna and take off. Destination: Oxford, Mississippi.

As Meredith and McShane make their way south, Vaught settles into the film room and begins to work. Two wins down, seven to go. In six days, the Rebels will face undefeated Houston.

6. THE FEDS ARRIVE

The players return from the game on their own, many going home for a night. On Sunday, they begin the trek back to campus. Buck Randall heads to Oxford from the Delta, through the flatlands, white cotton all around, waiting to be picked. He listens to music, not the news, and has no idea what waits on the other side. He has deep blue eyes, a boxer's nose, and a hard chin. Anger bubbles just beneath the surface with Randall, always, though he has trouble explaining it. When Buck was a kid, his father was in the pen, and Buck had to live with a high school teammate instead of his own family. He never walks away from an insult, large or small. Stories, some of them true, about him taking on two and three guys at a time, stacking 'em like firewood, make the rounds of Miller Hall, where the football team lives.

A bunch of the guys ride a bus back to campus from the airport, down University Avenue toward the statue of the Confederate soldier, honoring the students killed at Gettysburg. As they rumble toward the center of campus, quarterback Glynn Griffing stares out a window. Federal marshals have surrounded the Lyceum Building, the oldest structure on campus, where Meredith will register in the morning.

What are they doing here? Griffing wonders.

Players wander off to see what the commotion is all about. Sam

Owen, a wise guy lineman nicknamed Soup Bone, hangs around at the back of the crowd, taking in the scene. So does Louis Guy, one of the most popular players on campus. Jimmy Weatherly, a sophomore quarterback who is struggling with wanting to be a musician while everyone else wants him to replace Griffing, watches too.

Hundreds of students fill the circle of grass in front of the marshals who have gathered near the Lyceum Building. It feels almost like a pep rally, topped by a large dollop of defiance. Coeds ride on the backs of convertibles around the street in front of the building, Rebel flags flying from the cars. The familiar chants from the stadium ring out, albeit slightly altered:

> *Hotty Toddy*
> *Gosh Almighty*
> *Who the hell are we?*
> *Flim-flam*
> *Bim-bam*
> *White folks, by damn!*

And . . .

> *Two, four, six, eight . . . hell, no, we won't integrate.*

And . . .

> *Two, one, four, three, we hate Kennedy!*

As the sun sinks down, casting shadows from the tall oaks and magnolias, things begin to get really ugly. For some, nothing—not the campus, not the South, none of it—will ever be beautiful again. The marshals grit their teeth. Darkness settles over Oxford.

It will be a long time before sunrise.

7. A MOB SCENE

The players watch the madness unfold. Some join the mob. One player, a burly ex-boxer-turned-lineman named Don Dickson, disrupts an interview while a friend smashes the reporter's camera. Mostly, though, they stand to the side, some amazed, others frightened.

The violence increases, as if the dark offers absolution. First, it's a smashed camera. Then a tossed cigarette. The mob surrounds a Dallas television reporter, George Yoder, sitting in his station wagon with his wife in the passenger seat. Someone reaches in and grabs his camera, which is thrown at the marshals. Then the mob turns on Yoder's wife, reaching for her like a scene from a zombie movie, screaming, "N— loving Yankee bitch!" She is from Jackson, Mississippi.

Finally, after watching the scene with amusement, some state troopers lead the Yoders to safety. Later, their car will be flipped and burned. The mob closes in on the marshals. Missiles come from every direction, starting adolescent, slowly becoming more adult, from rotten eggs to firebombs. A construction site not far away is discovered, and bricks rain down on the white-painted helmets of the marshals too.

A group takes down the Stars and Stripes and runs up the Confederate flag. The chain snarls at half-staff, where the flag will remain throughout the night, the Stars and Bars a beacon heralding a long-gone moment when a bunch of college boys rose and charged from Seminary Ridge.

8. MASS INSANITY

Back at the Lyceum, it's a little after 7, and something has to give. A campus security official finds Vaught in the film room: Would the coach be willing to try to calm the crowd? Vaught wanders through the mob for a while, then rushes to Miller Hall.

At 7:30, Barnett goes on the radio to announce Meredith has been brought to Mississippi by force. Before signing off, he issues a warning to the marshals: "Gentlemen, you are trampling on the sovereignty of this great state and depriving it of every vestige of honor and respect as a member of the United States. You are destroying the Constitution of the United States. May God have mercy on your souls."

Twenty minutes later, Marshal McShane orders his men to put on their gas masks. More bricks. A bottle hits a marshal on his arm, and liquid splatters on him. It burns: acid from the chemistry building next door. A few minutes after that, as President Kennedy prepares to address the nation, a heavy length of lead pipe bounces off the head of a marshal, denting his helmet. The marshals grip their billy clubs tighter; the students at the front can see their knuckles turning white.

Jojo Wilkins, a senior wide receiver, standing close to the marshals, by a small magnolia tree near the sidewalk, hears someone shout, "Let 'em have it!" All hell breaks loose, the marshals spraying tear gas into the crowd, the rounds sounding like helicopter rotors turning. A haze covers the campus, and tears stream down everyone's face.

Nicholas Katzenbach, the deputy attorney general, picks up the open line to the White House inside the Lyceum. Robert Kennedy answers. "Bob," Katzenbach says, "I'm very unhappy to report that we've had to fire tear gas."

"I think I should really go tell the president about it," Robert Kennedy says. "He's just going on the air."

The attorney general runs toward the Oval Office, where his brother is about to go live. He arrives moments too late, just in time to hear the president begin. JFK's words carry over radios of cars parked near the Lyceum in Oxford, adding an eerie new soundtrack: the whoop of the tear gas guns, the screaming of the mob, the cloud covering the campus, with the voice of the president of the United States in the background, urging them to remain calm: "You have a great tradition to uphold, a tradition of honor and courage, won on the field of battle and on the gridiron."

No one listens.

9. "DON'T GO OUT"

With tear gas seeping into the team dorm, through the towels beneath the doors and windows, Vaught gathers his players. The sounds of explosions frighten them, as does a new sound: gunshots. Most are hunters, and they listen as the caliber of the rounds slowly rises. While assistant coaches patrol the halls, Vaught says, "We have to band together. We have a purpose. We must keep our poise."

The players get the message. Pull tight. Stay together, no matter what happens. The guys worry a lot that night, about the violence and about their season. Some try to sleep, but the explosions and gunshots make that hard. A few players help wash out the eyes of students who stumble into the dorm. Assistant coach Wobble Davidson, on patrol, keeps reminding the players, "Don't go out." For most people, the fear of Davidson, a former Marine who crawled into caves in World War II, is enough. They don't want to have to run up and down the 65 steps of the stadium, 10 laps in 10 minutes, or do it again.

But Buck Randall wants to go out. Telling him to stay put is like telling him not to eat ice cream. He slips into the night.

10. FACE-TO-FACE WITH THE CARNAGE

The battle is growing desperate. The marshals are running out of tear gas. Bricks and bottles and iron spikes rain down. Gunshots ring out. Thugs drive into town from Alabama and Arkansas and Tennessee and Louisiana, one carload sending two barrels of buckshot into the home of LeRoy Wadlington, the African American kid who lives off the highway leading into town. His father grabs his own gun and orders his family to lie down in the back of the house.

The Civil War has begun anew, and the North is losing. Later, the events of the night will seem impossible: an Associated Press reporter shot in the back with birdshot. A bulldozer and fire truck stolen and driven at the marshals. A French reporter is shot dead. So is a local resident. Dozens of marshals are shot or injured. A sniper sets up on the Confederate statue, first shooting out the lights, then turning his weapon on the Lyceum, pushing the marshals inside, high-powered deer rounds shattering the door and window frames.

During the night, Chief Burns Tatum, the head of security for the university, spots Randall in the crowd and pulls him into the besieged Lyceum, where Randall comes face-to-face with the carnage. In a corridor, shot through the neck, Marshal Gene Same from Indianapolis is bleeding out on the floor as his fellow officers kneel over him, helpless and frustrated.

"Where the hell's the doctor?"

"We're trying to get one!"

"Try, hell. This man's dying!"

Tatum tells the marshals that Randall plays football for the Rebels. That sends some of them over the edge. "Come on, son," a marshal snarls. "We've got something to show you." They push him real close to Same. "You see him? You see him? He's bleeding to death. You get out there and tell those bastards they've killed a man."

McShane decides to send the big football hero out into the mob. "Tell those people to disperse now," McShane says, "or we're gonna start shooting—students and all."

Randall heads to the Grove, calling for people's attention. Gorton, standing near the Lyceum, will remember, years later, what he saw: "Buck didn't give a 'speech.' He sought people out. He implored. There was a strange quality about that from a tough guy who looked haunted that night. Bear in mind that this was the toughest guy in the Delta. It was the end of an era. He must have lost his mind because Buck Randall was always in favor of mayhem and misery and murder. That's what he loved. There was some badass motherfuckers around. Of all the badass motherfuckers, I'd like to nominate

him for as mean as they got. Nothing on the face of the earth would
scare that guy. But that night did."

Scared or not, Randall tries to explain what they've done. "There's
a man in there dying," he says.

A crowd begins to gather, and people don't like what they're hear-
ing. Someone yells, "Pull him down!" Another yells, "Murder him!"
Every time someone challenges him, Randall snarls, "Come on, boy.
Come on. Try it. I'll kill you."

The people who know him, the students, don't get within a dozen
feet. The folks who came just to fight sense some major alpha mojo
because they don't mess with him either. But that doesn't mean they
intend to listen. They mock him. This goes on for 10 minutes. Finally, Randall gives up. The crowd separates to let him through, and
he walks back toward Miller Hall, alone, disappearing into the haze.

11. OCTOBER 1, 1962

Through the long night, the marshals wait for the U.S. Army regulars. The cavalry, in the form of the 101st and 82nd Airborne and an
elite military police unit, is on the way. Troops land in Memphis,
Tennessee, and head the 85 miles south to the Ole Miss campus. For
the first time in a century, the U.S. Army is invading the state of
Mississippi. Black families leave their homes and stand on the side
of the highway, silent, as if at attention, watching the Union army
speed toward Oxford.

On campus, the troops dismount and rush to rescue the marshals and local National Guardsmen, who are almost out of tear gas
again and scared of being overrun, 160 wounded, 28 of them by gun-
fire. The troops form a wedge and march past the sorority houses,
where girls curse and throw books. They march through a storm of
bricks and Molotov cocktails, never breaking stride. The precision
scares the rioters, as do the shining fixed bayonets. The sound of
hundreds of rounds of live ammunition being jacked into hundreds
of chambers echoes off the old white buildings, chilling the crowd.

The soldiers march toward University Avenue and, at last, the formation is within sight of the marshals, whose relief comes out as a long, loud cheer. By a little after 5 a.m., the troops have pushed the rioters off the campus. Students, the football team at Miller Hall, and Meredith over at Baxter, begin dressing for class, the smell of tear gas still heavy in the air. Marshals slump over in the Lyceum, surrounded by cigarette butts and bloody gauze. Others eat C rations under trees in front of the building. Two men, the French reporter and a local jukebox repairman, lie dead. The campus priest takes down the Confederate flag. The battle is over, and now a state, a school, and a football team have to pick up the pieces.

A light rain begins to fall.

II. RECONSTRUCTION

1. OCTOBER 1, 1962

Sam Owen wakes up early, slipping out of Miller Hall. The sun is up, shedding light on the destruction. The walk to the Lyceum takes only a few minutes. Around campus, little puffs of tear gas rise from the grass. It's hard to breathe. He feels as if he has walked into a swamp.

He sees the burned-out skeletons of cars, some of them flipped over, still smoldering, sending black smoke into the air. A bulldozer and fire truck rest at strange angles, as if tossed by a giant toddler. At the Lyceum, chunks of wood have been blown out by rifle fire.

He has never thought about segregation before. Not really. Never broken it down to its essentials: his people keeping another group of people from being free, by laws, by social order, and by violence. He has never questioned what he has been taught, that it is good for everyone. This is just the way things are done. He isn't for segregation—his high school had been integrated, which made his father livid—but he isn't really against it either.

But this? He didn't know segregation looked like this. For a moment, he just stares, his life divided into two parts now. On one side, this mystical thing: segregation, the Old Mississippi. On the other: the New Mississippi, an honest-to-god war zone, the physical manifestation of hate and fear. He looks back at his life and realizes a Rubicon stands here, and he has crossed it. The cars and the gunshots and the bleeding marshals, all of it works its way through his brain and into his heart.

After checking on his girlfriend, Judy, he finds a pay phone and calls his folks back in Tennessee. He tells them what has happened and that he is safe.

"Do you want to come home?" they ask.

Not a chance.

"We gotta play Houston," Owen says.

2. WILL THE SHOWDOWN GO ON?

The game is only five days away, and thousands of federal troops are camped out on Vaught's practice fields. More are camped outside town, one radio call away from marching on Oxford. Helicopters move men and equipment. Troops screen every car coming onto campus, and they will for months, looking in trunks and under seats for weapons. Meredith goes to class, escorted by armed guards, harassed the entire way. The first walk of the first morning brings frothing crowds. Someone gets right in his face and screams, "Was it worth two lives, n——!?" Meredith puts on his pope face.

Some politicians are demanding a total shutdown of the school. Straw polls estimate half of Mississippians want the university closed. There is really only one overwhelming reason not to shutter the place: the highly ranked Rebels. No school, no football. Few have more influence in Mississippi than Vaught. Robert Kennedy calls him after the riot: "Coach Vaught, I want you to do what you can to keep the situation calm."

Vaught certainly appreciates the call, the ego boost of the attorney general of the United States needing *him*. Vaught has a lot of good traits, but he is also vain. He is bald, and hates it, and always wears hats. The team calls him Slick, but only behind his back. He needs glasses but won't wear them. If it's sunny and he can wear prescription shades, he is a great game coach. If not, he can't see the action and sometimes doesn't know who is in the game or what plays are being run. "Vaught was a good organizer," Frank Kinard, a member of the '62 team and the son of assistant coach Bruiser Kinard, would say years later. "On the day of a game, he didn't know where he was."

Even if the school is to remain open, pressure is growing to cancel the Houston game. The government does the math: thousands of outsiders, pouring into town, gathering in one place, right next to thousands of the hated federal troops. Add in booze, and the passions of a game, and, well, they just tried that a few days earlier. Two plus two equals four.

The game is now only four days away, and Katzenbach wants it called off. Vaught argues with him, during several conversations, until finally Katzenbach flies to Washington to meet with Robert Kennedy. The news out of that meeting isn't good for Vaught: No way in hell is there going to be a public event on that campus.

The game is now three days away. Across campus, Meredith eats his first meal in the cafeteria. One student even walks over and shakes his hand.

The game is now two days away.

Among the players, the rumor mill is going wild. On Monday and Tuesday, they're told the game will be in Oxford. On Wednesday, they're told it will be in Houston. By the end of the week, after contentious negotiations with the government, Ole Miss–Houston is set for Jackson.

The game is now just minutes away.

Once again, the team gathers in the locker room, the same one from just a week before. Everything is different now. Vaught almost never gives pregame speeches, thinks they are silly. But this . . .

well, he needs to say something. Vaught feels like the entire university is riding on the backs of his team. He needs them to understand, these young guys. He needs them to see. "It is very important that we play this game, boys," Vaught says. "And we have to win it."

The team roars in response and rushes out of the locker room onto the field. Vaught gets chills watching them. The Rebels dominate undefeated Houston 40–7, with Griffing throwing three touchdown passes to Guy. But the most emotional two ovations of the day have nothing to do with the game.

One comes at the beginning, when Barnett enters his box. The other comes when the public address man announces other scores from around the country. Michigan, he tells them, has beaten Army, the hated invader of Ole Miss, 17–0.

3. OCTOBER 8, 1962

Two days later, about 6:30 p.m., Meredith heads for the cafeteria for dinner. Most of the students have eaten already and are milling around. A few more arrive, then a few more, until a crowd has formed. Meredith, accompanied by a marshal, sits at a table near a window, working his way through hamburger steak and potatoes. The crowd chants: "Eat, n——, eat."

A student throws a hand-sized rock through the cafeteria window; it lands three feet away, glass falling on the marshal and Meredith. Troops rush to the scene. The mob hurls the usual projectiles: lit cigarettes, rocks, bottles. Someone lets the air out of the marshal's tires. During the commotion, Meredith, shaken, is hustled out the back.

The insults continue, along with the constant cursing. Effigies hang from dorm windows. Mail pours in, more positive than negative, but the negative is truly vile. Meredith reads every letter.

Two students who eat dinner with him have their rooms wrecked, "n—— lover" painted on their walls with shoe polish. Later, a political science major, a girl named Judith Gardner, makes the mistake of sitting next to Meredith in class. Harassment grows so vicious that she is forced to leave school and her family is forced to move from the state.

One afternoon, two football players stand outside the old union, both boys from the Delta, watching the pretty girls go by. Along comes Meredith, with marshals in front and behind and soldiers nearby. One of the players starts fuming, getting jittery, one thought rolling through his head: "You know, it's sorry that damn n—— being up here with these white girls."

Stunning his teammate, the player jumps out in front of Meredith and hollers, "You black son of a bitch!" Then he rears back to hit Meredith, but a marshal grabs him. The player slugs the marshal and takes off running, through the dining area, bowling over a coed with an armful of books, heads for the back, swinging open the door, knocking back the soldier who'd been waiting for him. The guy runs for Miller Hall as troops search. Breathing hard, he tries to figure out what went haywire. He had never done anything like that before.

His teammate finds him back at the dorm. "Man, what the hell happened to you?"

"I don't know. That wasn't me. I went crazy."

He's far from the only one.

4. OCTOBER 20, 1962

A heavy, nasty rain is coming down, rolling off Vaught's coat, finally soaking through. The final whistle blows, the remaining fans rush to their cars, and Vaught starts the slow walk to the locker room, where he will shed layers of wet clothes. "Man, I'm glad that's over," he says of Ole Miss's 21–0 victory over Tulane on the sloppy field. Despite the one-sided whuppin', the Green Wave players are chatty after the game, talking about how the Rebels aren't as good as they were last year, how they aren't in the same league with Alabama and Texas.

Other observers seem to share those feelings. Ole Miss keeps winning, but the team continues its steady drop in the national polls, some voters citing weak opponents and lackluster performances. After the Tulane victory, the Associated Press poll lowers Ole Miss from fourth to seventh. After beating Vandy a week later, the team stays at seven, probably too far back to climb to No. 1. Mississippians wonder whether there aren't other reasons. An AP reporter was shot in Oxford, you know. Others believe—hope?—a victory over LSU will fix everything and put Ole Miss back into the thick of the national title hunt.

The LSU game is just a week away, and all the old anxiety is flooding back. LSU ruined three perfect seasons, in 1958, '59, and '60, and fans and players obsess over this pattern heading into Tiger Stadium. The '59 loss particularly haunts; many considered that year's Ole Miss squad one of the greatest college teams ever assembled. (Decades later, rankings guru Jeff Sagarin would call that group the third-best team between 1956 and 1995.) The night of that game, a 10-year-old from Drew, Mississippi, named Archie Manning cried himself to sleep. Yes, the losses have taken a toll on the psyches of football-loving Mississippians.

The stress of the coming game affects everyone. Vaught locks down practices and begins working on secret plays. On Monday night, students slingshot cherry bombs at the servicemen protecting Baxter Hall. One cherry bomb lands in a military police jeep, scattering several soldiers. When the marshals and soldiers give chase, other students repel them with eggs and bottles. The AP interviews a student leader who blames the chaos on a "general restlessness typical at Ole Miss before its football team plays Louisiana State."

Tuesday is worse. Someone throws a Coke bottle through the back window of the car transporting Meredith, and the glass cuts the face of a marshal. More cherry bombs land near soldiers.

Then there's the flier, several hundred of which flutter to the ground from a dorm window near Baxter Hall:

KENNEDY is out to destroy AMERICA, because he is a sick, sick communist. RED JACK KENNEDY intends to soon commit you to CUBA and Betray you there, just as TRUMAN betrayed the boys in KOREA. Red Jack Kennedy is the most DANGEROUS ENEMY AMERICA has ever had.

Finally sick of the abuse, the troops affix bayonets to their assault rifles and march through the dormitory halls. Two guns, a machete, a tear gas grenade, and a cache of fireworks are found. School chancellor J.D. Williams issues a new edict: Any further antisocial behavior will result in immediate expulsions. A pep rally scheduled for that Tuesday evening is postponed.

Two nights later, the pep rally is held. When the rally is over, some 200 students sprint toward Miller Hall, two blocks away. As they approach Baxter Hall, where Meredith lives, all the soldiers snap alert. One adjusts his gas mask and gets the tear gas gun ready to go. But the students race past Baxter and stand outside Miller Hall for a half hour cheering the team, desperate for the No. 6 Rebels to beat No. 4 LSU. For the first time in what seems like forever, Vaught is happy; he thinks this is the healthiest thing he has seen on campus since before the riots.

5. NOVEMBER 3, 1962

The Rebels gather at the tunnel. The concrete walls seem to amplify the noise of Tiger Stadium. Nearby, Mike the Tiger lounges in his cage and, without warning, lets out a hungry growl. Wilkins jumps. "It would scare the living shit out of you," Billy Champion will say later.

Jitters pass from one Rebel to the next like the flu. A stiff wind blows across the field, 15 miles an hour, coming in off the river. LSU, tough to beat here, takes a 7–0 lead with a little more than two minutes left in the half. Despite the buildup, or maybe because of it, the

Rebels look sluggish. Is it happening again? Another promising season lost in Death Valley?

Ole Miss starts a drive of its own but still seems a bit sleepy. Then one of LSU's defensive tackles pops all-everything lineman Jim Dunaway in the face, bloodying his lip. The sight and taste of his own blood awakens Big Jim, who bulldozes his man the rest of the night, opening up big holes. With 23 seconds left in the half, Griffing has his team at the LSU 10. After a couple of incompletions, Griffing hits A. J. Holloway, who juggles the ball but secures it just as two LSU defenders grab him at about the 3-yard line. As the clock ticks to zero, he breaks free, crossing the goal line. A missed extra point leaves the Rebels down 7–6, but at least they have life.

In the second half, with Ole Miss at the LSU 21, Vaught pulls out the trickery they'd been practicing all week. Chuck Morris swings to the right, faking a run, only to pull up short and toss the ball to Guy 18 yards downfield, the first completion of a halfback pass by the Rebels in four years. Two plays later, Griffing finds Guy to put the Rebels up for good. (They wouldn't beat a top-five team on the road again for 46 years, until last season's upset at Florida.)

As time runs out, the players run off the field, yelling, "We're No. 1!" The locker room is a madhouse. Vaught stands calmly amid the chaos. *What an effort*, he thinks. *Best I've ever seen.* He'd sweated through his shirt out there. This is what they'd worked for, what he wanted. He can't wait for the new rankings to come out. In such a tumultuous year, his Ole Miss Rebels are the best team in the nation. He is sure of it. A reporter asks whether he has any doubt how the wire service polls should go.

"None at all," he says.

6. NOVEMBER 4, 1962

The next day, the students awake tired, hungover but elated, ready to check out the polls. The news isn't good. The victory jumps the Rebels two spots to fourth, but undefeated Alabama and USC are still ahead of them. Both will have to lose for Ole Miss to have a shot at a national championship.

The team stays focused on the one thing it can control: winning. Among players walking to class or to practice or just sitting in front of their metal lockers, the refrain is always the same: "We ain't getting beat."

7. NOVEMBER 17, 1962

Two weeks later, a sliver of national title hope remains. Ole Miss is ranked third, with USC at No. 2 and Alabama No. 1. With all-everything quarterback Joe Namath dominating opponents, the Tide look unbeatable. Today, the Rebels have an easy game against the Vols, and Bama is taking on Georgia Tech.

Rain falls again before the game, hard, soaking the field. The Rebels are 10-point favorites but play not to lose instead of to win, clinging to a slim lead as the Vols are driving late in the third quarter. Nobody drives on the Rebels—they have the best defense in the country—but someone forgot to tell Tennessee.

Defensive back Guy lines up on the right side, worrying about yet another running play, when he notices the Tennessee receiver looking around. Guy thinks: *What's he doing?* He takes a few steps back, watches the end come out toward him, sees the ball coming, and eases in front of it, intercepting the pass 3 yards deep in the end zone. Some 103 yards later, Guy, untouched, reaches the end zone at the other end of the field, securing the victory. When he gets to the sideline, Vaught finds him. "God bless you, son," he says.

Meanwhile, Alabama, everyone's favorite to win it all, improbably loses to Georgia Tech. USC slides up to No. 1, with Ole Miss at No. 2. But the Rebels' good luck doesn't hold. A week later, as they sit idly at home—Vaught always caught flak for his weak scheduling—No. 3 Wisconsin beats No. 5 Minnesota and jumps the Rebels in the poll. A national championship seems impossible now. USC needs to lose to a weak Notre Dame team and the Rebels need to beat

Mississippi State to a pulp in their season-ending rivalry game to have any chance of sufficiently impressing skeptical AP voters.

8. DECEMBER 1, 1962

With time running out in the fourth quarter, Ole Miss has the ball just past midfield and is holding a narrow 7–6 lead against Mississippi State. On first down, Vaught sends in Weatherly, who is supposed to run a familiar play, with the back following a pulling guard. But Weatherly forgets they've changed a few details of the play—the tackle is supposed to pull instead of the guard—so he's out of position and misses the handoff to Dave Jennings, who hits the line without the ball. Everyone on the field is thinking fumble. But Weatherly still has the ball, safely tucked away, and as he sees State's defensive end crashing toward Jennings, Weatherly turns upfield. Ahead is an expanse of green, 43 yards worth, and it's empty of defenders.

Weatherly runs down the sideline, and it's one of the weirdest moments of his life because nobody in the stands catches on for a few seconds and he's running in silence. Finally, the crowd realizes he still has the ball and goes nuts. Weatherly scores, and when he comes back to the sideline, he's laughing. He can't believe what just happened. The first person to reach him is team trainer Doc Knight.

"Doc," Weatherly says, still laughing, "I missed the handoff."

"Don't tell anybody," Knight blurts. "Don't tell anybody."

Ole Miss closes out the game, another one way too close, 13–6. Sam Owen stands on the field as the clock counts down to zero, and their accomplishment hits him. They've gone through an entire season unbeaten and untied, something no Ole Miss team had done before. Louis Guy runs off the field toward the locker room, and on the way, a 14-year-old named Ray Mabus asks him for his chinstrap. Guy hands it to him, and Mabus takes it home, a treasured possession.

The locker room is quiet. A few hours later, they get the news. No national title. USC beat Notre Dame. The Trojans are 10–0, and they will face No. 2 Wisconsin in the Rose Bowl. The winner will be the national champion.

The Rebels' final game would be played for pride.

9. DECEMBER 7, 1962

A cold wind blows through campus. Students wearing sweaters and overcoats carry books past Meredith. They look away. Confederate flags hang from the windows, but no one screams at him. He isn't welcome—if he tried to hold the door open, most students would stand in place until he gave up—but the threats of violence have slowed to a trickle. A forced tolerance has settled over the campus.

At Baxter Hall, the living room in his suite is a marshal's command post, filled with smoke. His bedroom has bunk beds, one neatly made up in Air Force blankets, the other used for storing books and school supplies. There are two chairs and a set of drawers. He has three pairs of shoes and one pair of slippers under the bed. On his dresser is a nameplate with his name and rank engraved in both English and Japanese. Outside, the trees are bare and a fresh coat of white paint covers the Lyceum, hiding the bullet holes.

A few blocks away, at Miller Hall, the football team winds down, too, finishing the semester, waiting on the Sugar Bowl. Vaught sits in his office and worries about his team. A loss and this group of amazing young men will fade from memory, just another Ole Miss team to almost go undefeated. They are so close to perfection yet seem lethargic in practice, worn out. *Sports Illustrated* predicts the Rebels will lose to Arkansas.

Griffing heads to New York to be on the Johnny Carson show and attend a media function in the Empire Room of the Lexington Hotel, where the great DiMaggio lives in the penthouse suite. Shooting the breeze with a bunch of sports writers, Griffing gets a little taste of how the rest of the world views Mississippi. Indeed, when he and Guy come to the Giants' training camp in the fall, all anyone wants to talk about is Meredith—in the locker room, at cocktail parties, everywhere. Already the two narratives are becoming connected. Few will ever again talk about their 1962 season without also mentioning the riot.

10. DECEMBER 31, 1962

Five . . . four . . .

Bourbon Street's packed, the Ole Miss coaches and fans spilling out of the pregame media party at Antoine's on St. Louis Street to see the last seconds of 1962 tick away. The future is uncertain. How will Mississippi react to the changes that are coming? Will it embrace the future or become more isolated, open hatred turning to silent resentment, burrowing beneath the surface, unnamed? That storm is for tomorrow. Tonight, the *brûlot*, strong French coffee laced with brandy, keeps them warm.

Three . . . two . . . one . . .

It's pandemonium, with horns blowing and bells ringing, screams, kisses, laughs, and, yes, tears.

The next day the Rebels do not get upset. They win 17–13, and it's the Buck Randall show. He'll remember this game years later as one he almost lost. He fumbles a ball and gets beat on a pass play. Others will remember him as the hero. Randall hits the Arkansas quarterback harder than he has ever been hit before. In the third quarter, Randall knocks the guy out of the game for good. The Rebels have done it. They've put together a perfect season.

A few hours later, at the Sugar Bowl banquet, the team gathers in the Roosevelt Hotel, one of the oldest places in town, long a headquarters for Huey Long, and there's no expense spared. The players stare at ice sculptures on the tables. They're given Omega watches. A table is filled with glasses of bourbon. Piles of shrimp are everywhere. And more oysters than they've ever seen. The Rebels line up two and three deep around the oysters, knocking back dozens. They don't want this night to end, so many of the players spread out through the French Quarter, most landing at Pat O'Brien's.

The drinks keep coming, tall glasses filled with booze you can't taste, a dangerous combo, and some people will later remember the police bringing a horse inside to calm things down, but it's all so blurry, so who really knows. A few Rebels end up in the fountain, and Wes Sullivan loses his shoe. Finally, Sullivan and Billy Champion limp back to the hotel just off the French Quarter. The elevator door opens, and there's one person inside: Vaught. He looks at his ragged and wet players, Wes missing a shoe. "Where you been?" he asks. "Swimming?"

As soon as they can, Sullivan and Champ get off that damn elevator. The doors shut behind them, leaving Vaught alone. An early-morning flight back to Oxford lies ahead, he's certain, as do more championships, more big wins, more bowls. He rides the elevator up through the hotel, not knowing all of this will soon disappear, fading to a whisper, a distant memory of a different time.

III. CATCHING UP

1. JUNE 12, 1963

George Wallace is forced to back down and allow two black students to enter the University of Alabama. There will be no repeat of Ole Miss. That night in Jackson, Medgar Evers pulls his powder-blue Oldsmobile into his driveway. His wife, Myrlie, who had found herself singing "Dixie" a year before, waits inside. About 150 feet away, Byron De La Beckwith steadies his .30-06 Enfield, lines Evers up in the crosshairs, and pulls the trigger once.

The bullet tears through Medgar Evers's back, crashes through a window, and comes to a rest on the kitchen table. Evers staggers for about 30 feet before collapsing. Myrlie screams, "Oh, my God, my God!" She cradles his head as his kids bend over his dying body and beg, "Daddy, get up!"

All-white juries trying De La Beckwith twice fail to reach a verdict. He will finally be convicted 31 years later.

2. AUGUST 13, 1963

James Meredith and the other soon-to-be graduates march from the library toward the Grove, passing through the Lyceum, where all the violence had taken place just months before. The last few weeks of class, Meredith wears one of Barnett's Never pins upside down.

His parents sit in the crowd as he walks across the stage, including his proud father, Moses, the son of a slave. Myrlie Evers is there too. The commencement speaker tells the graduates the South is changing, more every day, and they need to take advantage and not be left behind. Two white women watch the graduates in their hats and gowns.

"Well, I'm glad he's gone," one says.

"There'll be others," her friend replies.

3. JANUARY 1, 1964

Another Sugar Bowl, another SEC title. But something seems different. Tailback Mitch Terrell, who'd transferred before the season, realizes that whatever they'd had at Ole Miss is falling apart. He has seen tension on the coaching staff; once, a coach he was close to came into his room and cried, distraught about the infighting. "I could see the house of cards, coach-wise, fixing to fall," Terrell would say later. "I knew there were strong personality conflicts there and it wasn't going to last."

Ole Miss hasn't won an SEC title in football since.

4. DECEMBER 5, 1964

The final score stuns those in the stadium: Mississippi State 20, Ole Miss 17. For the first time since 1946, State has beaten the Rebels, the final blow to a devastating season. Ole Miss began the season highly ranked but collapsed, losing to Florida, Kentucky, and LSU, finishing the season 5-5-1 after getting beat by lowly Tulsa in the Bluebonnet Bowl.

Weatherly gets much of the blame for the bad season. Fans lash out at the quarterback's well-known music career. To them, bad coaching or recruiting didn't derail the Rebels. Rock 'n' roll did.

5. NOVEMBER 6, 1965

In Texas, they call Houston halfback Warren McVea "Wondrous Warren." He is the first African American to play against the Ole Miss Rebels, and on this day, he is uncoverable: catching touchdown passes of 80 and 84 yards, leading the Cougars to a 17–3 upset of Ole Miss.

Robert Khayat, the kicker for the Washington Redskins, is watching the Rebels from afar. Not long ago he was the big man on campus: star of the '59 football team, elected Colonel Rebel, an honor given to the most popular male student. But he sees the Rebels refusing to recruit African American players and realizes the dynasty is fading. People won't remember Ole Miss for the dominant teams and the Miss Americas and the Sugar Bowl victories.

They will remember it for a long night in 1962.

6. MARCH 18, 1966

Robert Kennedy walks into the packed basketball arena on the Ole Miss campus. He has been invited to speak, and so many people want to listen that the administration had to move it here. When the crowd of more than 5,000 sees him, they give him a standing ovation.

During his talk, he makes fun of the bizarre phone conversations he'd had with Barnett. The crowd roars with laughter. Later, the former governor will lash out at Kennedy, claiming he lied about those phone calls. He calls Kennedy "a hypocritical left-wing beat-nik without a beard."

7. OCTOBER 17, 1970

The old program has one gasp left. With Archie Manning at quar-terback and a return to the Sugar Bowl the year before, Ole Miss is once again highly ranked, fourth in the nation, and undefeated through four games. They're talking national championship again. They've got historically weak Southern Mississippi next. But USM has an African American running back named Willie Heidelberg, who runs wild through the vaunted Rebels defense. Vaught calls the 30–14 loss the worst defeat in Ole Miss football history. He doesn't sleep that night, watching film of their next opponent instead. On Tuesday night, after three long days, he feels nauseated. "Boys," he tells his staff, "I'm sick. I've got to go home."

A few hours later, he turns to his wife in bed. "Something's wrong with me."

"How do you feel?"

"My arm's aching, and I have a nauseous feeling in my chest."

He is close to a heart attack, and he spends a week in a hospital in Memphis. After he gets out, the chest pains increase, so he goes back in. Except for a brief eight-game return three years later, Vaught's coaching career is over. The season falls apart, too, with Manning breaking his arm and LSU blowing out the Rebels 61–17 in Baton Rouge. There is no Sugar Bowl bid; Ole Miss has never been to an-other one. No national championships. Vaught returns to his farm.

He will never recruit an African American player.

That year, the Mississippi public school system is integrated.

8. 1973

Kenny Dill was the heart and soul of the '62 Rebels. Many blame the disastrous '64 season on his graduation; with him gone, there was no fire. No passion. He loved tough, hard-nosed football; he punched a teammate so hard during spring ball in '62 that he broke the guy's facemask, the guy's face, and his own hand.

Like many students, he learned something the night of the riot, a lesson about what politicians should do. He moved back home to West Point, Mississippi, after leaving Oxford and, in 1973, he runs for mayor. He wins, grabbing a chunk of the black vote—perhaps because black voters believe a young guy might be more willing to listen to their concerns.

Dill decides to be the mayor of everyone. He opens a dialogue with local NAACP officials, makes sure they know to call him anytime there is a concern. He goes about making West Point one city, not like other places in Mississippi, where integration will kill towns that don't know how to turn two communities into one. He restarts the Christmas parade, which had been canceled because whites didn't want blacks looking at their Santa. He brings basic services, such as roads and electricity, to black neighborhoods that have been left behind.

9. "MIDNIGHT TRAIN TO GEORGIA"

After college, Jim Weatherly leaves Oxford and goes out to LA. He takes along a band, and they play all the bars, the Whisky a Go Go and the rest, competing for gigs with bands such as the Doors. He does a USO tour of Vietnam with Nancy Sinatra and appears in a movie. Eventually, the band breaks up, and Weatherly is down to his last seven grand. He feels listless and makes plans, when the money runs out, to go back to Mississippi and become a football coach.

One day, through connections he made in his weekly flag football game, playing with movie star Lee Majors, Weatherly begins writing hits for Gladys Knight, and on October 20, 1973, one of his originals becomes the No. 1 song in America. He named it "Midnight Plane to Houston," but Knight wanted a different state and mode of transportation.

"Midnight Train to Georgia" remains one of the most popular songs of all time.

Years later, he'll be sitting in his home studio in Nashville, playing different versions of the song on the big speakers. Behind the keyboard, he takes my notebook and quickly draws the famous busted play from the Mississippi State game. Even now, he can see the look on the defensive end's face.

10. APRIL 22, 1982

John Hawkins is elected the first black cheerleader in school history. In an interview not long afterward, he says he will not carry the Confederate flag onto the field, as all cheerleaders have done before him. "While I'm an Ole Miss cheerleader, I'm still a black man. In my household, I wasn't told to hate the flag, but I did have history classes and know what my ancestors went through and what the Rebel flag represents. It is my choice and I prefer not to wave one. . . . I am a black man and the same way whites have been taught to wave the flag I have been taught to have nothing to do with it."

11. SEPTEMBER 30, 1982

Twenty years later, Meredith is invited to speak at Fulton Chapel on campus. The atmosphere is tense. During his speech, he says "Dixie" and the Confederate flags must be disassociated from Ole Miss. A large group of white students storms out of the speech and, outside, chants "Hotty Toddy" and sings "Dixie."

12. APRIL 18, 1983

Rumors are flying. The newly released yearbook contains a picture of white-robed Klansmen with Confederate flags. White students hear that black students are going to burn their yearbooks in protest. The yearlong debate about the future of the Confederate flag at

Ole Miss, one that brought the Grand Wizard of the Klan to a football game and students collecting signatures on a petition to keep the flag, is coming to a head. That night, about 600 white students march to Hawkins's fraternity house, waving Confederate flags and yelling racial slurs.

A bit of 1962 is in the air. The students chant the same words their parents chanted a generation before: "Two, four, six, eight . . . hell, no, we won't integrate."

University security and Oxford police officers break up the crowd before a riot can break out. The next morning, the student leader of the "Save the Flag" movement announces he no longer wants the job. Like many of his generation, he'd grown up believing the flag was a symbol of a great athletic tradition and school spirit. That night outside the Phi Beta Sigma house, he saw something darker, something Mississippians like to believe no longer exists.

The day after that, the chancellor holds a hastily scheduled news conference, announcing that the University of Mississippi will no longer be associated with the Confederate flag and that no one connected to the university will carry or display it, including cheerleaders. The chancellor receives death threats, and the next fall, it seems as if every fan in the stadium is carrying the Stars and Bars.

13. JANUARY 12, 1988

Ray Mabus is inaugurated as the youngest governor in the country and is featured in a *New York Times Magazine* story about the new guard changing the old Mississippi. He is the kid who wandered on the field after the 1962 Mississippi State game and asked Louis Guy for his chinstrap.

Afterward, Mabus will serve as ambassador to Saudi Arabia under Bill Clinton, but he never forgot his roots: He keeps an Ackerman, Mississippi, phone book on the coffee table in his office. Later, he will become a senior adviser to Barack Obama's campaign.

He still has the chinstrap.

14. APRIL 17, 2001

The issue is put to the voters: Keep the Confederate Stars and Bars on the state flag of Mississippi, or eliminate them? The man leading the crusade to eliminate is William Winter, the young politician who'd been so distraught the night Barnett spoke at the Kentucky game. He was governor of the state from 1980 to '84, when he started the first public kindergarten in Mississippi, fighting for civil rights for all its citizens. Covering the issue for *The Boston Globe* is veteran correspondent Curtis Wilkie, the Ole Miss student who received the letter from his mother urging him not to fight the Yankees.

On this night, when the results come in, Mississippi votes to keep the Confederate imagery, 65 percent to 35 percent. Mississippi is 61 percent white and 37 percent black.

Winter doesn't give up his dream of creating a Mississippi for everyone. At Ole Miss, the William Winter Institute for Racial Reconciliation does work all over the region, getting white folks and black folks to sit down and talk about the past and about the anger and the guilt that remain. He points to the 2008 presidential debate in Oxford as a sign that Mississippi is climbing out from the shadow of 1962. "We've been recovering all these years," he says.

The flag vote, though, is a sign of how much those old feelings still exist. In a recent political ad, one candidate for Senate attacked an opponent for supporting the removal of the Stars and Bars. Most Mississippians approve of having the Confederate Stars and Bars on the state flag.

"That tells you something about how far we still have to go, you know?" Winter says.

I want to believe we'll make it.

"Are we gonna get there?" I ask.

He smiles.

"Sure," he says. "We've come an incredibly long way from 1962."

TODAY

1. "WE ARE NOT LEPERS"

From his luxury box, Sam Owen is thinking about a night many years before, when all this was drenched in tear gas. His iPhone rings—he has ringtones from quacking ducks to the Ole Miss fight song. It's one of his three sons, Bryan, who played football for the Rebels in the '80s. The years have been good to Owen: He ran a complicated and large company, married that beautiful girl he went over to check on at the sorority house, took his boys to play the Old Course for Christmas one year, even wrote the poem that described the gift himself. He's got it in his will that the Ole Miss band will play "Dixie" at his funeral; when you write checks like Owen, you can pretty much get a university to do anything you want. He's still a funny guy, known for calling a teammate, telling a joke, then hanging up. He still wears that Omega watch team members got after their Sugar Bowl victory—had it sent to Switzerland to be cleaned—and sometimes, he'll Google "1962" . . . just to reminisce. These buildings, and this field, take him back, to a time when one South was dying and another was being born. Owen doesn't see that team as the end of an era. He sees it as a beginning.

"That was the bridge," he says. "I tell you what I believe. When you think about it, we were all raised under a system that we look back on now and nobody is proud of it. But guess what? Go anywhere else in this country, in any state, and they've got the same crap. I look at what Mississippi has done and how far it's come. Now you think about it. You walk into Oxford, and you'd never know there was ever a tear gas bomb thrown there."

About a dozen years ago, on a football Saturday, Owen and a group of guys from that '62 team stood around in the Grove, wondering why nobody ever seemed to bring up their perfect season, the only one in school history. "This is ridiculous," Owen remembers saying. "Everybody acts like we're the lepers. They ought to be talking about how we kept the university from closing. Nobody pays attention. It's like you didn't exist."

Right then and there, the guys conceived a monument to honor their team. In 1998, it was unveiled: an archway in the Grove that the team walks through every game day, another beloved tradition. It is called the Walk of Champions, and it was paid for by members of the 1962 Ole Miss football team. They are now remembered.

The players are older now and have drifted apart some. Many of them have new hips, new knees, chronic back pain. Owen recently canceled a vacation to Greece because his back hurt so bad. They've had diverse and mostly successful lives. Mayors. CEOs. A bunch of them went to Vietnam. Others became doctors, dentists, lawyers. They are the outgoing generation of power brokers in the South.

"There is the common thread that runs through here," Owen says. "These would be guys, if you had these fellows in your unit in the army, you'd take the hill."

2. THE LONG GOODBYES

Fred Roberts and Larry Leo Johnson are sitting in a golf club outside Jackson. Roberts holds a roster, with little marks next to some of the names. "We lost seven guys," he says.

The first to go was center Richard Ross, in a plane crash. Six others have followed, and the survivors always show up, stooped and a little wider around the middle, standing in dark suits at funerals, just as they once stood in light suits at weddings.

One afternoon not so long ago, Billy Champion's phone rang. It was Wes Sullivan, his old roommate and running buddy, Wes Sullivan of the Pat O'Brien's fountain, of hunting squirrels in the Grove. He'd been sick for a long time, a rare blood disease, and he'd fought it hard. Champion and Sullivan talked about the old days for about an hour, Sullivan sounding as good as he had in a while. They talked about the old games and the nights out together raising hell, about a time when both were young and invincible.

Champion hung up and turned to his wife. "I think Wesley just told me goodbye," he said.

Two days later, Sullivan died.

After his heart attack, Vaught stayed in Oxford, on his farm, playing golf, visiting with his old players when they'd come back. The stadium was renamed for him: Vaught-Hemingway. In 2006, at the age of 96, he died. His funeral took up the entire church and an adjacent building. Outside the South, the newspaper story said, nobody paid much attention.

3. HIJACKED BY HISTORY

The Mississippi they knew as children no longer exists. The little towns where they grew up have blown away, cracked open by the decline of agriculture and bled dry by a political system that disenfranchised a third of the state's citizens for a century. Integration meant a chance at equality, but for a lot of guys on the 1962 Ole Miss football team, it also meant that the world they knew as children no longer existed, an effacement of memory, a past shameful and best forgotten in a place where the past is the bedrock of identity. It has left a generation of Mississippians drifting. They have a hard time expressing this, knowing exactly how it sounds, careful with their words, lowering their voices and looking to see whether their wives are listening before whispering, "The blacks . . ."

When he returns to his hometown of Greenwood to visit, Buck Randall likes to drive around alone, past his old school, down the streets where he grew up and played. "Where I used to live," he says, "they're all black. Our whole neighborhood. Everything's gone."

Mitch Terrell sits in the lobby of the swank Alluvian Hotel in Greenwood, part of one Delta town's fight against the fate of so many other places in the state. Terrell is getting chemo after having some cancer removed. He's hoping to get his taste back; even the two or three glasses of Old Charter when the sun goes down taste dull. It's given him time, and license, to think. Done a lot of that lately. "All the little Delta towns are going," Terrell says. "Shaw, Drew, Shelby. It would break your heart to drive through Shaw, Mississippi. Back when I was growing up, it was a thriving place. Now everything's gone."

The guys from the '62 team want their state back, their youth. It's not segregation they miss—"I'm not a black hater," Terrell says—but a thriving place existing before the collapse of the rural economy. They're not economists. They haven't really thought about how segregation effectively ensured that Mississippi would have to claw its way into the 21st century. Instead of working to enfranchise black citizens quickly, many towns began figuring out new ways to segregate. Many towns opened all-white, private high schools. I went to one and never shared a classroom with anyone of color there. Problem is, my hometown of Clarksdale can't really support one successful school. Now it has two, and both struggle. Mississippi's children sink further behind, pulled down by the residue of past prejudices.

Sometimes I worry we've already made our decisions and have no hope of undoing them. There is just such a profound disconnect between whites and blacks from that era, and many have taught their children and grandchildren so many unfortunate lessons, handing off old ideas to the young. Even something as simple as "Dixie" creates an unbridgeable gap. I'll be honest. I like it when the band plays it. It reminds me of my daddy, and I cry a little bit when they play it slow. All the former players share that sentiment. "I have never thought one thing negative when I hear that," Owen says. "Just how much I love Ole Miss and that Grove and those trees." Then I talk to Wadlington, for whom the song brings back different memories: Ole Miss fans driving past his home after a game, blaring "Dixie," waving flags, screaming at his family. "I remember," he says. "I remember the cars. I remember the flags. I remember being the brunt of a lot of racial slurs."

The guys from that team have a hard time understanding the other side's point of view. They feel as if their past and their accomplishments have been hijacked by history, and it bothers them in ways they know better than to say aloud. They just want the little grocery stores and the guy pushing burgers off a griddle and the safe streets back. They want to remember when it was OK to be proud of Mississippi.

Terrell starts to cry, wipes his eyes, apologizes for getting emotional. "I hate to think what my grandchildren are gonna grow up in," he says. "I know you can't live in the past, but I sure like to recall it."

4. BUCK RANDALL: KNOCKED DOWN BUT UNBOWED

I pull up to Buck Randall's home in Clinton. This is my second trip here, and after hearing so many stories, I'm a little scared of him. He has done hard work since leaving football, including a stretch repossessing cars, carrying a piece for protection. The first time I met Randall, I had to help him stand up, his socked feet sliding on the floor, him sinking back into the couch. That made me sad. He'd been the most feared man in the Delta, but time hasn't been kind to Randall. He has had five operations on his knees, then had them both replaced, suffers from chronic back pain, had three heart attacks, had a stroke, has diabetes, wears a hearing aid. "I hurt every day," he says. One thing has remained untouched by time: His eyes are still a brilliant shade of blue.

I've returned to ask Randall a hard question. See, all the stories about the riot start with him being dragged into the Lyceum. There's no real explanation about why he was there or what he was doing. His teammates snicker when telling the story, hinting they know exactly what he was doing out there. Reporting a story makes you myopic sometimes, and I've come to believe that I need at least one member of that team to admit being an active member of that riot. Then I can ask whether they've repented, whether that night has changed them at all. My best chance, I figure, is Randall. Was he throwing bricks? Was he that football player the priest negotiated with? One history book says he was.

So I get to his house and see his wonderful wife, Sandra, who takes such good care of her husband. I talk with him about the old days. "Hell," he says, "it seems like I've been fighting all my life."

Finally, I ask him. What was he doing when Chief Tatum grabbed him?

"I went over there in front of Lyceum," he starts, "before the riot broke out."

That's as far as he goes, and sitting in his home, I stop too. The past few weeks have been hard on me. I found a photo of a young man screaming at Meredith. The face looks familiar. I think it's a family member. I show it to my mom; she says I'm wrong. I'm not sure. But I do not ask the relative; I do not press. There are questions that Mississippians won't ask because we are not prepared to hear the answer. So I decide, looking at Buck Randall, that it is unfair for me to demand a confession from him that I am not willing to demand from a family member. Some things seem best left buried.

5. THE SELF-PROCLAIMED MOST SIGNIFICANT MAN ALIVE

I pull up to James Meredith's home in Jackson. He raised cash for his house, in a middle-class neighborhood, by cutting down and selling those trees his father planted.

Time hasn't been that kind to Meredith either. He was shot in 1966 making a "Walk Against Fear" across Mississippi. Martin Luther King Jr. finished the walk for him. He's gotten a reputation for being a bit off. Tell someone you're going to see Meredith and you'll get a look that says: Have fun with that. He worked for Jesse Helms. And David Duke. Nobody could figure out what he was thinking there.

Sitting in a little room off the side of the house he has turned into an office, he says, "You see, what most people have never understood is why . . . the Ole Miss school thing, the white-black school thing, has such force and power . . ."

He is interrupted by one of his granddaughters, who wants some milk. Meredith finishes his thought—"it's about not accepting white supremacy"—then walks slowly to the house to get her a glass of milk.

When he returns, he holds forth, about the books he has read, about reading *War and Peace* in Russian, about Churchill, about the great moments of Western civilization, about Barack Obama. He says he has hope for Mississippi because his going to Ole Miss killed the tree limb of white supremacy and it has been dying ever since. It's still hanging on to the tree, he says, but it's rotted and hopeless. Mississippi will one day be different. As he talks, I think I understand the weirdness people associate with him, the grandiosity. He's not crazy. It's just that, in his mind, he's one of those people who've changed the course of history. When he talks about Churchill, it's not as if he's discussing some distant leader but, rather, an intimate. A peer.

He remembers his actions, and the wave they unleashed on the South, and, well, he has been chasing greatness ever since. What's the second act when you change the world at 29?

"Not only am I more significant than Barack Obama," he says, "I'm more significant than anybody living. I ain't never not thought that, but you are the first person, and if you hadn't told me you were from Clarksdale and 31 years old, I wouldn't have told you. You're the first person I've ever told that. It doesn't really matter after a time whether it's true or not. Tell you the truth, most of the things that guided me, I never knew if they were real or imagined. I got to where I couldn't tell the difference at all between a dream and something I thought up wide awake. To me, it was the same thing. Became the same thing."

As we talk, a roach crawls out onto the floor, headed toward his shoes, then moves away, making its way around the room. The weirdest thing happens. He doesn't mention it. Neither do I. My eyes stay straight ahead. It just seems unfair to make him stop talking about Churchill and his own historical significance to address a roach crawling around his small, cluttered office.

6. "NOTHING EVER LASTS FOREVER"

Glynn Griffing makes a familiar walk, from the dining area toward the Lyceum. The former star quarterback, who was born near my family farm, is wearing gray slacks, a blue shirt, and a blue tie. He's 68 now. It's a beautiful fall day, and the leaves are turning, the coeds showing their legs, the lights of the football stadium peeking above the tops of the buildings. He looks at the faces coming and going and can't believe he ever looked that young. An Ole Miss football player, a burly African American, passes him and doesn't pause to look at the older man sitting near the flagpole. Once upon a time, Griffing was the most famous person on this campus. Time marches on. "Nothing ever lasts forever," he says. "I knew it wouldn't last forever. But I never expected it to end as quickly as it did."

He remembers the night of the riot, the Confederate flag flying where he's sitting now, the tear gas. Now there are white and black faces here, walking together, going to the same classes, living in the same rooms. There have been so many changes. Robert Khayat, the former football star, is now the chancellor. One of the first things he did was make fans stop bringing the Confederate flag to the stadium. He, too, got death threats. He banned Colonel Rebel as the official mascot. He has overseen the university through millions of dollars in improvements and spearheaded the campaign to bring the presidential debate to Oxford. Understandably, Khayat is proud of the new Ole Miss.

Griffing stands, walks past the James Meredith statue behind the Lyceum that Khayat installed. There's a quote on it: "Yes, Mississippi was. But Mississippi is." That seems about right. He walks slowly, in color, not in black and white like those old photographs, a man who once knew glory but doesn't dwell on it. He's through talking to me about the past. The tear gas has faded away. He moves along the sidewalk beneath the oaks and magnolias. Nobody glances twice.

EPILOGUE

Reporting this story took me places I'm not sure I wanted to go. I've always loved Mississippi, but each new layer I unearthed made that love a more difficult and complex thing to maintain. I read James Meredith's hate mail. Not photocopies, the actual letters. I found my relative's name in the notebook, though never an explanation of why, and later, a photo of another great-uncle urging citizens to fight the feds. I realized for the first time how these symbols of Ole Miss football—the flag and "Dixie" and even "Hotty Toddy"—were once used as weapons. How for a third of my fellow Mississippians, those images bring back fear. I found myself wishing I didn't know any of this. That scared me.

But I did know, and now I had an answer to a question first asked in the library: What is the cost? I won't ever look at a Rebel flag the same again. Although I like "Dixie," especially when it's played slow, if it were never played again, I would be OK with that. Strangely, my biggest fear was that I'd be unable to enjoy Ole Miss football games, that I wouldn't be able to forget the images in my head from a time when these games served as a symbol of something else.

This past fall, the Rebels went a month without a home game, and that's when I did most of the library work on this story. I began to worry about the Auburn game. What if it was ruined for me? That morning, I got to my seats and searched inside for the first pangs of discomfort. I'm not sure what this says about me, but I still liked being there. Yes, it's OK to love Ole Miss football. It's part of me, just as the events of 47 years ago are. We are all of these things. They are our history. They are us. I didn't just feel shame researching this story. I felt pride in that group of guys, in Glynn and Sam and Louis and the rest. I am proud to have met them. I am fully aware that this will be the second story I've written ending with the Ole Miss band playing "Dixie." The first ran two years ago, an ode to Southern football, and that song made me think about my family. I still mean every word of that, as I do what I'm writing now, and believe that both can be true. Difficult and complex are not necessarily bad things.

Kickoff's close. I look up at the south end zone and see, in gigantic letters, "1962 National Champions." Seems some obscure poll voted the Rebels first. I read all the local coverage of that season, and there was no mention of this poll. But there it is, in huge letters. There's such a blurry line between fact and fiction about 1962 that nobody seems to mind that the university has rewritten history. Not only do we not like to talk about the past, but we like to rearrange it to fit with our own ideas of what should have happened. This strikes me as dangerous: If we don't look at our flaws and culpability and learn from them, we seem doomed. The truth? The 1962 team was good, really good, especially considering the obstacles, but that year, USC was better.

The sign also brings me to the final question: What is the cost of not knowing? Many of the students here have no idea what really happened that night in front of the Lyceum. They know what I knew: brushstrokes and a few comfortable anecdotes. Maybe their families are different, but in my family, it wasn't discussed. I suspect their families are not different. Students here mostly believe what their parents believe; it's the reason *The Daily Mississippian* was the only daily student newspaper in America to endorse John McCain. Thoughts are handed down like monogrammed cuff links and engraved shotguns.

The band starts playing "From Dixie with Love." The moment's coming, one that makes me cringe, for the black students who have to hear it and for the white ones who have no idea what they're actually saying. The song speeds up near the end, and the crowd shakes once more. I don't know when this began, or why, but as it finishes, many of the students, some of them the grandchildren of those here in the long fall of 1962, yell, *The South . . . will . . . rise . . . again!*

Shadow Boxing

Muhammad Ali fought 50 men. Only one disappeared.

MIAMI, FLA.—The old man opens the door and shuffles into a familiar room. The air smells of stale beer and discount-brand cigarette smoke. The tables are taken by men with no names. They are all friends. They are all strangers. A different journey brought each of them here, to the pool hall on Northwest 2nd Avenue, but that doesn't matter anymore. Their journeys are over. Most don't share the details, not even their last names. Some don't remember the year, or how long they've been coming here. They have no past.

The old man walks clumsily to a table. He has a story. The act of telling it, of having people hear it, keeps him from disappearing forever. One night, he says, he fought Muhammad Ali. Almost won, he brags. Some believe him. Some don't. Most don't care. He's just another wacko wandering the streets with some tale about how his life could have been different.

They ignore him, pretending he's not even there. He's got to show them.

The old man gets up and throws punches into the air.

The people around him laugh.

He sits back down, invisible again.

I. LOST

IN THE BEGINNING

The search began six years ago with a phone call.

The man on the other end is Stephen Singer, a New Hampshire

car salesman who collects things in his spare time. Most of all, he collects all things Muhammad Ali. It's a fetish. He prizes the light box he keeps on the wall of his office. With the flick of a switch, you can see an X-ray with a thin crack: Ali's broken jaw.

He tells me the story of the boxer who disappeared, starting by explaining his latest mission: collecting the signatures of all 50 men who fought Ali. The first 35 or so came easy. Singer got a professional autograph collector to help. Then, the pro came to a dead end; Singer decided to continue on his own.

He peered into another world, in which a brush with fame didn't grant immortality. One by one, he found them. Some took months. He searched dank boxing gyms and dusty public records. He found a man who'd given up the ring for a European carnival. He located a notarized letter from a fighter-turned-Mafia-hit-man. A rabbi acted as a middle man in a small Argentine town for the passport of a fighter who'd been dead since 1964. He was No. 49.

One fighter remained: Jim Robinson, who'd fought Muhammad Ali in Miami Beach on February 7, 1961?

Singer tried everything. He contacted boxing historians and even enlisted Ali's old trainer, Angelo Dundee. He found a boxer in Philly named Jim Robinson . . . who never fought Ali. Private detectives and former FBI agents helped. Robinson was a ghost. He had no known date of birth, no known full name. No known family. No ties. No public records linking him to a place or a time. In the exhaustively well-chronicled life of Muhammad Ali, Singer has stumbled into the one hole, a man who'd shared a moment in time and space with one of the most famous humans ever, only to vanish. An old Associated Press story said Robinson was from Kansas City, which is why Singer is on the phone with the local paper's feature writer, who happens to be me. He tells me there isn't much more information to build on; nobody has ever really thought to search for the fighter before. In a way, Jim Robinson didn't begin to exist until someone realized he was missing.

HOOKED

Singer asks me to help, so I collect everything already known about Robinson. Turns out, although sports people throw around the phrase "go down in history" a lot, in real life, history doesn't amount to much. Jim Robinson's name appears maybe a dozen times in print.

The night of the fight, he ran into the Miami Beach Convention Hall, carrying an old army bag full of his gear. The reason he seemed harried? He was a last-minute replacement, used to fighting for pocket change. The guy who was supposed to box that night, Willie Gullatt, didn't show.

Ali biographers figure Gullatt got scared. With good reason. Until that point, the old stories say, few considered Ali a great fighter. That all changed the day before he fought Robinson, when heavyweight contender Ingemar Johansson, in town training for a title fight with Floyd Patterson, invited the young Ali, still known as Cassius Clay, to spar.

They stepped into the ring, and by the time the men climbed out after two rounds, the history of boxing was forever changed. Ali threw a blur of punches, a jab, then two more, his feet dancing, a combination, right, left, right. Each punch landed—hard. Johansson lumbered forward, throwing a roundhouse right, which didn't come close, and the big heavyweight stumbled and almost fell.

Ali danced and talked in rhyme.

The next night, Gullatt, who also seems lost to time, didn't show up. Jim Robinson got the call, even though Ali outweighed him by 16½ pounds. Robinson came out fast, throwing wild punches, which Ali dodged, waiting for an opening. About a minute into the fight, he saw his chance. Bam! Bam! Pow! Pow! The shots to the head put Robinson down. He struggled to stand, but the referee counted to nine, then stopped the fight.

It had lasted 94 seconds.

Afterward, the New York *Daily News* wrote, "It was all a mistake." *The Miami News* wrote, "If promoter Chris Dundee had canvassed the women in the audience, he couldn't have found an easier opponent for Clay."

Three years later, Ali beat Sonny Liston in Miami to become champion, and the next night, a few miles up the road in a tiny auditorium, Robinson lost to a journeyman named Jack Gilbert. Robinson was already fading away. Boxing records show he kept fighting, losing much more often than he won, finally stopping in 1968.

There's been only one sighting since then. In 1979, a photographer shooting pictures for *Sports Illustrated* went to find Ali's earliest opponents. Michael Brennan located Jim Robinson, whom people down in Miami called "Sweet Jimmy." Most of what's known about his life comes from the brief blurb that ran with the photos. He lived off veterans' benefits. He claimed he was born around 1925. He claimed he was wrongfully convicted of armed robbery. Most days, he just hung out in the seedy Overtown neighborhood, at the pool hall owned by Miami concert promoter Clyde Killens.

The photos show a haunted man. His jaw juts out, like he's lost teeth. His eyebrows are bushy; once, they probably seemed delicate. A visor throws a shadow across his eyes. A deep scar runs along his left cheekbone. In one, he leans up against the wall of a Winn-Dixie. In another, he walks down railroad tracks, the skyline of Miami rising behind him. He never smiles.

Brennan shot the photos on a Friday night and a Saturday morning. Sweet Jimmy smelled of booze and Camel cigarettes. Brennan remembers the last time he saw him. It was in the morning, on the railroad tracks, and he slipped the old fighter 20 bucks. Sweet Jimmy turned and walked off, negotiating the cross ties. He never looked back.

"Tell Clay I ain't doing too good," he said.

THE PAPERLESS TRAIL

We all live parallel lives on paper.

Long after we're gone, the details of our existence will remain part of the public record; in time, they will be all that's known about us, a skeleton of facts, the human whys long decayed. That's what made Sweet Jimmy's disappearance strange. It's hard to disappear. Search engines record everything: our arrests, the amount we paid for our house, the times we've defaulted on a credit card or paid our taxes late. No piece of our past is truly private. The love of a wedding day is public record, as is the hatred of divorce. Public records allow me, in less than two minutes, to learn that Muhammad Ali has a home or office at 8105 Kephart Lane and that his wife has owned a Lexus, license plate LA1, with an AM/FM cassette player and a standard tilt steering wheel. The invasiveness can be scary but also strangely reassuring. Someday, through these strings of ones and zeroes, people will know we were here. It's impossible not to leave a trail. Finding Jimmy, I was sure, would take a day. Two, tops.

That was six years ago.

I stuck with the search, first while with *The Kansas City Star*, then at ESPN. Everywhere I turned, I found pain and loss, a procession of wasted lives, people who never fought Ali and, thus, won't ever have someone come looking for them. Did any of these men hang in the pool hall, too, never knowing someone a few feet away shared the same name? A James Robinson born in 1929 was shot a few blocks from the pool hall in 1984, his murderer yelling, "I told you I was gonna kill me a black son of a bitch." A James Robinson died of a gunshot to the head in Overtown in 2007, likely a suicide, but he turned out to be just 54. A Jimmie Robinson was beaten to death under an overpass near the pool hall in 1991. He had an old arrest for being in a park after hours, and his only address was the Camillus House, a local homeless shelter. His date of birth made him too young to have fought Ali in 1961. The Miami medical examiner's office said 227 people have died in Miami since 1980 and never been identified. Any of them could be Sweet Jimmy.

I ran hundreds of searches, through every imaginable database, called every Miami boxing authority still alive. Dundee helped by going through his wealth of boxing sources. The VA struck out, as did the military records center and the Social Security office. Current and former law enforcement officers tried to help. The police union sent Sweet Jimmy's picture to old beat cops. The county and city cold case detectives searched. They found no J. Robinsons who were African American and the right age. The Florida Department of Corrections said it had never had custody of a Jimmy, Jim, or James Robinson who fit the description.

Finally, I began to realize that I was looking for Jimmy all wrong. I was looking for him the way I'd look for myself. He'd lived off the grid, managing to go through life and, according to society just out of reach around him, never exist.

It was pointless to look for Sweet Jimmy in my world.

I had to go search in his.

STARTING OVER

The first stop is in Miami Beach at the Fontainebleau hotel. Elvis and Sinatra stayed here. Bond spied on Goldfinger's card game here. The man I've come to see stands ready to grab my luggage—an old bellhop, name tag reads Levi. Yes, that's my guy, Levi Forte, an old boxer who fought with Sweet Jimmy. He's been here 44 years, and the tourists whose bags he carries have no idea that he once stood in the ring with champions, just like most folks didn't know that Beau Jack, the old man who shined shoes downstairs, had headlined Madison Square Garden 21 times, more than any fighter before or since.

I show Levi the photograph. He studies the drooping chin, the delicate eyelashes, the wild beard. "That's him," he says. "I haven't seen that guy in I don't know when."

The last time was about 30 years ago, and both men were passing by the famous 5th Street Gym. Levi thought Jimmy would turn and go up the stairs. When he didn't, Levi stopped him.

"You Jimmy Robinson?" he asked.

Jimmy seemed surprised and pleased. The question made him real again, briefly.

"You know me?"

"You fought the Man," Levi said.

The tourists pile out of their cars as I step back into mine. Before I can put it in drive, I hear a knock on the glass. Levi fills my window. He's got a story. One he needs to tell me before I'm gone forever. "Don't forget," he says. "I was the first guy to go 10 rounds with George Foreman. December 16, 1969."

A LINE IN THE WATER

Next stop: Overtown.

Though it's just a few blocks from the downtown AmericanAirlines Arena, the home of the Miami Heat, you can feel the world changing as you turn off Biscayne Boulevard, each street bleaker than the one before, buildings giving way to boarded-up facades giving way to empty lots. People walk toward my car when I stop at traffic lights. Minor laws and small courtesies don't apply; a cop had advised me to run the red lights. People huddle beneath the overpasses. Drug lookouts in white T-shirts eye me warily from corners and the rooftops. Nobody enters Overtown undetected.

It didn't always feel like this. In the '60s, when Sweet Jimmy fought Ali, blacks-only hotels and nightclubs filled each block. The best musicians in the world—who could play, but not stay, on Miami Beach—saved their best and wildest sets for Overtown. Everybody came, booked by promoter Clyde Killens: Sam Cooke, Aretha Franklin, Count Basie, B. B. King, John Lee Hooker, everyone. That time and place is as lost as Sweet Jimmy. "You get off 2nd Avenue," says Gaspar González, a documentary filmmaker who made a movie about Ali's time in Miami, "and there's a hopelessness there. It's an island. There's no sense the world is bigger than that. People are desperate in a way you can't communicate. You're behind God's back."

Driving through the streets, I finger a stack of homemade posters I brought, each with Sweet Jimmy's photo and a local 305 phone number I set up. I explain on them that ESPN is looking for this man but don't include his name. I tape them up around the neighborhood, and I drop them off at all the restaurants, shops, and liquor stores. I email them to the secretaries at the local churches; nobody sees or gossips more. If Sweet Jimmy is alive, he's probably in Overtown. Finding a focal point is both satisfying and heartbreaking. All this time, Singer and I didn't know where to look for Jimmy, who never knew anyone was looking.

It's as if he was shipwrecked.

A MESSAGE IN A BOTTLE

Three days after I return home from my first trip to Miami, my phone starts ringing.

The first caller, Melvin Eaton, claims, "I've been knowing old Sweet Jimmy for years."

He says the last time he saw Jimmy was five or six years ago, and that Jimmy never stopped reminding people that he fought Muhammad Ali. He'd shadowbox and brag. "That's all he talked about," Melvin tells me. "That's all he talked about. 'I'm the one who fought Ali. I'm the one who should have been the greatest.'"

A few days later, a woman calls. Her name is Brenda. "I see him every day," she says. "He's my friend. He be in Overtown around 12th Street and 2nd Avenue every day. He be on the street and asks for a dollar for a soda or a beer."

I ask her to go to that corner and put the phone in his hand. "They told me he just walked off," she says later, and I'm not sure whether she really knows Jimmy or just wants to feel like somebody with a mission, with a purpose, even if just for a few thin moments.

These calls point me to the door of Jimmy's world. I go back to Miami. As I'm sitting in the medical examiner's office, waiting to read the files of a few dead James Robinsons, a private investigator suggests checking Camillus House.

It sits on the edge of Overtown, a gateway. Miami has 994 people living on the street, and almost all of them end up here at one time or another. Outside, a man and a woman push a stroller toward the shelter door. Another man steps inside holding a baby rattle. I walk up to the front desk, holding a flier. "I'm looking for someone," I tell the lady manning the desk.

Her name is Patricia. As she studies the photo, sadness darkens her face, as though a cloud is passing overhead. She slumps. Every day, unwanted people come through that door, and now, finally, someone has come for one of them—and it might be too late. "I never forget a face," she says. "He is homeless."

"Is he alive?" I ask.

She shakes her head. She doesn't know.

II. THE WORLD WHERE NO ONE EXISTS

GHOSTS OF THE POOL HALL

The pool hall is boarded up, its secrets buried inside. The past is gone. It never happened. No sign of the white father and son who ran a watch repair business here until the '50s, when the son got polio. No sign of Killens, who took over the building; no sign that it once attracted the best sharks passing through Miami; and no sign of Jackie Gleason, who liked to stand atop the tables and sing.

It's the only building left on the block. Once, Ferdie Pacheco, Ali's fight doctor, had an office next door, but it burned in the 1980 riots. Crime took over the avenue. Cops often found themselves at this address. One night, they found a police motorcycle in the back that someone had stolen. As the years passed, fire and the wrecking ball cleared out the rest of the block. The promoter Killens died in 2004, but not before heroin took his son. At the end, Killens sat in his home around the corner with the shades drawn. He stopped listening to music.

The pool hall was condemned in April 2005. Killens's daughter made some poor business decisions and lost the property. It's been empty ever since. Rolling doors, like smaller versions of a garage's, are locked shut. Cinder blocks fill the upstairs windows, where a few apartments used to be, and boards cover the glass painted with the address: 920.

The current owner lets me inside. The tables are gone. The room's painted orange and turquoise, the colors of the Dolphins and nearby Booker T. Washington High. There's a toilet out in the open; the interior walls have been ripped out. The floor's been ripped up. A homeless person lives in the back room, with a basket of clothes and cardboard boxes spread out to form a bed. There's a pile of trash in the corner with a shoe sitting on top. There's a welcome mat.

There is no sign of Jimmy.

OVERTOWN 101

Overtown surrounds the empty pool hall, split north and south by I-95 and east and west by I-395. The concrete canopy is a daily reminder of what the neighborhood used to be, what it's become and why.

Building the interstates in the late '60s forced thousands from their homes, destroyed a vibrant business district, and further cut them off from the rest of Miami. Population declined, from 40,000 to where it is today, just more than 10,000. A new kind of economy rules the neighborhood now. A beer or two for a bath. Penicillin or tetracycline might buy you a place to sleep for a night. A crack rock buys just about anything.

The zip code, one of the poorest in the country, has more sex offenders than any other in Florida. It's a dumping ground for addicts, pedophiles, and the insane. In the shadow of a booming downtown, people live invisible lives. Near the corner of Northwest 3rd Avenue and 11th Street, I talk to a group gathered beneath I-95. They're looking for cops.

"Police tell us to go home," one guy says, eyeing me suspiciously. "It's martial law in Overtown." There's one woman in the group. Her arms are disfigured with scars, like she's been in a car wreck. In a way, she has. I'm told later: infections from years of heroin use. She's seen my fliers and asks if I could help her too. She wants to find out about her daddy. She gives his name. Any little bit of information will help her reconstruct the past, and a past is at the core of our humanity. A story is what makes us real.

Under the overpass, they talk about Sweet Jimmy, whom they haven't seen in a while, and about how people down here just vanish. "Give an emergency contact number," the woman tells her friends. "Let somebody know your name in case you go missing."

They go back to sitting around, their words muffled by the whine and hum of the car tires overhead. They're waiting, for the next hit, the next drink, the next meal, the next green mattress at the Camillus House, waiting for someone to come save them, for their body to end up at the morgue with a tag that reads "Remains, Unknown," for the cops to tell them they can't stay here any longer. They're waiting for tomorrow, which will be just like today. The concrete shades them from the hot South Florida sun, and if you stand in just the right spot, sometimes a breeze blows nice and cool on your face.

They're waiting on the breeze.

LESSONS OF THE STREET

It takes a while, but eventually I make friends in Overtown, and their help opens the neighborhood. Smiles replace stares. The barriers fall away. One morning, local social worker Al Brown and I walk into a barbershop on Northwest 3rd Avenue.

"Gentlemen, gentlemen, how are you?" Al says. "I got a gentleman here who's looking for a guy that fought Muhammad Ali. Called him Sweet Jimmy."

A voice calls out from a back room: "Sweet Jimmy's dead."

One of the old barbers introduces himself. "My name's Payne," he says. "I used to cut Jimmy's hair, and the guy in the back used to cut his hair. When he was walking the streets, before he went to the homeless shelter."

"Do you know what happened to him?" I ask.

"He got involved in drugs and walked the streets awhile," Payne says.

"Did he have a job?"

"No job. The street, man. He became an addict, and whoever he knew from the past he would rely on."

Payne knows a guy named Mr. Big, who was friends with Jimmy. He lives down the street in a squat, turquoise building, across from the empty lot where the old Harlem Square Club, the site of Sam Cooke's famous live album, used to be. Al knocks on Mr. Big's door until he steps out into the sunlight, squints a bit, then tells us he thinks Sweet Jimmy left town.

"How long ago?" Al asks.

"A good while," Big says. "Back in the '80s."

Finally, I am learning some things. I learn most people here didn't really know Jimmy; they just saw Jimmy. They didn't know his last name or his hometown. None actually saw him fight Ali. He moved silently through their lives, as two-dimensional to them as he was to those who read his name in the old boxing records and yellowed newspapers.

I learn there are two groups of old-timers who live here. There are those who held down jobs, like Big and Payne, and there are the hustlers. Both groups knew Jimmy, but as the years passed, he seemed to spend less and less time with the people who kept a foot in the real world. Irby McKnight, a local organizer who's helping me look, moved into the neighborhood the year Jimmy quit fighting.

"When I first met him," he tells me, "he used to be loud and obnoxious, but he was well-dressed. I used to say: 'Where'd this man get these old clothes from?' And people would say: 'That's Sweet

Jimmy.' 'You ain't telling me nothing.' 'Oh, you don't know him. He was a boxer, and he fought Muhammad Ali.'"

I learn a third thing, too, more slowly than the other two. I learn about the people searching with me. In the beginning, I wondered why they were doing it. I thought about that a lot, especially when I left them in Overtown every day to go back to my fancy hotel, and finally I understood: As long as they help me look, they are a part of my world and not of his. As long as they help, they exist to me.

"HE FORGETS ABOUT TOMORROW"

We keep looking for people who'd remember, driving every street in Overtown, Mr. Big and Al pointing out the former sites of flophouses and restaurants and nightclubs where Sweet Jimmy spent his days. One by one, they vanished. Wrecking balls took some; riots and fires took others. Sweet Jimmy's world tightened until, finally, only the pool hall was left. He outlived his neighborhood. Old-timers moved or died. Not many folks who knew him are left.

"I tell you who would know," Al says. "Shorty, who used to work at the racetrack."

"Yeah," Big says, "Shorty, he'd know about it. Shorty saw him fight."

"Whatever happened to Shorty?" Al says.

"Shorty around," Big says. "I saw him yesterday. He hangs around the corner here by Payne's. Catch him around here in the evening time. Racetrack Shorty."

The next day, we're parked next to an apartment building when Shorty Brown comes outside, a faded hospital bracelet on his arm. The skin hangs loose around his neck.

"Is Sweet Jimmy dead?" I ask.

"If he died, he didn't die here," Shorty says. "He didn't die in this town. If he'd died in this town, you'd know."

Jimmy hustled for money, Shorty explains. Worked his angle, a game with a belt and a pencil, and he was good at it. Shorty is the

first of many who try to explain this quaint street hustle, and no-
body can do it. Is it real? Is Jimmy real? Did Shorty ever actually see
Jimmy? "He used to come to the racetrack and break everybody," he
says. "Out at Gulfstream. The last time I saw him, him and Sonny
Red screwed with everybody on the racetrack. They put him in jail."
"Who was Sonny Red?" I ask.
"Sonny Red was one of those little hustlers. They go around swin-
dling people. Sweet Jimmy liked that life."
Guys like Shorty, and Jimmy's friend Benny Lane, who called after seeing the flier, paint a picture. The kids made fun of Jimmy's
heavy, heel-first walk. He always carried a deck of cards and dealt a
mean three-card monte. He laughed at his own jokes when no one else
did. He shadowboxed when the fellas would yell, "Sweet Jimmy!" A
guy punched him one night at the pool hall after Jimmy kept on about
the man's wife. By then, Jimmy couldn't fight back. "He was always
looking to tell a joke or get a joke or say something funny," Benny
says. "Get a laugh. A short laugh. Not a long laugh. That's Jimmy."
The years passed. More teeth fell out. He put up his game with
the belt and pencil, shedding another thing that made him different
from the faceless men and women who wander the Overtown streets.
"He wasn't in the best of shape," Benny says. "He drank kinda heavy.
And, uh, his mouth was kinda raggedy. Kinda like mine."
Sometimes, Benny and Jimmy would talk. About women, about
whatever current events led the news, about home. Now Benny can't
remember where Jimmy was from. He thinks Jimmy says he went to
school in Kansas City. Sometimes, Jimmy'd pack up and leave for a
month or so. He said he had a brother. "He talked about his family,"
Benny says. "He didn't forget about them."
This picture of Jimmy is the saddest. Not some historical foot-
note, but Jimmy the man, making it as best as he could. A man who
thought about his family and missed his home. Benny tells me that
Clyde Killens and a few others who'd made money off Jimmy's fighting watched over him. "Sometimes they cash his check," Benny says,

"and give him an allowance because he liked to gamble, and he didn't care. If he gets in a game, he forgets about tomorrow."

As we are about to pull away, Shorty comes running after my car. He's remembered one last thing. "Sweet Jimmy was a disabled vet," he says. "He gets checks from the army. He gets a check every month. We used to gamble it out of him every month. He said, 'I'm getting 740.' He always told us, 'I get 740.'"

Shorty remembers the check. Benny thinks that Jimmy might have used Killens's address. The current residents remember mail showing up every now and then for a Robinson.

The last letter arrived about a year ago.

IS ANYTHING REAL?

The stories go on as long as you care to listen, and they mirror one another mostly, though the few contradictions make it impossible to know what's fact and what's a cocktail of real memory and decades of street life. One guy who fought Jimmy twice claimed Sweet Jimmy was an impostor, that he didn't fight Ali. I'm as sure as I can be that he's wrong, but I can't be positive. In a way, that's perfect: The possibility exists that the only things people know about the man who was called Sweet Jimmy are made up. Brenda, who claimed she still sees him, turned out to be high, crazy, or running a scam.

All the twists and turns add up to one thing: I didn't get to him in time, and he's probably lost forever.

I keep asking whether anyone actually saw him leave, or saw his dead body, or went to a funeral. Nobody did. One person thinks they remember a program from a funeral, but it's gone too. It's comforting to those here to imagine him packing up and moving away. The alternative is horrifying: that he died unnoticed, surrounded by people who used to be his friends. That he's in the potter's field down on Galloway Road.

"A lot of people remember him, but they can't remember the last time they saw him," says James Hunt, who managed the pool hall from 2002 until it closed in 2005.

Sometimes, Jimmy seems close enough to touch, sitting patiently in the pool hall every day, while Singer and I and everyone else look for him in other places. I can see him hiding in the smoke and the shadows, no past, no future, wearing charity clothes they gave him down at the Camillus House. I see his beard, and I imagine the long-forgotten passions that birthed his deep scar. I am close enough to know what his mouth looks like, to see the teeth disappear, and then, he's gone, too, swallowed, a figment of the fractured memory of Overtown. Watching someone be forgotten is like watching them die, and the more people forget, the more it's like he never existed at all. *He used to tell some story*, they say, *but I really wasn't listening*.

In those final years, he got quieter, an outsider even here. Regulars shooting pool wouldn't let him in on games. "If he got some money," Hunt says, "he'd play a few games of pool and claim he could have been one of the world's best. When he said things like that, a lot of people ignored him. He always said he could have beat Ali, but he got in the way of the punch."

He didn't like to be called homeless. "I pay rent," he'd say. Nobody remembers where, or if that was even true. Maybe it was a defiant act of pride in a life full of compromises. He walked in the moment the pool hall opened, earlier if Hunt came to clean. Sweet Jimmy would help for a few free games and a soda. He liked Pepsi. People gave him their leftover food. First of the month, he shot a few games of pool, 50 cents a rack, and bought tobacco. He rolled his own cigarettes. Sometimes, Hunt would ask him why. Jimmy would smile and say, "So I can make 'em as big as I want." The folks who'd loaned him money would line up then too.

"Jimmy," Hunt would say, "when you get through paying out, you won't have any left."

"No," Jimmy would say, "but I can make it."

"He always said, 'I can make it,'" Hunt remembers.

Then the pool hall closed.

He never saw Sweet Jimmy again.

III. WHERE THE HELL DID HE GO?

THE THING WITH FEATHERS

The most important thing in a search isn't a database or contacts or cops. It's hope, and Overtown is methodical in its assault on hope, just as it is unforgiving in its ability to chip away at reality. Sometimes, people are lost for big reasons; sometimes, they are lost because of a typo.

I am in the Miami library, reading through all the issues of the African American paper when I see an item that mentions the name of the man originally scheduled to fight Ali on February 7, 1961: Willie Gullatt. I know immediately why I've been unable to find him. The white papers, and later books and magazine articles, misspelled his name.

He's in the phone book.

The next afternoon, I am sitting under his carport as Willie, who has just lost a leg to surgery, holds court with his neighbors. He's beloved, with folks crowding around to hear stories and others honking when they drive past. They call him Big Willie. I want to believe that somewhere in America, in a similar fashion, Sweet Jimmy is telling neighbors about the night he fought Ali. Seeing what his life could have been makes me mourn for him and makes him seem both closer and farther away than ever before.

"I'll be 75 October 6," Willie says. "And still getting me some unda-yonda."

He grins, and his audience falls out.

"I ain't did nothing since I had the operation," he says, "but she gonna get right after a while."

After some small talk, I finally get to ask the question: "What happened that night?"

Money, he says. Promoter Chris Dundee, Angelo's brother, offered Ali $800 and offered Willie only $300. He told 'em where to stick it.

"What did you do instead?"

He smiles wistfully, remembering an army duffel bag full of bootleg whiskey. "Got drunk," he says.

Looking back, he's got a lot of regrets. "If I coulda, woulda have left that women and that drinking alone," he says, "I believe I could have had a shot at the championship. But I didn't have the sense I have now. If I'd have had the sense, I'd let that booze alone. Left that damn liquor alone and went out there and had a shot at the championship."

But that's all in the past. Now the triumphs are more modest. The folks in the neighborhood want to throw him a barbecue for Labor Day.

"Sunday?" one asks.

"Every day is Sunday with me," he says.

CSI: MIAMI

Hope is good.

Hope keeps the city of Miami's cold case detectives in business. They sit in a small office with a green door. Files fill the room, each a different victim, people like Sandra Jackson, who await closure inside a brown expandable folder, her entire existence reduced to the details of her death: *found at empty lot . . . 3-23-85 . . . 14:34 . . . 1255 NW 38th St.*

Inside, Andy Arostegui helps me run Robinsons through the system again. Nothing. There's an internal database of information that doesn't rise to the level of public information but might be useful to them one day. Among other things, it tracks nicknames. He gets the officer who manages that system to search Sweet Jimmy. Nothing.

Sitting with Andy and me are two cops from Daly City, California, in town to find witnesses for a murder case. I explain that I've been in Miami for a long time looking for a missing boxer. Frank Magnon and Al Cisneros dictate notes back to their home office to help me search another law enforcement database for Jimmy.

"This isn't even a state," says Frank, who's worked down here before. "It's an island of a country. It's like a vapor. They walk in and they're gone."

I fill them in on the search: the fliers and the phone calls, the people in Overtown, the pool hall and barbershops, Mr. Big and Racetrack Shorty.

"His world kept shrinking and shrinking and shrinking," Frank says, "until there was nothing left for him. Some of these guys just drop off the face of the earth."

"And don't want to be found," Al says.

"There was nothing left," Frank says. "He might have decided to just not wake up one day. Sometimes people just say, 'I've had enough.'"

A woman circles the office, pouring the little plastic thimbles of café cubano for the detectives and me. All the homicide guys in the bullpen outside the green door get a midday shot of caffeine too. Andy finishes his last possible search. Sweet Jimmy's not here. In the beginning, I wanted to sit across from Jimmy and have him tell me about his life. Now, near the end, I just want to find a body.

"I got a feeling," Andy says, "you're gonna find him at the medical examiner's office."

NAMING OUR DEAD

It's time to meet Sandy Boyd.

We've spoken on the phone many times; she's the cold case detective of the medical examiner's office. Naming the dead is one of our human responsibilities, she believes, and she is tireless in her work.

Her office is like Andy's, terraced in files. These are the people who died alone, who died with nothing in their pockets, who died in horrible fires or in dark waters or, improbably, both: A few they found in burned-out cars buried in silt at the bottom of the canal. These are the people who died seeking a new life, like the body who fell from the wheel well of an airplane, and those who died running from their old ones, like the young suicide victim who broke into a half-built skyscraper and jumped. Scratching out "Remains, Unknown" and writing in a name is a triumph. "One day, I'm gonna solve all these cases," Sandy says. "Little by little, day by day, these cases are gonna get solved. They are someone's loved one."

The folks at the ME help me narrow the search. Elise Bobbitt, who runs the indigent burial program, says Sweet Jimmy isn't in one of the city's potter's fields. Sandy figures that there's been only one unidentified African American body in the right age range found since the pool hall closed. The captain of a river detox boat saw him floating in the Miami River on December 8, 2008, and fished him out. His body's still downstairs, waiting on a name.

Sandy walks me through the morgue, past the autopsy room. "You don't want to see in there," she says.

She explains the logistics of death. When a body comes in, it goes to Cooler 1, which has big stainless steel doors and looks like a restaurant walk-in. The bodies with names and family go to Cooler 2 after autopsy to await funeral home pickup. Cooler 3 is for bodies they're still trying to identify. Cooler 4 provides extra storage space.

She takes me through the doors to another building and opens the door to the Decomposed Autopsy room, and the smell of death almost knocks me down—a combination of really strong blue cheese and old buttermilk. This is where Cooler 5 lives. There's a person on the table. He's got a tag on his left big toe. Bleached spots dot his body, and his skin is sloughing off in sheets.

Down the hall is Room M164: the bone room. She opens the door. There are rows of metal shelves with cardboard boxes. "These are all unidentified," she says.

Most contain full skeletons. One is from 1957. She opens a box;

the skull inside is missing a few teeth. It's waiting on a name. In the back are the boxes from 2004 on.

Could any of them be Jimmy?

Back at her desk, she goes through the computer system. Of the 14 unidentified skeletal remains found since 2005, all can be eliminated, for one reason or another. And we also eliminate a final loose end.

"I can show you the guy from the river," Sandy says.

She digs out the file and hands me a Polaroid. The body is shrouded in blue so only the face is visible, offering the dignity in death he never had in life. His eyes are closed, and his nose looks as if it's been broken. He's got a slight overbite, and his front two teeth just stick out on his bottom lip. He doesn't have a scar.

Case 2008-03065 is not Sweet Jimmy.

He's not here.

OUT THERE . . . SOMEWHERE

Sweet Jimmy is gone. He didn't leave a record. He doesn't exist on paper, just in the minds of those left in Overtown. He won't even exist there much longer. I walk into James Hunt's home one Saturday morning, and he tells me the news.

Three days earlier, Racetrack Shorty died.

"They're dropping like flies," James says.

Instead of getting closer to finding Jimmy, I'm getting further and further away. The old boxer grows more elusive every day. There is more talk about a brother who supposedly came looking for him. Some people say the brother took Jimmy home. Others say the brother never found him.

I ask everyone the question: Where did he go?

"I think Missouri."

"He might be in Clearwater."

"St. Pete."

"His brother took him to Tampa."

"They say he took him up to Louisiana and he died in Louisiana."

"New Orleans."

"I heard he went to Belle Glade."

"He went to Texas."

"He had an accent that would be more Georgia."

"Georgia, Alabama, I don't know."

"Ohio."

He's everywhere. He's nowhere. He's both.

EVERYTHING IS EQUIVOCAL

Al Owens lives north of Liberty City, in a house on a corner. He fought Jim Robinson twice. He looks at the photo on the flier.

"That ain't him," he says.

The first time they fought was three months before the Ali bout, the second seven months after. When he got into the ring the second time, he says it was a different guy. He remembers the night because a crowd of hustlers from 2nd Avenue screamed for Al to kill Jimmy. "They wasn't following him to see him win," he says. "They was following him to see him get his ass whupped."

It was a long, hard fight, and Al says he repressed the memory of it until an autograph collector began writing him letters. Al says he knew Jim Robinson, and he knew Sweet Jimmy, and he claims he saw them together. Then, he says, Jim Robinson quit boxing to join the army and the street hustler Sweet Jimmy began fighting under his name. "He had the same beard," he says. "He had the scar already. He wore the same visor. The visor was the thing for the guys playing three-card monte."

But Al is a strange character, too, and his memory doesn't stand up to scrutiny. The timeline he lays out is, simply, impossible. He, too, has lost pieces of himself along the way.

I send three photos—two of a young Jim Robinson in boxing gear and one taken by Brennan—to a lab in England for scientific comparison. The Centre for Anatomy & Human Identification uses a six-point scale, ranging from "Lends No Support" to "Lends Strong Support." One means they are absolutely not the same person; six means they absolutely are. Their report:

> There are numerous morphological and proportional similarities between the man in image 1 and the man in images 2 and 3. There are no apparent morphological or proportional differences which cannot be easily explained by the effects of 20 years of aging, or the differences in camera angle, lighting and resolution; hence, there is nothing to indicate that the man in image 1 is not the same man shown in images 2 and 3. However, these same factors (time, difference in angle, lighting, expression, resolution, etc.) also make it difficult to be more conclusive.

On their scale, they give it a four: Lends Support.

Even science is equivocal. Nothing in the strange search for Sweet Jimmy is certain. Everything is gauzy, covered in a haze of mights and maybes, his disappearance a mirror held up to his life.

GOING HOME

One stop remains before I step out of Sweet Jimmy's world for the last time and return to mine. On my final Sunday morning in Miami, I show up for my shift volunteering in the Camillus House kitchen. After slicing four hams and dicing a crate of onions, I make my way to the exit. I see a familiar face coming in. Two minutes either way, I'd have missed him.

His name is Shelly. He's 80. He's weathered smooth, like a piece of driftwood, with milky eyes. His rap sheet reaches back to the '70s, with busts from trespassing to auto larceny to drug possession. I met him yesterday, in the street, and he told me he saw Sweet Jimmy leave town. He said he and Jimmy were close, hanging out in the

pool hall together. But he seemed out of it, and in a hurry, and standing in the middle of an Overtown street isn't the place for an interview. I thought I'd never see him again.

"Shelly!" I say.

He tries to place me. I remind him we'd spoken yesterday, and he
seems to remember.

"Do you need anything?" I ask.

"A Pepsi," he says.

I return with two sodas, and we sit in the courtyard, surrounded
by other homeless men and women. They are gathered around a radio, listening to gospel and R & B, the old soul hits, staring intently,
as if the music has the power to take them away. The tops of some
waterfront luxury condos rise high above the shelter, and hidden
behind them is the AmericanAirlines Arena, its outdoor jumbotron
flashing messages from another dimension.

"I miss Jimmy," Shelly says.

We talk for an hour and a half. He tells me the story again, and
it's the same as he told it yesterday. That's what makes me believe
him, because the streets have left his mind fractured, full of images
he can't order. I don't think he is capable of remembering a lie.

He says he arrived here 10 years ago: March 15, 1999. He repeats
the date over and over. Later, he says he's been here 20 years. I know
for sure he was arrested here in 1973, so who knows.

He tells me about his parents, back in Atlanta, who left one day
to go to the store and never came back. He tells me about the pool
hall regulars trying to hang together after it closed but ending up
scattered, about Clyde Killens making sure they all had something
to eat and about the last day he ever saw Sweet Jimmy. They were
sitting in the pool hall.

"He told me a long time ago," Shelly says, "his brother was gonna
come for him, you know. But I didn't know when. Jimmy said he had
a brother. I didn't believe it until I saw him. His brother came and
got him and took him home. I'm probably the only one who seen him
get in the car. Everybody know he left town, but I was there when he

got in the car and hauled ass. Shook my hand and every damn thing. Shook my hand. Said, 'I'll see you when I come back.' I never saw him no more."

He points up at the perfect blue sky. "I'll see him again."

A deformed pigeon, large tumors growing off its head, pecks around the concrete patio for crumbs. A crackhead stops throwing himself into a chain-link fence and crawls around under my chair, checking every stray cigarette butt for leftover tobacco. A man who looks too healthy to be here leans back in his chair, closes his eyes, and sings along to the music: *From the bottom of my heart, it's true . . . I wish I could take a journey.* Shelly sits quietly with the addicts and the sick, all huddled together, unwanted. Shelly takes a sip of his Pepsi and thinks about all the people who've come and gone.

"They disappear like the wind," he says.

EPILOGUE

The journey ends where it began. Six years after he first called, Stephen Singer leads me back through his office until we're standing in front of what he calls the masterpiece: two large frames six feet across containing a collage of photos, programs, ticket stubs, and, of course, 49 signatures. There's an engraved plaque: "Jim Robinson's whereabouts unknown . . . autograph missing."

He's no longer searching for Jimmy. "I moved on," he says. "I haven't really thought about it for a couple of years. I'm way past that. I've got real work to do."

It's easy to believe the journey of Sweet Jimmy is unique. It's not. Singer's collection is a reminder of how a boxing life often goes completely off track.

Tunney Hunsaker, the first opponent, spent nine days in a coma after a bout.

Trevor Berbick, the final opponent, was beat to death with a steel pipe.

Herb Siler went to prison for shooting his girlfriend.

Tony Esperti went to prison for a Mafia hit in a Miami Beach nightclub.

Alfredo Evangelista went to prison in Spain.

Alejandro Lavorante died from injuries sustained in the ring.

Sonny Banks did too.

Jerry Quarry died broke, his mind scrambled from dementia pugilistica.

Jimmy Ellis suffered from it too.

Rudi Lubbers turned into a drunk and joined a carnival.

Buster Mathis blew up to 550 pounds and died of a heart attack at 52.

George Chuvalo lost three sons to heroin overdoses; his wife killed herself after the second son's death.

Oscar Bonavena was shot through the heart with a high-powered rifle outside a Reno whorehouse.

Cleveland Williams was killed in a hit-and-run.

Zora Folley died mysteriously in a motel swimming pool.

Sonny Liston died of a drug overdose in Las Vegas. Many still believe the Mafia killed him.

"That's the saddest one," I say to Singer.

"They're all sad," he says. "They're all sad in their own way."

Even finding Sweet Jimmy isn't certain to provide any answers about his life; he might not remember he ever fought at all. Many old fighters end their lives stripped of their memories. The night Jimmy fought Ali, the main event was a light heavyweight title fight between Harold Johnson and Jesse Bowdry. Today, Johnson lives in a Philadelphia VA nursing home and has good days and bad days. His memory is going. Bowdry's wife answers the phone in their St. Louis home. "He's not gonna remember," she says. "He has dementia."

Even Ali is a prisoner in his own body, a ghost like Sweet Jimmy, lost in a different way. He paid a price for his fame, just as the men who fought him paid a price for their brush with it. Nothing is free. Confronting the wreckage reminds me of an old magazine story, written by Davis Miller. There's a haunting moment, in 1989 when things were turning bad. Ali stands at the window of his suite on the 24th floor of the Mirage hotel in Las Vegas. His once booming voice comes out a whisper.

"Look at this place," he says. "This big hotel, this town. It's dust, all dust. Don't none of it mean nothin'. It's all only dust."

A fighter jet lands at an Air Force base out on the desert. Ali watches it through the glass, the lights on the strip so bright it seems like they'll burn forever.

"Go up in an airplane," he says. "Go high enough, and it's like we don't even exist."

DECEMBER 2009

Here and Gone

The strange relationship between Lionel Messi
and his hometown in Argentina.

ROSARIO, ARGENTINA—In the imagination of guidebook writers, who see places as they should be but rarely as they are, there is a passionate love affair between the city of Rosario and its famous progeny, global soccer star Leo Messi.

I know this because it said so, right there on page 179 of the *Lonely Planet*, which I thumbed through during the three hours of countryside between Buenos Aires and Messi's hometown. An Irish ex-pat named Paul, my translator and friend, drove. He'd agreed to help me act on my obsession with Messi, who is one of the world's most famous—and most unknowable—athletes, a combination of which sucked me in. I'd been reading everything I could find, watching Internet videos of him scoring one ridiculous goal after another for Barcelona. Other players seem to chase the ball, while Messi moves in concert with it, full speed to full stop. Then, when the game ends, the fire inexplicably goes out: vanishing eye contact, single-syllable answers—a flatline. The more I read, and the more I watched, the less I understood. Maybe in Rosario, where he was born, that might change.

Pulling into town, Paul and I searched for some sort of acknowledgment, casually at first. You know what I mean. Billy Cannon's Heisman Trophy is on display in a Baton Rouge rib joint, and there's a bar-turned-shrine in Brett Favre's hometown. Signs all over the world let those who happen to rumble past know that this piece of dirt once produced greatness: a football hero, a rock star, an astronaut. Our first day in Rosario, we didn't see a thing that indicated Messi grew up here. The next morning, eating gas station empanadas, we noticed a sports bar across the street, just a few blocks from Messi's old neighborhood. On the windows, there were big photographs of Muhammad Ali, Maria Sharapova, and Rafael Nadal. No Messi. In the coming days, the pattern would repeat itself around town. You'd never know he was from Rosario. Not even at the first pitch where Messi ever played, which we found as the sun set on an urban moonscape of Soviet-style apartment blocks and howling dogs. On the wall outside, in bright colors and abstract lines, someone had spray-painted a graffiti mural. The headband and face looked familiar. Holy hell. I laughed. That's Keith Richards. Then I saw enormous lips next to Keith, as another out-of-context face came into focus: Mick! On the spot where Messi first played, the Rolling Stones capture the imagination more than him. Baffled, and certain I'd missed something obvious, I described what we'd found—or, rather, hadn't—to a local youth coach who knows Messi and his family. I felt better. He saw Rosario the same way we did, and he imagined how he'd react if his hometown spurned him. "You don't feel it's the city of Messi," David Treves said. "If you are the best player on the planet, and you don't even get the most miserable bit of love from your own people, most would say, 'Go to hell. I will stay in Barcelona and just keep filling my wallet.'"

Finally, we carried the guidebook into the local tourist office.

"We are interested in Leo Messi," we told the young man behind the counter. "Is there anything in town we can visit?"

One of his co-workers chuckled.

The guy said no.

Before we left, he remembered one thing. Messi's family owns a bar called VIP—the local pronunciation rhymes with "zip"—and it was just down the road on the waterfront, with the blue umbrellas, in the shade of a willow tree. The low-slung building arches with slick glass and vaulted ceilings, trendy in a suburban and soulless way. There wasn't a single mention of Messi inside. It was Sunday afternoon. Across the ocean, Messi and his Barcelona teammates were kicking off. The game was being broadcast all over the world, but not in Messi's own bar. I looked up at an enormous high-def television, which at the moment was tuned to a cooking show called *Clasico Shawarma*.

DRAWING BLOOD FROM A STONE

Beyond the lack of visible acknowledgment, we soon found something more bitter than mere ambivalence. Late one night, walking back from dinner on Pellegrini Avenue, the town's vibrant restaurant row, Paul and I ducked into a dark, dimly lit pool hall. Everyone looked up for a moment, checking us out. The walls were bare, cigarette-stained, chipped plaster. Smoke hung in the air. A battered espresso machine hissed. No music played. Old men circled the billiards tables, while others sat in small groups, holding cards, fingering dominos. Two thick-ankled women talked with the bartender. One of them wagged her finger at a guy shooting pool. Later, he'd tell us he worked in America for the mob, once moving 16 kilos of cocaine up the Eastern Seaboard in a car. In some detail, he described what it's like to have your fingernails ripped out with pliers. Paul, ignoring my signals to shut his damn mouth, asked if he's ever killed anyone, and he said no. Then he winked. We ordered a few liters of beer, shot a game of pool, and brought up Messi to the old man serving our drinks.

"He hasn't won anything for Argentina," he said.

Just as we saw little of him in Rosario, many of its citizens see little of him in themselves. Messi is as unknown to the people of his hometown as he is to me, sitting in my office watching his famous goal against Getafe over and over on YouTube. They don't understand how he plays, or how he acts, and they don't see a clean cause and effect, no X + Y = Z, that would explain either. Diego Maradona, they get. He grew up violently poor, in a slum named Villa Fiorito. His entire life was a fight to escape the facts of his own birth, and when he succeeds, and even when he fails, his countrymen recognize his struggle. They understand the wellspring of his talent and his demons. Everything Maradona has ever done can be explained by the rough streets of Fiorito.

Messi, now 25, plays like no one they've ever seen. His talent can't be easily explained by biography: a middle-class kid from a stable and ordinary family. Until he became a superstar for Barcelona, seemingly overnight, most people in his hometown had never heard his name. His greatest accomplishments in Rosario came for a youth team. They lost one game in the four years they played together. In the small world of people who follow local children's sports, they became known as the Machine of '87, after the year they were all born.

There was a problem, though, an ocean separating potential and realization. When Messi was 9, he stopped growing. Doctors discovered a hormone deficiency and put him on a regimen of daily injections, which he gave himself, carrying around a little cooler when he went to play with friends.

"Will I grow?" a teary Messi asked.

"You will be taller than Maradona," his doctor, Diego Schwarzstein, told him. "I don't know if you will be better, but you will be taller."

His soccer club, the local professional powerhouse Newell's Old Boys, agreed to help pay for the drugs, but, as costs mounted, it eventually stopped. Frustrated, his father found someone who would pay: Barça. So when Leo was 13, after the Machine of '87 won its final championship, he and his dad, Jorge, moved to Spain. Before Messi left, he stopped into his doctor's office to say goodbye. Schwarzstein wished him luck, and Messi handed him his Newell's jersey, tiny, with the number nine on the back. He autographed it, then rode with his father to the Buenos Aires airport, trading his old comfortable life for an unknown new one.

His mother ultimately stayed behind with his siblings, dividing the family, and Messi, always shy, struggled. When he cried, which was often, he hid. He didn't want his father to see. His whole family revolved around his future; Barça even agreed to employ Jorge while Leo trained at the club's famous youth academy. He went to class, reluctantly, but really he was a professional athlete by the age of 13. Four years passed. During this time of loneliness, when he was a child supporting his family, he changed from Lionel into . . . *Messi*. He grew. Schwarzstein was right. Maradona is 5-foot-5. Messi is 5-foot-7. The next time people in Rosario heard his name, he was a star. "It is difficult to be a hero in your own city," explained Marcelo Ramírez, a family friend and radio host who showed us text messages from Messi. "He didn't grow up here. It's like he lost contact with the people. He is more an international figure than a Rosarino."

The Argentine national team coaches found out about him through a videotape, and the first time they sent him an invitation to join the squad, they addressed it to "Leonel Mecci." In the 2006 and 2010 World Cups, playing outside the familiar Barcelona system, he struggled, at least in the expectant eyes of his countrymen. His coaches and teammates didn't understand the aloof Messi, who once went to a team-building barbecue and never said a word, not even to ask for meat. The people from Argentina thought he was Spanish, and in the cafés and pool halls, they wondered why he always won championships for Barcelona but never for his own country. They raged when he didn't sing the national anthem before games. In Barcelona, Messi inspired the same reaction. People noticed he didn't speak Catalan and protected his Rosarino accent. He bought meat from an Argentine butcher and ate in Argentine restaurants. "Barcelona is not his place in the world," influential Spanish soccer editor Aitor Lagunas wrote in an email. "It's a kind of a *laboral* emigrant with an undisguised homesick feeling."

In many ways, he is a man without a country.

"He is fully Argentine in Barcelona but not completely one in Buenos Aires, since he came to Spain as a child," continued Lagunas, whose magazine *Panenka* devoted an entire issue to exploring

Messi and Rosario, "and the contrast between his amazing games with Barça and the not-so-good with his national team also helps this strange vision of the Argentine people. Unlike Maradona, who shows an ultra-typical Argentine personality, Argentine people find it difficult to recognize themselves in this little, shy, introverted, silent boy."

Messi never reveals anything. When *Sports Illustrated* sent star profiler S. L. Price to interview him, Price got 15 minutes of bland, semi-annoyed answers. An Italian journalist named Luca Caioli wrote an entire biography of Messi that contained basically one revelation: friends and family admitting that Messi is unknowable even to the people closest to him. "When he's not doing so well," close friend Cintia Arellano told the writer, "Leo is a little bit solitary. He retreats. He withdraws into himself. He was like that even with me sometimes. It was like drawing blood from a stone trying to find out what was going on inside."

WITNESSES

Messi's old youth coach slipped an off-brand cigarette from a pack and pinched the filter. He smiled wistfully, a look layered with happiness, wonder, and regret.

"Messi is guarded in a crystal box," Ernesto Vecchio said.

He led us through the Newell's Old Boys football school, past picnic tables of parents watching children in baggy shirts. Newell's is the most historic professional club in Rosario, and like most soccer teams it has a vibrant youth system. Messi trained on this pitch, on days like this one. The skies were tall and blue, a late-winter chill in the air. Off to the side, kids kicked a ball, dodging the row of leafless trees between the bleachers and a fence of sawed-off highway guardrails.

"They all want to be like Messi," Vecchio said with a sigh.

For years, he resented his former player. Something happened here at this school, a bit of magic, and Vecchio played a role. Many people did. There should be some acknowledgment. Instead, they're known as the short-sighted fools who let a legend walk away. The former Newell's team official in charge of Messi's growth hormone payments still carries around receipts, which seem like forgeries, trying to prove that he didn't make the dumbest decision in the history of professional sports. Burn scars remain. Vecchio couldn't even see his former player. Two years ago, talking to a reporter from a London tabloid, he offered the lament of all jilted launching pads: Messi forgot his roots.

"It's over 10 years since we spoke," he said then. "It's a shame kids forget some things when they find success. In 2006 I heard he was in Rosario and I went to his house to catch up with old times. They told me he wasn't there, but it was a lie. He must have been afraid I would ask him for something. Money changes people a bit."

We sat down at a table in the school's café.

"When was the last time you spoke to him?" I asked, fishing for the expected answer. He didn't give it.

"One year ago," he said.

Once again, he had heard Messi was in town, holding court at VIP. By now, Vecchio surely knew the truth. He hadn't been a shaper of Messi's talent, merely a witness to it. Vecchio went to the bar and found a local policeman guarding the door. "When I arrived," he said, "there was a world of people of all ages, trying to get close to him, trying to get photographs taken, looking for autographs. I told the guard who I was and that I wanted to speak with him."

Vecchio waited for an answer in a crowd of sycophants.

Messi said yes. The guard escorted him to a table with Jorge and Leo, who smiled and stood to give his old coach a hug. Messi did not mention the old newspaper quotes. Vecchio kissed his cheek and said how much pride he felt every time he watched a Barcelona game. He thought his former player was happy to see him, but he didn't know for sure. Messi said little. Jorge dominated the table. Vecchio felt the clock ticking as he spoke, surrounded by a jockeying crowd. Little distinguished Messi in Barcelona from Messi in Rosario. He lived in a bubble of fame. It had been this way for years; he'd gone from being alone to always surrounded, which are sort of the same thing. Vecchio asked Jorge if they imagined it would ever get like this. Jorge said no. Vecchio's five minutes ended, and he worked back through the chaos, replaced by another supplicant.

Sitting with us in the café, Vecchio said he hadn't asked for anything. But three months after those five minutes, Jorge Messi hired him to work for the family's foundation. Vecchio's job is to discover the next Leo Messi.

A GLIMPSE BEHIND THE WALL

With each person we met, Messi's inner circle came more into focus.

"It is small and very closed," explained the radio host Ramírez when Paul and I quizzed him one afternoon about the particulars. There is a group of people in Rosario with whom Messi speaks, by phone or text, almost every day. There is another, larger group who hear from him less often, on holidays or special occasions. He spends his time with his aunts and uncles, with his cousins, with his brothers, and with a small group of friends. His mother will excommunicate anyone seen to be taking advantage. Messi is fine with friends bringing other people to hang out with him, as long as they don't ask for anything. He hasn't made a new friend in a long time. Most of his confidants were teammates on the Machine of '87. He texts them before they play big games in Argentina.

The goalie from that youth team, Juan Cruz Leguizamon, one of Messi's oldest friends, met us one evening. He chose a local café called El Cairo, a faded, literary place, an airy room with tall glass windows and a high ceiling. It's one of those time machine bars you find in South America. A Brazilian band played, a 10 piece, and we shouted at one another over the noise. Finally, they took a break and we could talk. Leguizamon is athletic, a goalkeeper now for Central

Córdoba, a small local club. He's got blue eyes and delicate eyelashes. I asked him what part of Messi's life he wouldn't want. He laughed. "As I just said to him, the only thing I wouldn't want is his face." When Messi is home, we're told, he likes to play soccer, both in backyards and on video games.

"Is Messi always Messi?" I asked.

"He is always Barcelona," Leguizamon said, smiling, "and he makes himself the captain."

Messi's friends are a little in awe of him. Years ago, he was better than them, but the difference now is exponential. Leguizamon saw a photograph of Messi screwing around at Barça practice, playing keeper. His form was perfect, naturally, like he'd been playing the position forever. Leguizamon even called and asked if the picture was real. "Yeah, he's Messi," he said. "We are conscious of the fact that we have the best player in the world in front of us, but there is a certain confidence in the feeling we are all equal. We speak about the lives of everyone. We mess around. There are jokes."

"Like what?" I asked.

"Many things," he said, grinning. "His ears, for instance."

Messi, he of the goofy ears, knows what is going on in their lives, and the conversation picks up easily, no matter how much time passes between trips. Usually, Messi and his friends hang out at one another's houses. When they want to go out—he likes a restaurant on Pellegrini called Club de la Milanesa, and a few nightclubs—Messi calls ahead to alert the place. Hearing the stories, it's clear his friends love going out with Messi in part because he attracts so many beautiful women. Sometimes they travel with guards. Leguizamon laughs thinking about the funny moments—the things that happen when your boyhood friend becomes rich and famous. "He asked the security guys to accompany him as he had to go to the bathroom," he says, describing a night out at a bar. "He asked me to go with him. So all the security guys were protecting him, and I was behind, and then another group of security guys protected me, and well, for me, it was silly. They were protecting me—and I'm nobody."

CLOSING IN

We circled the city, moving from address to address, knocking on doors, looking for members of the family. We searched for hints at whatever might be going on inside Messi. Nobody who is great at something is normal. They are all pushed, or pulled, by things that rarely break the surface. Often those things are memories of who they used to be, and where.

On a recent trip to Buenos Aires, to give an example, I wanted to visit Maradona's boyhood house. That sounds simple, but it took days of logistical planning, trying to find someone who could guarantee safe passage into Fiorito, which is home to some of the world's largest cocaine kitchens. Basically, he grew up in New Jack City. Finally, I agreed to pay a local charity $60 to walk me there. The hotel arranged a car to the woman's house. Rolling through the outer slums, the black Mercedes-Benz felt like a spaceship. "It's like going on vacation to Syria," the driver said.

We parked and walked through the streets. A workers protest echoed through a tinny bullhorn a few blocks away. Finally, we stopped in front of a blue-brick hovel, the front yard filled with semi-organized trash. A huge bin of cardboard boxes, a barrel of broken Heineken bottles. The fence sagged. Maradona's distant relatives lived here, squatters, really, making a living by digging through dumpsters. A neighbor told me to leave. She knew Diego as a boy, was friends with his grandmother. "*No viene,*" she spit. He never comes here.

What about Messi? What's his connection to the neighborhood, and the house, where he grew up?

His dad spends a lot of his time in Barcelona, but they have a family compound outside of town. He moved his mother out of their old, simple home, buying her a place in the fanciest building in Rosario, a tower of mirrored glass and buffed metal called Aqualina. It looks like a skinny cruise ship standing on its stern. Messi's mom lives on the entire 26th floor, we're told, with four bedrooms, two terraces, and a small apartment for servants. She just left, the doorman said.

The drive from his new life to his old one took us down along the riverfront, past the port. We turned right off the highway toward the south of town. On Sunday, men built a shanty on the sidewalk off the exit. On Monday, children's clothes hung from a washline outside. Grain elevators peeked above rooflines, out of place, like oil pumpjacks in the middle of West Texas parking lots.

His aunt and uncle still live in the same house. There was a sleek black Audi sports car parked inside the gate. The garage area looked familiar; then I remembered. I saw a video of Messi playing soccer here with his young nieces and nephews, dodging and feinting, moving the tiny ball with his feet, the kids unable to take it away. The look on his face is the same as when he plays in front of millions of fans. There's something innocent about him with a ball. His friends laugh about how Messi seems somehow less than himself without one. Leguizamon told us a story. The last time Messi came to visit, they hung out in a backyard, and they watched him, uneasy, antsy. Finally, without even realizing he was doing it, he pulled a lemon from a tree and juggled it mindlessly with his feet, whole again.

The Internet is full of tribute videos with some version of the title "Messi doesn't dive," a trait rare in a sport where players roll around on the ground like gunshot victims when an opponent so much as breathes on them. Theories abound about why Messi won't fall, about his character or his respect for the game, but I think it's much simpler. If he dives, he loses the ball. The boy forced to grow up fast is only happy at play. He laughs when he scores. He pouts when he loses. He gets moody. When he was young and got kicked out of practice, the coach saw him with his face pressed against a fence, the longing palpable even from a distance. When he got ejected from a match as a pro, he wept. A common adjective emerged: childlike. He acts remarkably like a 13-year-old boy.

We pressed the buzzer. The street was middle-class. A man

answered, probably Messi's uncle, and said his aunt would be back in a few hours. We left a note. I stood outside a bit more before heading back to the car. This is the house where, on Christmas Eve a few years ago, a fan from Sweden stopped by and was greeted by Messi himself, who invited him inside. They talked in the hallway for a half hour. Messi sometimes seems oblivious, like he doesn't realize he's famous. There are videos, taken on shaky cell phone cameras, of him waiting for his own luggage at baggage claim, or walking toward the taxi line, followed by fans. He makes millions of dollars a year and waits for luggage and usually flies commercial, and you get the sense that it isn't because he is trying to stay humble but rather because he doesn't know any better. He seems to sleepwalk until a ball is at his feet. Then he comes alive.

LIONEL IS NOT HERE

We learned the Messi family never sold the old house.

It's on Estado de Israel Street, hidden in a maze of one-ways. After turning at the blue Laundromat painted with the white bubbles, we followed the numbers, counting to 525. The first time, before we figured out how to drive here, we parked and walked. The street seemed to dead-end into a house, and we followed a narrow alley off to the left that led back onto the street. The Messis' yard backs onto the home of Cintia Arellano, who was quoted about blood from a stone. She still lives there. A block away, Argentine funk, called *cumbia*, bumped out of an open window, heavy with bass thuds and loud horns. It's Messi's favorite music. An iPod and earbuds can take him home.

The house looked basically like the other houses on the block, just a little bigger, with a few modifications, including a tall fence, a security camera. It was white, in need of a paint job. The awnings over the small terraces on the second floor were made of sheet metal. Wood shutters covered the windows, which were mirrored.

We stood at the gate and listened. It sounded like someone was home. Paul rang the bell. A woman answered.

"Lionel is not here," she said. "He is in Spain."

The woman said she was a cleaning lady and that nobody lives in the house anymore. The Messis have all moved up in the world, but they like the house to remain clean, as if they might all return to this street and resume the life abandoned when Leo left to become a star. The music echoed off the concrete houses. The cleaning lady wouldn't tell us why a family maintains an empty house. As I stood there listening to the music, an idea began to take shape.

Maradona grew up poor and has spent his whole life running from the blue-brick hovel, never looking back, never able to escape. Maradona has done his best to forget Fiorito, but Messi has done the opposite. He, or maybe his family, clings to the past, as if preserving the modest house at 525 Estado de Israel will preserve something more important and harder to define.

A PILGRIMAGE

Messi isn't known as a deep thinker, or even really as a thinker at all, so it's fair to wonder if he's capable of existential longing. Many recycling bins of column inches have been devoted to the debate about his bland public persona. Is he incredibly well managed? After all, many thought Tiger Woods was unknowable too. Is Messi—how should I put this?—stupid? An idiot savant? What if he's not guarded so much as empty? All those debates are just different ways of asking if he lives a second, interior life. Are there things inside Leo Messi—fears, desires, hopes—that he doesn't share?

There is a European newspaper story I read that strikes me as relevant. A few months ago, he took a private jet to Dubrovnik, Croatia, where a car took him across the Bosnian border into the town of Medjugorje. There's a shrine there, drawing pilgrims from around the world, because in 1981, six local youths claim to have seen the Virgin Mary, and some of them claim to still communicate with her. Messi was the guest of one of the visionaries, as they are known.

Ivan, his host, has received nine secrets from the Virgin that he has never shared. He says he sees Mary every day. She has rosy cheeks, blue eyes, and an oval face. She wears a gray dress. Most people come to have their mind, body, or spirit healed. The visionary wouldn't reveal the reason for Messi's pilgrimage, so we're left to wonder. What is broken inside Messi that he wanted to fix? What can't he buy with his millions or his fame? Of course, it's possible he just thought it might be a cool scene to check out. Maybe the visionary made up the whole thing. Maybe the paper did, or papers, plural, since the news appeared in multiple places, in multiple languages. Maybe we believe it because we want there to be unseen layers of Messi. We want there to be an explanation for his miracles even if we never hear the explanation ourselves. Just knowing it exists would be enough. That's certainly why I was in Rosario, driving around, knocking on doors.

YOU CAN'T GO HOME AGAIN . . . RIGHT?

Late one afternoon, we saw three young men hanging outside Messi's old house. A sleek black Audi sports car with limo-tinted windows sat parked on the sidewalk. Paul and I walked over to them.

"How fast does it go?" I asked, nodding at the car.

"Two hundred and something," Matias Messi said.

Matias, the middle brother, looked like a professional footballer: tracksuit; rakish beard; spiky, gelled hair; big diamonds hanging off each ear. He resembled Cristiano Ronaldo more than Leo. It's his job to manage VIP. Next to him was Rodrigo Messi, the oldest, who usually lives in Spain. He wore a hoodie pulled up over his head. The third guy was their cousin, whose mom we left messages for. The whole scene was bizarre. Even though they have other places to

be, they have returned to hang out at their old home. Not *in* the
home, just on the street outside. An hour or so ago, Barcelona had
finished a game in Spain.

"Two goals from Messi," Matias said.

That's what he called him. Not Leo, or "my brother." *Messi*. Matias did most of the talking, while Rodrigo and the cousin picked on
each other like children.

"What are you looking at?"

"No, I am just looking at you, you idiot, I'll break your head."

"No, you idiot, I'm going to hit you, seriously."

The only time the others really engaged was when Paul mentioned Ronaldo, the flamboyant striker for Real Madrid and Messi's
main rival.

"That's a bad word around here," Rodrigo said. "Ronaldo here is
a bad word."

"Excuse me," Paul said.

"Watch out with that," Rodrigo said.

"I understand," Paul said.

"That's right," Matias said, laughing. "I don't know another that's
so vain like that."

They described the house as the emotional center of a scattered
family, and when the brothers looked up at the peeling paint, Matias
muttered a Spanish expression that translates as, roughly, "this
piece of shit." In the years since Leo moved to Spain, Matias said,
the tangible pieces of home have become more important to Messi
than to the family members who never left. This house, and especially his aunt's house, which Matias describes as a "refuge" for his
brother, the big Sunday meals with the family, even the teammates
he's known since childhood—Leo longs for these things when he's
away. He's trying to fill a hole, this boy who was born in Argentina
and came of age in Spain. He never liked robots or toy cars, just
kicking a ball. He traded his childhood for the game he now plays
with a childish joy. Growing up in Rosario might not have shaped
him, but leaving it certainly did.

"What would happen if you sold the house and didn't tell Leo?" I asked.

"No," Matias said emphatically. "Because, you know, we were all brought up here. We grew up here. For this more than anything else, we still have it."

A CONSTRUCTION PROJECT

Messi keeps returning to Rosario, pulled by obligation, to be sure, but likely by something else too. He works at maintaining connections to his hometown. It starts with the way he talks. I grew up in Mississippi, but as I moved around, I left the guts of my Southern accent in the Midwest. Paul's Irish lilt has been blunted by time and distance. But Leo never lost the very specific Rosarino accent, and he's lived in Spain almost as long as he lived in Argentina. That's a choice.

After an injury, when he needed a month of rehab, he came here to do it. And though tabloids once connected him to one supermodel after another—he's not so childlike that he doesn't know how to do that—he has settled down with a girl he knew growing up. Her family knows his family, and vice versa, and she is now pregnant with his first child, due in October. Newell's has already made plans to present the child with a special club membership card.

His long public feud with his old club, and the club's with him, is ending. He funded a new gym and the construction of a dorm inside the stadium to house youth players. Two days before it opened, I walked through the bowels beneath the grandstands, surrounded by the buzz of saws and the echo of hammers, creating the same sort of academy where he trained in Spain. Maybe, if it's done right, some future boy with talent won't have to move across the ocean alone. Five months ago, the club added two small framed photos of Messi in the café beneath the stadium, one of him as an adult with his arm around Maradona, the other in his Machine of '87 uniform, his eyes focused on the ball, which is actually bigger than his head. A month later, in the lobby of its office, Newell's added a picture of Messi, next to one of Maradona. This season, for the first time, a group of fans brought a Messi banner to home games. We arrived in the midst of a change, and I wondered what someone repeating my journey in five years might find.

Even in the Barcelona locker room, his mind is often in Rosario. After a recent game—the one we watched at VIP—Messi's former doctor, Diego Schwarzstein, texted him. He sent the message soon after the whistle. Ten minutes later, Messi replied. All these things, and the many more I could cite, are the actions of a man searching for something. Whatever his motivation, Messi is actively building a relationship between himself and the city that was, for so long, his hometown in name only. It goes beyond simply returning. He is creating roots.

He's kept the same friends. He's kept his old house, which Ramírez confirmed is in the family because of Messi. "Lionel does not want to sell it," he said. "As some kind of memory, he wants to keep it."

He keeps coming back, even when it's inconvenient. A while back, Ramírez told us, Messi and the Argentine national team were training at the team's facility near the Buenos Aires airport. Practice finished one night at six, and Messi got straight into a car and rode three hours to Rosario. He had dinner with his family, went to sleep, and got up the next morning and rode back to Buenos Aires in time to step onto the field.

"Why does he do it?" I asked his old doctor.

We sat in Schwarzstein's office, where he'd just read me the text messages from the day before. He paused, searching for the right English words, speaking in English, trying to articulate an idea about Messi and the reasons he returns home.

"It was very hard for him, leaving Rosario," he said finally. "He suffered a lot."

There it is, at last, beneath a lot of layers: the familiar sight of cause and effect. Something about the pain of Messi losing his childhood seems to make him always be looking for it—or even still living it—whether he's got a ball at his feet in a packed stadium, or visiting the town where that childhood was lost. I read an interview not long ago with Bruce Springsteen where he said he spent years driving past the house where he grew up, night after night, and a psychologist told him he was trying to go back in time to change the things that happened in that house. Does Messi come back to Rosario because it's normal for someone to miss his family, or is he subconsciously trying to change something about his past, or is he simply stuck at age 13?

FOREVER YOUNG

Past 1 in the morning, at the end of our trip, we crowded around a table in a dark corner of a Rosario hotel. It felt like Havana, haunted by a sort of faded gentility. Juan Cruz Leguizamon sat with us. We'd been talking for almost three hours. It was late.

"What do you think Leo is scared of?" I asked.

"To leave football," he said.

"I can't imagine a 50-year-old Messi," I said.

"The truth is," his close friend said, "me neither."

HOME AGAIN

Leaving town, Paul put on a Pogues record. He sang along, thinking of home, and I looked out the window at the roadside stands selling oranges and trucker food. Route 9 parallels the gently meandering Paraná River, which irrigates endless rows of green soybeans. Pastures of cattle stretched to the sky. This is the road that took Messi away when he was a shy, homesick boy and the one that brings him back now that he's a star. Flags flapped in the wind. Old women hawked produce. Sheet metal windmills pumped water, and

I pictured the 13-year-old Messi making this drive with his father. Everything about the exterior of his life changed after that moment, at first for the worse, later for the better, but we can never know what happened inside. We settle for glimpses, like Messi retracing that long-ago drive, three hours each way to spend a fleeting night, chasing the things he lost on this road.

OCTOBER 2012

The Last Ride
of Bear and Billy

Thirty years after Coach Bryant's last season at Alabama,
the man who knew him best struggles to remember.

TUSCALOOSA, ALA.—Each rising sun takes a little more from the
couple who live in the small brick home southwest of downtown.
Something important is being lost. Billy Varner has been married to
Susie for 57 years, and as her life was once spent waiting on him to
get home from a job that didn't know hours or days off, now it's spent
managing his dementia. Each day brings its own reality. On the
worst, Billy, who is 76, doesn't recognize Susie. He'll dress in the
middle of the night and try to leave, his pajamas rolled up in his
hand. Regularly, he refuses to believe that his old boss isn't at home
waiting for a ride. Billy was Bear Bryant's driver, bodyguard, and
valet, one of the few remaining people who knew him as a human
being. As Billy's memory fades, that knowledge disappears with it,
widening the gulf between truth and imagination.

Billy tells Susie that he talks to the coach. Sometimes Bryant
visits.

"Coach Bryant isn't dead," he'll say. "Don't tell me he's dead."

"Billy," Susie tells him, "yes, he is."

Bear Bryant surrounded himself with people he could trust, and he
trusted nobody more than Billy Varner, a tough, barrel-chested
African American. Billy was always just *around*, in the office, on the

road, on the sidelines. Over the years, various accounts have given him different titles, but essentially, he was a fixer. He took care of business, and he kept everything to himself, even after Bryant died.

"We knew he'd been offered a lot of money to write a book or help make a movie," says Linda Knowles, Bryant's longtime secretary, "and he would have none of that. And no one knew Coach Bryant better than Billy. Even Mrs. Bryant didn't know him as well as Billy did. He was with him almost 24 hours a day."

Billy picked him up in the morning. He dropped him off at night. Sometimes they talked. Sometimes they didn't. Often, Coach read the paper aloud. Once, when a state trooper clocked Varner speeding, Bryant stuck his houndstooth hat in the back window. The patrolman understood and backed off. Billy saw him weak and insecure. He drove him to Birmingham one year before Christmas because Bryant got a letter from a sick girl and he wanted to surprise her. He saw him cry. When Paul took his grandson fishing, Billy came along.

Varner never felt comfortable enough to strike up conversations with Bryant, but he could poke at the Legend of the Bear. Driving through Mississippi one night, they stopped at a catfish house. Bryant bought seafood dinners for everyone there, and Billy cracked later, "It was like you were handing out loaves and fishes." At the end, when Bryant was sicker than anyone knew, Billy heard the private coughs.

The roots of this bond, like many things with Bryant, are full of mystery, myth, and misinformation. Earlier this month, a retired Alabama assistant coach sat at his kitchen table and gauged how much he could reveal.

"What do you know about the story where Coach Bryant and Billy met?" Jack Rutledge asked carefully.

Rutledge played for Bryant's first team and was an assistant on his last, and when he realized that he would be sharing new information, he clammed up.

"Well, we don't hardly know the details," he said finally. "It was so quiet."

The official records show Varner started working for the university police in February 1976, but he'd been around for a decade or more by then, floating in the shadows. "There's not much really you can talk about Billy," Rutledge said. "His life is as concealed as Coach Bryant's life."

The 1982 Liberty Bowl was to be the last game of Bryant's career, and when the college football media arrived in Memphis, Tennessee, Billy became, for a brief moment, a reflected celebrity. They hoped that through him they might better understand the coach. A few days before the game, as a television crew interviewed him, Bryant walked by and cracked, "Don't rush yourself, Billy, I'll bring the car around."

They'd known each other for more than 20 years by then. They watched the moon landing together, hung out with Bob Hope together. They reached the end together, sitting in a 14th-floor suite of the Memphis Holiday Inn. Bryant grew reflective. He looked out the window at the river and the bridge to Arkansas, which led eventually to the place where his journey began: a four-room house without electricity or running water. He poured a drink and chatted with guests. As always, Varner stood in the background. After an hour and a half, Bryant, looking tired and old, walked into his bedroom. He said he had to rest. Billy was worried. "I just don't know what's going to happen to him," Varner told a reporter. "He won't make it without coaching."

After the game, on December 30, Varner drove Bryant back to Tuscaloosa. They made small talk in the car, nothing about the life's work that had just ended. Twenty-eight days later, on a Tuesday night, Billy's phone rang. Coach was at Jimmy Hinton's house and didn't feel well. Varner drove over, helped get Bryant to the hospital.

The next morning, on January 26, Varner ran errands, taking Bryant's daughter to the hospital and dropping off a to-do list at the office for Knowles. Billy told her not to worry about Coach. He'd eaten some sausage, and it upset his stomach is all. In his hospital room, Bryant was joking with the nurses.

Knowles began canceling the next two weeks of Coach's schedule. Varner went home to rest, and that's where he was when the phone rang again. He rushed back to the hospital, and when he saw the look on the team trainer's face, he knew. Bear Bryant had died, and as the news went out on the radio—the man's voice cracked when he said, "Ladies and gentlemen . . ."—Varner stood in the hallway of the Druid City Hospital with nowhere to go.

The local paper interviewed him, and Billy cried. "He could eat pheasant under glass with the president," he said, "or he could eat cheese and crackers with the boys out by the caddie shack, and he'd enjoy it all just the same. That's the man I'll always remember."

He took a month off, trying to figure out how Coach Bryant would tell him to deal with his grief. When he came back, he was a regular campus policeman. They put him on night traffic, and that first winter, he caught pneumonia. He worked security at games, no longer inside the circle. In 1996, 14 years after Bryant died, he retired from the University of Alabama Police Department. He never talked about the private things he'd seen. The director of the Bryant Museum approached him about writing a book. Varner told him no.

Susie Varner answers the door. Billy is asleep.

The living room takes up the front of the house, with a television at one end and, on the wall, a poem about footsteps in the sand, which ends with God telling a follower: "The years when you have seen only one set of footprints, my child, is when I carried you."

It's lunchtime. The lights are low, and the house sits in cool darkness. Susie is short, 77, with gray hair and a walker she pushes around. Her voice sounds exactly like that of comedienne Wanda Sykes, and Susie, in real life and in the pictures around the house, wears a little smirk, as if she knows something you don't know.

"Billy had a stroke in 1996," she says, "right after he retired. Sometimes his mind is clear as a crystal. Sometimes it cloud up and rain."

She sits down and tells the story her husband can no longer tell. They married right out of high school. She was 19. He was 18. Four years later, Billy was bartending at the Tuscaloosa Country Club. That's where he met Alabama's new football coach, and when Varner took the same job at the Indian Hills Country Club, where Bryant lived off the third fairway, they became close. Most afternoons, Bryant would slip into the bar and play cards with friends. When the bar was empty, the two men talked. That led to jobs, bartending at parties and running errands, and by the late 1960s, around the same time the coach traded his brown fedora for a hat with black-and-white checks, Billy began working for Bryant full-time. You want a window into Bear Bryant's power in the state of Alabama? He got his bartender a badge and a gun.

Neither man spent much time with his family. Susie would come home—she worked with mental patients in a local hospital—and see Billy's traveling bag gone. Later that night, she'd get the inevitable call.

She'd always ask: "When y'all coming back?"

He'd always answer: "I don't know."

The coach visited this house once. They were traveling, and Billy said he needed to get home for supper. Bryant asked whether there might be enough for him. Billy found a phone and called ahead, telling Susie to make her good corn bread. She shot back: "I thought all my corn bread was good!" They sat in the kitchen down the hall and ate and laughed. She liked Bryant, thought he had a good heart, even if he did almost always call her Sally. After one trip, when the men went to a horse track, Billy came home with an envelope from Coach. Bryant got the name right; "Susie" was scrawled on the outside. Inside she found $500 and a note. *Buy what you want*, he told her, *not what you need*.

"I always did want me the old-timey ice-cream freezer," she says. "I went and bought me one of those. I didn't use it but one time. But I got it. We made ice cream, one time. Sure did."

These are the stories she can tell. About how Billy left her alone a lot of the time, how he gave up his life like Bryant did and how Billy never got to enjoy his retirement either. She laughs some, with only a little bitterness, about what was gained, what was spent, and what remains. All he has to show for two decades of service are his memories, and even those often hang just out of reach. Susie can tell you what she saw, but that's it. "He never told me anything personal about Coach Bryant," she says. "Nothing."

As she talks, there's a noise down the hall, a rattle of movement and the thump-thump of a cane on the floor. The sound gets louder.

"That's him," she says, standing so he can sit.

"Come here, hon," she says softly.

Billy shuffles into the room wearing gray pajamas and black slippers. A diamond of belly shows through the puckered front of his shirt. His voice is deep and trails off when he's unsure.

"Too many football games," he says. "I ended up playing football."

"You didn't play football," she says.

Billy sits up, his voice and cane rising at the indignity.

"What do you mean, I didn't play football?"

"You didn't play no football," she says. "Uh-uh. No, no. That's a no-no."

Billy deflates, his voice and his body sinking back down into the chair.

"She knows," he says.

She picks back up the conversation about Bryant, and Billy sits across the narrow room, listening. She answers for him when he seems lost.

"You was at the hospital when he died," she says. "Do you remember?"

"No," he says.

———

Something remarkable happens when Billy figures out where the den is located—at first, he stood in the living room confused while Susie called his name over and over—and inches down the hall, through the kitchen where Coach sat one time for supper, into a room decorated with photographs of Bear Bryant.

He remembers.

It happens slowly but clearly. His voice becomes higher-pitched, quick but not rushed, with confidence in the direction of the words, without the long pauses to read the maps inside his mind. All his memories are still in there, somewhere, only much of the time he can't translate them into words. Today he can. The pictures seem to anchor him. The walls are covered with certificates and mementos of his service. He's an honorary assistant coach for the 1975 season. He's a 1978 national champion. To his left, surrounded by the small frames, is a large photograph of Bear Bryant at the 1982 Liberty Bowl, sicker than anyone but Billy and a few others knew, bundled tight against the cold. To his right is the famous painting "315" that shows Bryant on the sideline as he breaks the all-time wins record, and down the wall from that is a pencil-and-ink drawing of Bryant as a young man.

"There's Coach Bryant," Billy says.

That's what he called him, like it was a Southern debutante's double name. Always, Coach Bryant, just like Mary Wilkes or Sarah Catherine: *Coachbryant.*

"That looks like him over there," Billy says.

"That's him too."

He focuses on the shot from the Liberty Bowl. Billy always walked a few feet in front of Bryant, for reasons he's trying to recall.

"That's him up there," he says. "Right there with the hat on, in the middle. I'd travel with him to the games. I remember all of them. We'd go to the stadium. I'd drive him. I'd park the car. He'd get out.

We went to the dressing room. I walked in front of him. To shoot him, they had to get me first."

He forms his right hand into a pistol, and Susie laughs, but then he starts to get lost again. His voice loses its pitch and clarity, sort of like he's got a mouth full of pea gravel.

"Shoot them I always thought."

His eyes get wide, bulging, like they do when he's confused. Gaps open between the words, and sentences turn staccato. He laughs at himself when he recenters. His voice ticks up a few notches.

"Coach Bryant used to be the coach at Alabama," he says. "I keep trying to call that the Indian Hills football team. It was the university football team."

He looks back at the Liberty Bowl photograph. Today his memories seem to orbit around the idea of protecting Bryant from some unseen enemy.

"He's there in the black," he says. "The white hat. There he is. He's following me. We're going into the stadium. He's following me. I always felt if somebody was after him, they'd come at him from the front. I was a big guy"—Billy sits up in his chair, and his face becomes menacing; he bows up his shoulders and arms—"and by the time those bullets go through me, he's gone. We had some guys behind us. I always thought about that. Somebody comes up to do something to Coach Bryant, they're gonna have to get me first. They're probably dead themselves because I was a fast gun. He told me one time, if somebody comes up and shoots me, they're gonna shoot you first. I looked at him like, 'What the hell you think I'm here for?'"

He laughs and claps his hands. Four loud slaps. A half hour or more has passed. His clarity comes and goes. The pictures on the wall hold him. To his right, in the corner of the room, there's the pencil-and-ink drawing, a fresh-faced Bryant, without the deep lines in his face.

This is a portrait of Paul.

"He's young all the time here," Billy says.

The price for memories is regret, and somewhere in the middle of all this, Billy considers how he spent his life. Nobody ever has a plan. A man looks up and he's 76 years old, with memories he can't touch and not much else. Like his boss before him, Billy Varner has come to the place where he must consider what he did with his time. "There was so much going on," he says. "So little coming out of it. You start thinking about what you could have been doing. You get a job out there you would have made $50 more a month. If I'd changed jobs, I would have been making $50 more a month. Oh, shit, $50 wasn't worth it. You had more fun on that job. You can reach up and feel it. When things happened, and you were there."

The pitch of his voice starts to drop again, wavering between the treble of here and the deep bass of gone.

The man Billy Varner is remembering has very little in common with the Bryant who is beloved by so many Alabama fans. Bryant's inner circle, those who knew the man, is surrounded by reminders of this. A few weeks ago, as Linda Knowles took the elevator up to the fourth-floor office where she works for the Alabama faculty senate, a car with a houndstooth paint job drove past her building on Paul W. Bryant Drive, past Bryant-Denny Stadium, past the Paul W. Bryant Museum, which is filled with what can only be called relics, then past the Bryant Conference Center. A houndstooth car is just the beginning. The university sells houndstooth beach balls and houndstooth pool floats, which you can enjoy with an adult beverage kept cold by a houndstooth huggie. Croakies to hold sunglasses, cuff links, purses, both the kind with handles and clutches. Even Knowles sheepishly admits she has a houndstooth umbrella. It's a cult.

Bryant's son, Paul Bryant Jr., remembers his father's birthday more than the anniversary of his death, but for most Alabama fans, everything changed "the day Bear Bryant died." There's even a song named that. This isn't a celebration. It's a deification. Yes, Bear died, but He is risen. Before every Alabama home game, the big video board plays clips of Bryant talking, sounding like he ate a carton of Chesterfields. Fans stand and cheer. Knowles cries every time. There is, always, a disconnect between the few people who miss Paul and the legion who worship The Bear.

The Bear, the rough-faced legend on the video board, was predestined to be great. Paul, who rode in a mule-drawn cart from Moro Bottom, Arkansas, and in the back of Billy Varner's crimson Buick LeSabre, struggled, season after season. Paul never forgot the middle-class kids pointing and laughing at his mother. The number of people left alive who knew *that* Paul is small. It grows smaller all the time. Close friend Jimmy Hinton died a year ago; former assistant and confidant Clem Gryska died last month. The Bear wore houndstooth. Paul started reading a devotional in the final two years of his life that read, in part, "When tomorrow comes, this day will be gone forever, leaving something in its place I have traded for it."

Knowles has walked through the museum about 10 times. She settles in front of the exhibit of his office, the soft black-and-white couch players hated because they'd sink farther and farther down, the white telephone, the wide wooden desk. In real life, biographer Allen Barra reports, Bryant had a copy of Philip Roth's masturbation-heavy literary masterpiece *Portnoy's Complaint* on his shelf. That's been scrubbed for posterity.

Knowles and Varner cleaned out the real version of this office after Coach died. Standing before the exhibit, she can hear his voice all around her, literally, from the museum's video displays. His voice might be what affects her most. At home, she keeps the microcassette of the last letter he dictated, the day before he died. She plays it sometimes. As she stands by the office exhibit, the speakers to her left loop audio of Bryant reading part of that devotional: "What I do today is very important because I am exchanging a day of my life for it."

She stands still, surrounded by the strangers who've come to genuflect, and she thinks, "If they only knew." And yet they don't, and they almost certainly won't. Bryant's family and friends fiercely guard his legacy, but this omertà brings with it an accidental cost. Missing in the houndstooth beach balls and paint jobs is a person. Barra wrote the best biography of Bryant, *The Last Coach*, and even in his book, there is a Paul-sized hole at the center of the narrative. We get hints. "I know I've made this journey," he told a reporter just before his final season. "I'm not sure I've enjoyed all of it. You miss a lot of things you shouldn't miss."

When an assistant coach told him in 1970 that Vince Lombardi had died, Bryant spoke of regrets, and it shocked his friend. It was the first and only time he heard Bryant talk like that, and he realized that maybe his boss was a lonely man. There is certainly regret in Bryant's choice of devotional. "I wish I'd read this 30 years ago," he told a friend. "I wouldn't have wasted so much valuable time." He collapsed once from nervous exhaustion, chain-smoked cigarettes, ripped the filters off ones he bummed, passed out on couches, checked into alcohol rehab. There are actions that tell of unseen turmoil and doubt, but Bryant is never revealed.

Barra found himself attacked for describing one bender at the 21 Club in New York City. This urge to protect, probably born from seeing the *Saturday Evening Post* erroneously accuse the coach of fixing a game, is also erasing something. We know Lombardi from David Maraniss's biography, *When Pride Still Mattered*, and he comes across as smaller and therefore larger in the retelling, because his humanity is on every page. He is a *man*.

Thirty years after his last season, Bryant's humanity lives only in his family and a few aging friends, in former employees such as Knowles, in 72-year-old assistant-coach-turned-athletic-director Mal Moore, and, perhaps most of all, in Billy Varner. Paul W. Bryant is dying for the second time, and one day, in the not-so-distant future, only The Bear will remain.

He's gone.

Billy's voice drops back down, and the words press together, a slurry of confusion and rearranged thoughts, part truth, part fiction. Whatever order was brought on by the photographs disappears.

He pauses. His eyes get wide. He spends a long minute staring at the remote control, trying to figure out how to turn up the volume. Finally, he asks for help. Susie is in and out of the room, doing laundry, listening to gospel music. Bear Bryant looks down from four or five different places.

"I don't ever talk to him now," Billy says.

He says something else, his voice deep, the sentences trailing off. "I don't know whether he died or what" is what it sounds like he says. "I never did hear about him dying."

He smiles and clacks his cane. He puts a finger over his lips and says, "Shhh." On the wall, there's a candid shot of Paul and Billy in what looks like a living room. There's the framed photograph of Bryant on a football field for the final time, with a "Thanks for the Memories" sign in the background. Billy sits in his big brown chair and looks at an oddly familiar man.

"Is that him?" he asks.

MARCH 2012

Urban Meyer Will Be Home for Dinner

A football coach tries to balance the kind of man
he wants to be with the kind of man he is.

I.

Before you join Urban Meyer, who is walking toward the exit of the Ohio State football office, there's a scar you need to see. A few years ago in Gainesville, his middle child, Gigi, planned a celebration to formally accept a college volleyball scholarship to Florida Gulf Coast University. It was football season, so she checked her dad's calendar, scheduling her big day around his job. As the hour approached, she waited at her high school, wanting much, expecting little. Some now-forgotten problem consumed Meyer, and he told his secretary he didn't have time. He wasn't going. His beautiful, athletic, earnest daughter would have to sign her letter of intent without him. Meyer's secretary, a mother of four, insisted: "You're going."

Eighty or so people filed into the school cafeteria. Urban and his wife, Shelley, joined their daughter at the front table, watching as Gigi stood and spoke. She'd been nervous all day, and with a roomful of eyes on her, she thanked her mother for being there season after season, year after year.

Then she turned to her father.

He'd missed almost everything. *You weren't there,* she told him.

Shelley Meyer winced. Her heart broke for Urban, who sat with a thin smile, crushed. Moments later, Gigi high-fived her dad without making eye contact, then hugged her coach. Urban dragged himself back to the car. Then—and this arrives at the guts of his conflict— Urban Meyer went back to work, pulled by some biological impera- tive. His daughter's words ran through his mind, troubling him, and yet he returned to the shifting pixels on his television, studying for a game he'd either win or lose. The conflict slipped away. Nothing mat- tered but winning. Both of these people are in him—are him: the guilty father who feels regret, the obsessed coach who ignores it. He doesn't like either one. He doesn't like himself, which is why he wants to change.

Meyer strolls through the Ohio State football parking lot with his 13-year-old son, Nate. Years from now, when Urban either succeeds or fails in remaking himself, he will look back on these two days in June as a dividing line. On one side, the past 18 months of search- ing, and on the other, the test of that search. In the car, he turns right out of his new office, heading some two hours north. There's vital business at hand, which requires him to leave the football bun- ker on a summer afternoon.

Road trip!

"All right, fun time today," he says, amped and smiling at his son.

Fun? Smiling? Urban? There's gray in his brush cut, weight back on his hips. The radio in the car, as always, is tuned to 93.3, the oldies station. "I Got Sunshine." Tomorrow he will meet with the 2012 Buckeyes for the first time, beginning the countdown to the first practice, the first game, the first loss. Today he's driving to Cleveland to take Nate to an Indians game.

In front of him is a second chance. Behind, there's his old dream job in Florida, which he quit twice in a year, and the $20 million he left on the table, unable to answer the simplest of questions: Why am I doing this? During the break, he studied himself for the first time in his life, looking for a new him or maybe trying to get the old him back—the person he was before a need for perfection nearly killed him. At least he can laugh about it now. During one of his many recent visits to a children's hospital in Columbus, he told a group of nurses on an elevator, "My wife's a nurse."

They turned, and he said, "A psych nurse," which is true.

He paused.

"I'm her patient," he said.

Like any man who destroys himself running for a finish line that doesn't exist, Meyer often longed for the time and place where that race began: Columbus, 1986. As a 22-year-old graduate assistant for the Buckeyes, right down the road from his hometown of Ashtabula, Ohio, each day brought something new. He romanticized the experience; in later years, when the SEC's recruiting wars got too dirty, he waxed about the Big Ten, where it was always 1986, which was just another way of hoping he could look in the mirror and see his younger, more idealistic self. After Jim Tressel resigned in shame a year ago, a joke passed among SEC insiders: "Who's gonna tell Urban there's no Santa Claus?"

It might have been genetic. His father, Bud, idolized Woody Hayes, who died a year after Meyer arrived in Columbus. Bud Meyer thought Woody offered the perfect template for a man: Hard work solves every problem. Never accept defeat. Stay focused on the future; reflection is weakness wrapped in nostalgia. Urban grew up in a house free of contradiction. Bud Meyer believed in black and white.

"No gray," Urban says.

Bud studied three years to be a priest before he met Gisela, who escaped Nazi Germany as a child. They raised three children and never missed a game or a recital. A chemical engineer, Bud enjoyed Latin and advanced mathematics, but when his son struck out looking in high school, he made him run home from the game. The Braves drafted Urban after his senior year, and when he tried to quit minor league baseball, realizing he wasn't good enough, Bud told him he no longer would be welcome in their home. Just call your mom on Christmas, he advised. Not only did Urban finish the season, he told that story to every freshman class he recruited. His whole life had been unintentionally preparing him to coach; after baseball, he played college football at Cincinnati, and the stern men in whistles seemed familiar. Some boys rebel against demanding fathers. Urban embraced his dad's unforgiving expectations, finding a profession that allowed him to re-create the world of Bud Meyer: the joy of teaching, the lens of competition, the mentoring, the pushing—the black and white.

He discovered more than a calling in college. He met a beautiful woman named Shelley, and after he got his first job in Columbus, she moved to town. Once, a possum peeked its head over the television, and Urban and his roommates screamed and stood on the couch, yelling for Shelley, the Ohio farm girl, to do something. Urban made less than his rent. He lived on happy hour egg rolls. Staying up all night during the season, he cut 16-millimeter tape, nursing a six-pack of beer through the tedious job. He loved it. To make ends meet, he picked up shifts at Consolidated Freightways, driving a forklift. Shelley calls it his "Archie Bunker job." He bought steel-toe boots, and three or so nights a week during the off-season, he pulled the graveyard, getting off at 6 a.m., showering, and heading to the football office. At the warehouse, they got a breather about 2 a.m., those callow faces yellowed in break-room light, eating peanut butter sandwiches, maybe a bag of chips. He looked around and saw the same question on every face, one he knew they could see on his: *Why am I doing this?*

In 1986, he knew the answer.

Often he lets in only what he wants; you can watch him listen to a story and pick certain details, turning the facts into an allegory that either confirms some deeply held belief or offers a road map to one he'd like to hold. For instance, there's a book he loves, written for business executives, called *Change or Die*, which shaped his ideas about altering the behavior of athletes. He has talked about the

book in speeches, invited the author to Gainesville, handed out copies, and never, not once, did he realize the book almost perfectly
described him.

"I know," Shelley says, laughing. "He didn't have any self-
awareness at all."

In the car on the way to Cleveland, he is reading a paragraph
from page 150:

Why do people persist in their self-destructive behavior, ignoring the blatant fact that what they've been doing for many
years hasn't solved their problems? They think that they need
to do it even more fervently or frequently, as if they were doing the right thing but simply had to try even harder.

Meyer's voice changes, grows firmer, louder. "Blatant fact," he
says.

He pauses. A fragmented idea orders itself in his mind. "Wow,"
he says.

He asks to hear it again. "Blatant fact," he says. "It should have
my picture. I need to read that to my wife. I'm gonna reread that
now. Self-destructive behavior?"

The car is quiet. Those close to Meyer say he lives in his head,
with a constant interior monologue, which is why he'll zone out
at dinner with his kids or start calling people he knows by the
wrong name.

"Wow," he says. "This is profound stuff. Profound. Now as I sit
here talking about it, I know exactly what happened."

II.

He lost things one at a time.

He lost 15 pounds during every season as the head coach at Bowling Green and at Utah, unable to eat or shave, rethinking things as

fundamental as the punt. Purging the weak, he locked teams inside a gym with nothing but bleating whistles and trash cans for their puke, forcing the unworthy to quit. The survivors, and their coaches, were underdogs, united. His children often asked why they kept moving. Shelley always said, "Daddy's climbing a mountain."

His desire to mentor battled with the rage that often consumed him, a by-product of his need for success and his constantly narrowing definition of it. He threw a remote control through a television. Players whispered about Black Wednesday, about Full Metal Jacket Friday, about a drill named Vietnam. His own body rebelled against the intensity; during his time as an assistant, a cyst on his brain often sent crushing waves of pain through his head when he was stressed. He kept coaching, moving up, each rung of success pulling him further away from his young wife and kids. A voice of warning whispered even then. "I was always fearful I would become That Guy," he says. "The guy who had regret. 'Yeah, we won a couple of championships, but I never saw my kids grow up. Yeah, we beat Georgia a couple of times, but I ruined my marriage.'"

At Bowling Green, at Utah, and finally at Florida, the teams celebrated with something he called Victory Meal. They'd gather after a win, eating steak and shrimp, watching a replay of the game. They'd hang out, enjoying the accomplishment. Players and coaches loved Victory Meal, and Meyer often sat at the front of the room, glowing inside.

Then he won the 2006 national title.

Bud Meyer joined him in the locker room. They hugged, cried, and before Urban left, he took his nameplate from his locker as a souvenir. Back at the office, he gave his secretary his credit card and told her to buy everything she could find from the game. She spent around $5,000 on blown-up photographs. Urban essentially scrapbooked, collecting mementos of the success he couldn't really enjoy. There was something melancholy about it. Truth is, he loved reflecting—his favorite song, Jimmy Buffett's "One Particular Harbour," is about someone who imagines an escape, dreaming of being an old man able to look back—but he'd learned that reflection is weakness, so he didn't indulge beyond the pictures on the wall and those moments in the locker room with his dad.

He lost even that.

Success didn't bring relief. It only magnified his obsession, made the margins thinner, left him with chest pains. After the 2007 season, he confided to a friend that anxiety was taking over his life and he wanted to walk away.

Two years after he cried with his father, Urban Meyer stood on the field with his second national championship team, the 2008 Gators, singing the fight song. After the last line, he rushed into the tunnel and locked himself in the coaches' locker room. He began calling recruits as his assistants pounded on the door, asking if everything was OK. Back in Gainesville, his chronic chest pain got worse, and he did test after test, treadmills and heart scans, sure he was dying. Doctors found nothing, and the pain became another thing to ignore. "Building takes passion and energy," Meyer says. "Maintenance is awful. It's nothing but fatigue. Once you reach the top, maintaining that beast is awful."

A few months later, during the 2009 SEC media days, a reporter asked what it felt like knowing anything but perfection would be a failure. Meyer tried to laugh it off, but he walked away from the podium knowing the undeniable truth of the question.

Success meant perfection.

The drive for it changed something inside him. For the first time, Meyer needed an alarm clock. Shelley called his secretary to ask whether he was eating. Unopened boxes of food sat on his desk. He lost even when they won, raging at his coaches and players for mistakes, demanding emergency staff meetings in the middle of the night. He stopped smiling. Days ended later and later. He texted recruits in church. He ignored his children, his fears realized: He'd become That Guy.

The tighter he gripped, the more things slipped away. *The blatant fact.* The Gators beat Georgia, another step closer to perfection.

He'd been skipping Victory Meal, heading straight to his office to watch film, but after that win he stopped in. The room was almost empty.

"Where the hell is everybody?" he asked.

His strength coach and friend Mickey Marotti didn't want to answer.

"Where the hell is everybody?" he repeated.

"Coach," Mickey said, "they don't come."

The unbeaten streak reached 22 games.

Four days before the SEC title game against Alabama, Meyer got an early-morning phone call: Star defensive end Carlos Dunlap had been arrested and charged with drunken driving, threatening the perfection, triggering the rage, which had always been connected for Meyer. He wanted order, and this desire had turned him in a circle, or, more accurately, a spiral: Losing filled him with loathing, for himself and everyone connected to the loss, and over time his personality came to define losing as anything short of perfection. His rage was the exhaust of whatever hidden motor turned inside him. After the campus police officer delivered the news about Dunlap, Meyer went to the office, overcome, driving in the dark. That week, everything came apart.

He popped Ambien but couldn't sleep.

The morning of the game, early in a quiet hotel, Meyer waited to do an interview, and when his public relations guy, Steve McClain, saw Meyer gaunt in the television lights, he felt panic. Meyer's pants sagged off his thin hips. McClain called Shelley Meyer and asked her to come down: They needed to talk. An intervention loomed. That afternoon, Florida lost to Alabama, and afterward, the cheers from the Crimson Tide echoed in the concrete halls of the Georgia Dome. Meyer limped to the bus, ghost white, settling next to Shelley in the front right seat. His head slumped. An unopened box of chicken sat on his lap.

He'd lost 35 pounds that season.

Six or seven hours later in Gainesville, around 4 a.m., Meyer said his chest hurt, and he fell on the floor. Shelley dialed 911. She tried to sound calm, but a few shaky words gave her away. "My husband's having chest pains," she said. "He's on the floor." "Is he awake?" the operator asked. "Urban," Shelley pleaded. "Urban, talk to me. Urb." Meyer lay on his stomach, on the floor of his mansion, his eyes closed, unable to speak. Soon he'd resign, come back for a year and resign again, but the journey that began with hope in Columbus in 1986 ended with that 911 call and the back of an ambulance.

Urban Meyer won 104 games but lost himself.

Meyer didn't just give up a job. He admitted that the world he'd constructed had been fatally flawed, which called into question more than a football career. Follow the dots, from quitting to asking why he'd lost control to trying to understand himself. *Who am I? Why am I that way?* When the facade fell down, the foundation crumbled, too, so he needed more than a relaxing break. If he came back and allowed the rage to consume him again, his quitting would have been meaningless. He didn't need a piña colada. He needed to rebuild himself. His dad sneered at the weakness when he quit, leveling his stark opinion: "You can't change your essence."

Five months after retiring, Meyer woke up early in a hotel near Stanford University, there for his new job as an ESPN analyst. His chest didn't hurt; a doctor finally thought to suggest Nexium. Turns out esophageal spasms mimic the symptoms of a heart attack. That morning, he went for a run, on a whim grabbing a book he'd started the night before: *LEAD . . . for God's Sake!*

He ran with the book in his hand, stopping on campus to sit and read. He ran an hour, read an hour, back and forth. The sun climbed, and he couldn't turn the pages fast enough. He finished that day and emailed the author from his phone, saying, "That is the most profound book I've ever read."

The novel tells of the winningest high school basketball coach in Kentucky, a man consumed by success. When players make a mistake, he punishes their weakness, destroys watercoolers, but he doesn't understand why his star breaks his hand punching a wall. *They skipped Victory Meal because I did.* Finally, his family fades away. The character's son begs him to shoot baskets, and the coach can't make time. When things collapse and his team can't win, the man is forced to ask, "Why do I coach?"

"That hit home," Meyer says. "That was in my backyard. Even closer, that was in my living room. It brought me back to 1986 and why I made a decision to get into coaching, as opposed to what was going on in 2009—chasing perfection. Never one time did I say, 'To go undefeated at Florida.' All of a sudden, every step, every time I had a cup of coffee, every time I woke up in the morning and shaved, it was all about somehow getting a team to go undefeated at Florida."

The coach in the book forms a relationship with the school janitor, a mystical Christ figure, who becomes a spiritual guide in his search for himself. Meyer left Stanford looking for his own guides. "Without anyone really knowing it," he says, "I went on a yearlong research project. How can you do both? How does Bob Stoops be a good dad and husband and still have success?"

Meyer traveled to Norman, Oklahoma, and met with Stoops, who said, "Live your life. When you go home, go home."

He flew several times to Texas to sit with Mack Brown, who told him to remember when he loved the game. Before you wanted a perfect season, before million-dollar homes and recruiting wars, once upon a time you loved a game.

Meyer and Nate visited West Point, stayed in coach Red Blaik's old house. He sat with Army coach Rich Ellerson in the little café behind the cemetery, in the shadow of General Custer's grave.

Holding hot cups of coffee, they talked about the essential truths often hidden by the contradictions, the things obscured by money and success. Ellerson told Urban that football itself helped nurture and protect its values. The snippets of life lived between the snap and the whistle could purify everything bad that people did to the game. "It clarifies," he said. Meyer, who'd seen the lines blurred in the SEC and within himself, said he wasn't sure. Ellerson offered his sermon on MacArthur and the Corps and the West Point mission: "To educate, train, and inspire." Urban stared at him. "Wait a minute," Meyer said. "You really believe this." They talked about why they loved a game, following the question: *Why do I coach?* At Bowling Green, he'd loved tutoring his players in math. Could he have that back again? The game was the problem, but maybe it could be the solution too.

West Point came in the middle of a 13-day road trip with Nate, maybe the best 13 days of Urban's life. The two helicoptered to Yankee Stadium, hung out for almost a week in Cooperstown, where they held Babe Ruth's bat. "I was 7 years old again," he says.

Back home, Urban slept in. Shelley couldn't believe it, getting up around 7:30 to work out, leaving Urban in bed. When he finally dressed, he'd walk a mile to a breakfast place he loved, lounge around and watch television with the owner, then walk a mile back.

"His mind shut off," Shelley says.

Shelley begged him to do this forever. She'd never seen Urban so happy. He coached Nate's baseball and football teams. He played paintball. The family went out for dinners, and Urban was *present*, cracking Seinfeld jokes and smiling.

But he still felt empty. He'd ask, "Is this it?" He missed the ability to make an impact; he'd gotten into coaching to be a teacher. A challenge grew from his trip to West Point: What if he could have the feeling of Bowling Green on the scale of Florida? What if he could answer the question posed in the novel: Why?

Yet beyond the intellectual journey, he missed football on an almost biological level, deep down in the place where his ambition—where his love and his rage—hibernated. In early November, he stood on the sideline at Bryant-Denny Stadium in Tuscaloosa. The crowd roared. God, he loved the crowd. Sometimes, when it felt as if they'd never lose again at the Swamp, he'd slip his headset off just for a moment and let the noise cover him like a hot rain. In Tuscaloosa, with LSU and Alabama waiting to take the field, the stadium lights bright on the green grass, something awoke. The person standing next to him looked over to find the old Urban Meyer, eyes dark and squinted, arms crossed, muttering, "I miss this."

In late November, Meyer wanted to accept the Ohio State job. Shelley demanded a family meeting. They had all gathered around Thanksgiving in the Atlanta apartment of their oldest daughter, Nicki, who played volleyball at Georgia Tech. Shelley told the kids to ask anything. He heard the fear in their voices: How could he be sure he was ready to go back?

"We wanted him to make promises," Shelley says.

During the fall that Urban spent searching, as the rumors circled about his return to the game, Bud Meyer was slipping away. Lung disease had left him frail and weak. Urban used his freedom to visit whenever he wanted. Around the LSU-Alabama game, Urban and Bud watched a television news report about the open Ohio State job. Urban's picture appeared on the screen.

"Hey, you gonna do that?" Bud asked.

"I don't know," Urban said. "What do you think?"

Bud turned to face him, gaunt in the light. An oxygen tube ran to his nose. Twenty seconds passed, the silence uncomfortable. Thirty seconds.

"Nah," Bud said. "I like this shit the way it is. I don't care who wins or loses."

His response couldn't have been more out of character. Never before had Urban asked his dad for his opinion and not gotten direct, blunt advice: "I think you should . . ." In his father's answer, there was a measure of absolution—maybe for both of them. Sometimes walking away isn't quitting. Sometimes, when the fire burns too hot, walking away is the bravest thing a man can do. Bud offered the best mea culpa he could, in his own way. Maybe he knew this would be one of their last conversations. Ambivalence was his final gift. Whatever Urban chose to do with his future, he could walk through the world knowing he had his father's blessing. They never discussed coaching again.

Two weeks later, Bud Meyer died in his son's arms.

Meyer accepted the Ohio State job three days after his father's funeral, five days after his family demanded promises. During his first news conference, he reached into his suit jacket and pulled out a contract written by Nicki, which he'd signed in exchange for his family's blessing. These rules were supposed to govern his attempt at a new life, as his father's example had governed his old one. So much was happening at once, and as he said goodbye to the man who molded him, he began undoing part of that molding.

He went to work.

Meyer unpacked his boxes, setting up little shrines on the blond-wood shelves of his Ohio State office. To the right, positioned in his most common line of sight, he placed a blue rock with a word etched into it: BALANCE. Behind the rock went a collage of photographs, the orange of a sunset from his lake house—his particular harbor—and of his old church in Gainesville. The shrine was a gift from his pastor in Florida, a prayer from people who love him that he won't lose himself again.

Framed above his desk hung the contract he signed with his kids, written on pink notebook paper.

1. My family will always come first.
2. I will take care of myself and maintain good health.
3. I will go on a trip once a year with Nicki—MINIMUM.

4.   I will not go more than nine hours a day at the office.
5.   I will sleep with my cellphone on silent.
6.   I will continue to communicate daily with my kids.
7.   I will trust God's plan and not be overanxious.
8.   I will keep the lake house.
9.   I will find a way to watch Nicki and Gigi play volleyball.
10. I will eat three meals a day.

III.

Seven months later, Meyer drives through the outskirts of Cleveland, 60 miles from Ashtabula, past the refineries and smokestacks, his son Nate in the back seat. They're almost at the Indians' stadium, where Urban is scheduled to throw out the first pitch in a few hours. Meyer's living his life, keeping the promises he made.

"I've really been working on that," he says. "I'm gonna do that in the fall. I'm gonna go home. I'm not gonna bring my work home with me and not be able to sleep at night. I'm not . . .

"That's easy to say now."

The season is still a few months away. He hasn't lost a game yet. That's what pushed him into the darkest corners of his own personality. He squeezes the steering wheel.

"Can I change?" he asks.

The question hangs in the air. In public he talks a good game, but he knows how hard the next year will be. Maybe, deep inside, he already knows the answer. The skies darken. Rain will soon land on the windshield with heavy thumps.

"TBD," he says. "To be determined."

Father and son play catch in the rain, standing in shallow left at Progressive Field, the bowl of seats empty around them. Urban smiles when Nate backhands a grounder, a schoolboy grin, the one

that believed what the girls whispered in the hall back in the day.
Meyer's enthusiasm is as powerful as his rage. Halfway is for other
people. When he took his girls to Rome and Israel for nine days, they
begged to sleep in just once. Nope. "We attacked Rome as hard as
you possibly can," he says, and then mimics his own stern voice: "'We
are gonna have fun on this vacation!'"

Urban throws one high into the air, watching as Nate settles
underneath it, the scoreboard right on top of them, thunder clapping
in the air, the drizzle coming and going.

"I can't believe they're letting us do this," he says.

These are the things he lost in Florida and the things he's
found in Ohio. He's missed only one or two of Nate's baseball games
since taking the job, an astonishing change. Nicki is entering her
final year at Georgia Tech, and her coach scheduled Senior Night
on the Saturday of the Buckeyes' bye week. Urban will walk onto
the court with Nicki, a walk he's made with other people's children
but never with his own. He's eating, working out, sleeping well,
waking early without an alarm clock. On the night before the 2012
Buckeyes gather for the first time, he's playing catch with his son
in Cleveland.

"Bucket list," Urban says.

The Indians arrange for Nate to throw out the first pitch with
Urban, and in the dugout, the team gives Nate a full uniform, No.
15, with MEYER on the back. Urban pulls out his phone and takes a
picture, sending it to Shelley. He follows his son into the clubhouse,
calling out in his best announcer voice, "Leading off for the Cleveland Indians, Nate Meyer."

Two hours fly past, and they're led back onto the field. Now the
bleachers are full. The speakers echo their names. Urban loops it a
bit, but Nate throws a bullet for a strike.

"What a night, Nate!" Urban says, turning to the Indians guy
following them with a camera. "Get me those pictures. I'm gonna
blow them up. My man brought it!"

They find their seats. Nate holds a slice of pizza. Urban pours a cold Labatt's and digs into a bowl of popcorn. The sun sets over the Cleveland skyline, and the lights shine on the grass. Urban's mind and body are in the same place. Urban and Nate recite favorite movie lines and list the ballparks they've visited. "I'm melting inside," Meyer says finally. "You can't get this back. Remember That Guy? I'm not That Guy right now."

The next morning begins back in Columbus with heavy-metal music grinding out of the weight room. Shouts and whistles filter in from the practice field. No other place in the world sounds like a football facility, and the effect is seductive, pulling anyone who's ever loved it back in, like a whiff of an ex-girlfriend's perfume. Outside, hundreds of youth football campers run around like wild men. This week, Meyer's constant nervous pacing—"I'm so ADD," he says—includes laps around the camp, taking pictures with parents, urging moms to make their meanest faces for the camera. He spots Godfrey Lewis, one of his former running backs at Bowling Green, who's now a high school coach.

"What's up?" Meyer asks, beaming.

"You," Lewis says. "That's what's up, Coach."

"You look good," Meyer says. "You got kids?"

"My son is over there," Lewis says.

"Make sure I meet your son. Where's he at?"

"Alex!" Lewis yells.

A boy at the water station turns his head, finding his dad standing with Urban Meyer.

"Alex!" Meyer yells. "Hurry up. Let's go. Let's go."

Alex Lewis runs over.

"Your dad played for me," Meyer says. "He was a great player. Good father, good guy, right? How old are you?"

"Twelve."

"Can you run?"

"Yes," Alex says.

A cocky, curious kid comes over, too, poking his head into the conversation, popping off about how he's faster than Alex. A look flashes across Meyer's face, his eyes bright. He cannot help himself.

"Right now!" he barks.

Meyer calls to Lewis. "Godfrey," he yells, "this guy says he's faster than your boy! We're gonna find out right now."

Godfrey is wired too.

"Right now!" he says.

"Right now!" Urban yells. "Right now! You ready?"

He calls go, and the kids break, Alex Lewis smoking the opposition. Urban and Godfrey stand together, elated, a messy world shrunk to a 10-yard race. Someone wins and someone loses, and there's no ambiguity, no gray. The heat makes the air smokehouse thick. The morning smells like sweat and rings with whistles and coach chatter, the game always the same no matter how much the men who love it change, a simplicity that waits day after day, beautiful and addictive.

Meyer grimaces and wipes a streak of sweat off his face with his shirt. Lunchtime racquetball is war. The football ops guys know to ask Meyer any difficult questions before the game, because losses blacken his mood and rewire a day. It's a running joke: Did Coach win or lose? Today Meyer's playing Marotti, his friend and strength coach. Best of three, tied at one game apiece. Meyer works the angles, lofting brutal kill shots that just die off the wall. Marotti smacks the bejesus out of the ball. Muffled curses echo through the glass door. Meyer chases after a ball and doesn't get there. He cocks back his racket, about to smash it into the wall, but he pulls back. *Be calm.* The end is close, a few points away. Shoes squeak, and the ball pops off the strings, laid over the backbeat of Marotti bellowing, "Fuck!" Meyer loses another point, then another. About to lose the match, he grimaces, flexing his racket to slam the ball off the floor in disgust, then checks his rage. *Be calm.*

———————

The football facility pulses with the rush of building, and through a series of decisions and coincidences, Meyer has somehow managed to go back in time. He feels like he felt in the beginning: unproven, energized by the challenge. Beneath the surface is the idea that maybe this time, with his father's absolution and the lessons he's learned about himself, he could return to 1986 and not make the mistakes that led him to 2009. There's joy in starting a climb, for a 48-year-old coach and for the newly arrived freshmen sitting in the team meeting room, waiting for Meyer to welcome them to Ohio State. The recruiting class, Meyer's first, is nervous, unsure what to expect. He senses their fear and stands at the podium relaxed and calm. All their dreams are right there, waiting to be grabbed.

"I've seen life-changing stuff happen," he tells them.

He describes walking across a graduation stage, your family in the crowd crying, and when you reach out to shake the president's hand, there's a fist of diamonds: championship rings. Meyer bangs his fist on the podium, asking if they've ever heard how much noise five rings make when they hit something.

"I'll do it for you sometime," he says. "It's loud as shit. Some guys get to do that. I've seen it."

Eager faces stare back. He does not tell the story about his dad threatening to disown him for quitting. Reflect, he says. Look around this room.

"These guys will be in your wedding," he says.

They will come back to Columbus as grown men, bringing their sons and daughters to this building, walking the halls. They will point at old photographs, smile at out-of-style haircuts, telling stories about 2012.

But even in his new world, nostalgia must be earned. Contentment must be bought with work, with sacrifice, and, since competition is still black-and-white, with wins.

"That team that goes 4-and-7, how many reunions do they have?" Meyer says. "How many times does that senior class come back? You never see 'em."

This is the difficult calculus of Meyer's future, of any type A extremist who longs for balance. They want the old results without paying the old costs, and while they'll feel guilty about not changing, they'll feel empty without the success. He wants peace *and* wins, which is a short walk from thinking they are the same.

"How about that 2002 national championship team?" Meyer says, his voice rising, the players leaning in. "All the time. When they hit their hands on the table, what happens? It makes a lot of noise. It makes a lot of noise. Let's go make some noise."

Another coach is on the phone, asking for advice about a player who got into trouble. Meyer gives his honest answer, a window into the murky, shifting world of big-time athletics, into how nobody emerges from the highest level of anything with every part of himself intact.

The first year at Bowling Green, Meyer tells him, he'd have cut his losses. His fifth year at Florida, when he needed to win every game, he'd have kept him on the team.

The caller asks about the Buckeyes. "I like it," Meyer says. "I don't know how good we're gonna be, but I like it. We've got one more week, and then we get on the ship to the beaches of Normandy."

On the northwest side of town, Shelley Meyer sits in their new house, praying, literally, that this time will be different.

He's made promises before.

She believed his first news conference at Florida in 2004 when he said his priorities were his children, his wife, and football—in that order. She believed in 2007 when she told a reporter, "Absolutely there's a change in him. There's definitely an exhale."

She wants to believe today. His willingness to admit the possibility of failure is oddly comforting. He knows he could end up back in

2009, which is worth the chance to reclaim 1986. "There's a risk," he says. "What's the reward? The reward is going back to the real reason I wanted to coach."

There's confidence in his voice. She's heard it, seen how calmly he handled the arrest of two players or his starting running back getting a freak cut on his foot.

"Man, I just feel great," he'll say.

"But you haven't played a game yet," she'll remind him.

Shelley moves to the bright sunroom overlooking the golf course, with pictures of the girls when they were little, grinning with Cam the Ram, the Colorado State mascot. There's a Gator on the table and Ohio State pictures on the walls. Another room contains a helmet from every school where Urban has coached and all the memories, good and bad, evoked by each. Once they sat in a gross apartment with a possum over the television, young and in love, wondering where their journey would lead. It's led here, to this dividing line. All the things they want are in front of them. So are all the things they fear.

"I've seen enough change already," Shelley says. "I'm convinced. We still have to play a game, though."

She bites her fingernail and sighs.

"The work he's done," she says, "the books he's read, people he's talked to. He's gonna be different."

She stops between sentences, little gulfs of anxiety.

"He's gonna be different. I totally believe it. I'll just kick his butt if he's not."

One more hopeful pause.

"But he will be."

The door shuts, and his last meeting of the day begins. For the first time, the freshmen and veterans gather, the 2012 Buckeyes in full. Meyer sits calmly at the front of the room, as composed as the crisp lines on his shirt. A quote on the wall is from Matthew, 16th chapter: "What good is a man that gains the world yet loses his soul?" Behind him in his office, there's a blue rock and a pink piece of paper. He's been at the facility almost 12 hours. Breaking No. 4— working no more than nine hours a day—couldn't be helped. Meyer lived up to all but one of his promises today.

His calm lasts until a player giggles.

From the back of the room, it's not clear who laughed, or why exactly, only that the players were making fun of a teammate while an assistant coach gave a speech. Meyer listens, waiting for the coach to finish, stewing, simmering, slowly beginning to burn. If he were transparent, like one of those med school teaching dummies, maybe you could see exactly where his rage lives and how it spreads. In imagination, it's a tiny, burning dot, surrounded by his humor and love for teaching, by the warm memories of 1986, by his desire to grow old and gray with Shelley, and the dot spreads and spreads until there's nothing but fire.

Meyer rises and interrupts the flow of the meeting, looking out at his team. His voice holds steady, but he says he's struggling not to climb into the seats and find the offending giggler. The fire is growing. He paces, back and forth, back and forth, waving his finger toward the center of the room. The air feels tense. Nobody makes a sound. There is one voice.

"Giggle-fucks," he says.

He slips, his language rough and mean, giving himself over to his rage: f-bombs, a flurry of curses, pounding on the soft and the weak, the unworthy who'd rather giggle than chase something bigger than themselves.

In 43 days, he says, Marotti will hand him a piece of paper with a list of names. "Grown-ass men," he says. That's who belongs on his team. No "giggle-fucks," he promises, pointing toward the big pictures of Ohio Stadium to his right.

"We're talking about our season," he roars. "We're going to that place."

His mind is there already.

The players will gather in the tunnel, walking out in scarlet, sunlight blinking off their silver helmets. He'll raise his fist and call the first-team defense. He can see it, a personification of his hopes and fears, of his contradictions: first the grown-ass men moving as one, then the giggle-fucks who can destroy what he spent months building. The sun will shine on silver helmets. The crowd will roar. The band will play. Maybe he'll slip off his headset for a moment, feeling the hot rain. Nothing else will matter. The helmets will sparkle, and the Buckeyes will advance, an army of gray. Standing before his players in the meeting room, he can smell it, hear it—feel it even, in places he doesn't understand and can't control. Nobody makes a sound. Meyer's shirt is wrinkled, untucked a bit. Thick veins rise on both sides of his neck. He squints out at the team, his eyes dark, hiding everything and nothing at all.

AUGUST 2012

The Losses of Dan Gable

Wrestling's most famous winner is taking on one final battle:
To save his sport and all he's ever been.

FEBRUARY 12, 2013, IOWA CITY, IOWA

On the morning the IOC announced it would drop wrestling from the Olympics, Dan Gable was a continent away, fast asleep. It was dark outside. His wife, Kathy, sat at the computer, waiting on the coffeemaker to start. She scrolled through the Iowa wrestling message boards, and one thread caught her attention. When she finished reading, she hurried to the bedroom. Dan was on the left side of the bed, on his stomach. That sticks in her mind, for some reason—him peaceful, unaware. She tapped him, asked if he knew anything about the Olympics getting rid of wrestling in 2020. He mumbled something and kept sleeping for a few moments, until the information traveled through his subconscious and he rushed to the computer. The news rearranged his world. Sitting by himself in the dark, Gable struggled not to cry. He called the head of USA Wrestling and blurted, "Tell me it isn't true!"

Gable's phone started to ring. One by one, his four daughters called. They said they loved him and that he could save wrestling. His oldest, Jenni, called from her home up the road and described the look on her son's face when she told him. He's 9. An unspoken dream seemed to die in his eyes. This hurt Dan most of all. As the sun rose, he pushed away his pain to do the thing he did best: fight.

Dan Gable paces suite No. 8 at Wells Fargo Arena in Des Moines, trying to decide whether he can watch the last Iowa match of the

NCAA wrestling tournament. It's March. The Hawkeyes, whom he hasn't coached in 16 years, are having a miserable weekend, with no national champions. Just the other morning, a former Iowa wrestler saw Gable punishing an unsuspecting elliptical machine in the hotel gym. When the machine had asked his age, Gable, who is 64, typed in 29, as always, and began attacking the pedals, grinding out frustrations about the IOC and the collapsing Hawkeyes.

"How you been?" the wrestler asked.

"I've been better," Gable said.

Now, in the last hour of the tournament, a scowl anchors his face. His eyes jump from side to side, scanning the mats. The arena sound system pours out decibels, sludgy bass lines and screaming guitars. Derek St. John, the Iowa 157 and the last hope to salvage a national title from a tournament gone wrong, crouches at the center of the mat. Gable pumps his feet and looks like he might get sick.

"I don't think I can sit here," he says, stepping out of the suite into the hallway.

His life has been one of victory: He went 64–0 as a high school wrestler, 118–1 in college, won an Olympic gold medal in Munich without surrendering a point, won 15 national titles in 21 seasons as the Iowa coach. Outside in the concourse, feeling weak, then feeling guilty about feeling weak, he knows what must be done. Gable triumphs again—over himself. He swings open the door and steps back inside. "I'm gonna watch," he declares, then almost to himself adds, "I can't be such a chickenshit."

St. John pushes his opponent into the mat. "Ride him like a dog!" Gable yells. The first two periods pass. Sometimes Gable just mouths words, intense, forgetting to speak. St. John is tied with 48 seconds left. The Penn State fans in the next suite are peeking over at the red-faced, bald man losing his shit. At rest, Gable looks like a retired math teacher, but under the influence of anger and adrenaline, he transforms. His eyes seem to shift from a soft hazel to a dull black, the color of an alien, subterranean element. Given the right stimuli, like a vital Iowa match, he seems a good sweat from his final wrestling weight of 149. The eruption arrives. Watching Gable melt down is like watching Picasso paint. He shakes and strains, a rocket on the pad. The flying spit and sudden fits of decorum, like "Jiminy Christmas!"—Tourette's in reverse—are followed by growling, intense curses.

"SONOFABITCH!" he roars down into the fulcrum of noise.

St. John bucks and twists, and with 38 seconds left, he breaks his opponent's grip and takes a 3–2 lead. He is going to win the national championship. Someone says, "This match is over," which pushes Gable to the edge. "No, it ain't!" he yells, his voice sounding like a gut-shot deer looks, ragged from days of this. "It's not over!"

"Four . . . three . . . two . . . one," a friend counts down, and the horn sounds. Everyone in the Gable suite celebrates, except Gable himself, who is almost panting, his eyes glassy. Without anyone noticing, he slips out the door into the concourse. Leaning over, with his head down, the tears come. Soon he is sobbing, his back to the suite. His shoulders heave up and down, shaking. A former Iowa wrestler stops to swap war stories, then suddenly backs up, a look of horror on his face. Mackie Gable, Dan's youngest daughter, steps outside and finds her father weeping.

"I've never seen him like that ever," she says.

Gable doesn't say anything. What would he say? Not even he really knows what's happening to him. Mackie seems unsure, taking a step toward him, then a step back. She doesn't know what to do. She ducks into the suite, scans the room, and calls, "Mom?" Kathy Gable comforts Dan, talking softly to him, and soon he returns, drying his eyes, trying to explain something he doesn't understand.

Later that night, some friends sit around the hotel bar, just as baffled as Mackie. Why was the hardest dude on the planet crying because a wrestler he doesn't coach won a match? Most of the guys at the table are young, and they see Gable as superhuman. But an old friend, Mike Doughty, has known Gable for decades.

"Every once in a while," he tells them, "I'll be traveling with Dan and things like that will hit. He has these things locked in trapdoors

and *eeeek*"—he makes the creaking sound of an old hinge opening—
"they start coming out."

1955, WATERLOO, IOWA

People think Dan Gable isn't afraid of anything, but that's not true.
He is deeply afraid of one thing. Hidden in his past, before he ever
wrestled a match, there's a story most people don't know. Even his
four daughters have never heard it. When he was a small boy, his
parents drank, and they fought. The Gables always seemed to be one
bad night from breaking apart, leaving Dan without a family: alone.
So when Mack and Katie went out on the town, young Dan would
make his way to the front of the house. He would station himself in
the big picture window, scared that they'd come home and get di-
vorced, or maybe not come home at all. From time to time, he'd
suck his thumb. All night, he'd peer down the street, looking for
headlights.

Back home, he's got a 45-acre spread he's put together in pieces over
the years, a place to live out his uneasy retirement. This is where he
was before the wrestling tournament and where he would return
when it ended. Today, a month after the IOC decision, he sinks down
into his hot tub, which overlooks a wide yard of snow, downrange
from the two cement deer that, on occasion, real deer like to hump.
Gable thinks this is hilarious. He's soaking after his intense daily
workout. There's a sign above his head that reads: WHATEVER HAPPENS
IN THE HOT TUB STAYS IN THE HOT TUB.

Gable sighs, a look of mock resignation on his face. "Nothing's
ever happened in the hot tub," he says.

It's late afternoon at the compound, near sunset. The buildings—
the main house, his clubhouse with a sauna and gym, the barn with
his axes and Everlast heavy bag—look like they belong in a Nordic

postcard, all dark wood and peaked rooflines. He jokes that the set of *Rocky* was stolen from him.

He's focused on overturning the IOC decision. When the news broke, Gable invited a reporter to his home outside Iowa City and to the NCAA wrestling tournament, which remains a holy week in his family. He's still the most famous person in the world of wrestling. A Des Moines newspaper reporter once wore an Iowa hat to a Russian village during the Cold War, in the mountains near the Siberian border, where an American had never been. A young man stepped out of the crowd, pointed toward the hat, and said one of the few English words he knew: "Gable."

He sinks down farther into the water. The heat helps him think. He's been doing a lot of that lately, out here by himself, looking back at a life of competition and pain.

Steam rises off the water.

"I never wore a mouthpiece," he says suddenly.

He sticks out his tongue. Gouges and divots cover the bottom, like a target-practice soda can, deep scars and even holes, dozens of them. Wearing a mouthpiece would have prevented the holes and the mouthfuls of blood he swallowed and spit out, but it would also have made him weak, made his jaw slide, made him feel vulnerable. He welcomed the hurt. Now he clenches his teeth. He's always punished weakness with suffering, putting on a war mask for the world and for himself. His face hardens, his mouth curving into a frown, his muscles firing, looking like a weapon.

"It makes you strong!" he roars.

Gable leaps from the hot tub and dives into the drift of snow.

"Ahhhhhhhh," he moans, a cloud of vapor exploding as bare skin hits cold ground, moving his arms and legs back and forth, carving out wedges. Gable is spread-eagled in his backyard making goddamn snow angels. Just as quickly he jumps back into the hot water, his body temperature skyrocketing, the snow melting off.

"It burns," he says, gritting his teeth, and he sounds supremely happy.

His journey has consumed all of their lives.

For years, if you saw Gable at a wrestling event, you saw his wife, Kathy, and his four little girls. At Carver-Hawkeye Arena, they sat in section NN, seats 1–6, the first two rows. If you've seen him at a match lately, they're still there, grown up, screaming down at poorly performing wrestlers, questioning their manhood, urging a coach to "slap the shit" out of one who celebrates a poorly wrestled match. Forget winning an Olympic medal. Are you man enough to marry a Gable? His daughters are funny, pretty, and intense. All ended up with former athletes, and only Molly lives outside the state of Iowa. Jenni and Annie both live in Iowa City. Mackie's just up the road in Dubuque, and they get together as much as they can, mostly around wrestling events. During a speech not long ago, Gable laughed about the rolling circus that travels with him. "My wrestling and family go together," he said. "It's always been that way, from day one with my mom and dad, my sister, my wife, four daughters, grandsons, son-in-laws. They're all here." Some coaches ignore their families on their climb to the top; Gable needed his to be with him, as Sherpas, eventually as fellow climbers. His career molded his family, then welded it together. Wrestling kept his daughters from sitting in a window looking for headlights.

Kathy Gable knew he needed to build his family around wrestling. A blue-eyed Iowa girl, hilarious but fierce in defending her family, she found a soul mate in Dan. She lived with the storm of his career because she loved his willingness to devote himself fully to something. Even now, she alone seems capable of seeing through the shell into the real Dan Gable. He turns to her for the simplest of questions, such as: "When did my mother die?" They first met at a party. She lived in Waterloo then, in high school, and Dan, at Iowa State, sometimes trained in his hometown. For their first date, two years later, he invited her on a bike ride. Between that ride and their wedding some 12 months later, in 1974, he called her every

night. The calls came from his desk at the Iowa wrestling office, after he'd finished coaching.

The Gables measured time in seasons, their world growing as
small and insular as Dan's. Until high school, or maybe even college,
Mackie thought the John Lennon song "Imagine" was written especially for a 1992 wrestling highlight video. She thought it was *about*
wrestling, she admits sheepishly. Dan's obsession became theirs.
Even though he chose this life and they did not, that distinction became smaller and smaller until it ceased to matter at all. "He brought
his work home with him a lot," Mackie says. "His life was his wrestling. When my dad was coaching, there would be some nights at
home when it was scary."

He threw a mug through the Christmas tree. One night they
heard a loud crash; Kathy had asked Dan why he wouldn't kick a
wrestler named Rico Chiapparelli off the team if he was causing so
many problems, and Gable flipped over the kitchen table. The girls'
bedroom doors had holes in them; they'd slam and lock them, and
Dan would punch through them. Boyfriends getting the tour would
see the holes and make a mental note. The girls never actually felt
in danger, just that they needed to stay clear. Before a match with
main rival Oklahoma State, the girls knew not to talk to their dad,
and if they saw him in the tunnel, not to expect a hello. They all
shared the cost of his obsession.

Then, in 1997, burned out and with chronic pain in his hip,
he quit.

Without wrestling, he felt something missing. So did his family.
Mackie cried during the final news conference. Even though she
says their relationship improved after he quit, since he suddenly had
time to watch her play soccer, she also wanted him to keep coaching.
It's hard to explain, this dichotomy, but when he gave up that job,
they all lost something.

"I still don't think I have forgiven him," she says.

They needed the clarity of Gable's obsession. Without it, they
were a different family. Mackie was in elementary school when he

quit. She wanted to wrestle in junior high school, but her mom wouldn't let her join the boys' team. Instead, she volunteered to be the high school wrestling manager, staying after practice to clean the mats. Her reasons are her own, but it's hard not to see a girl trying to keep a world intact. They followed him on his journey and counted his successes as their own. "Our gold medal," Mackie starts to say one day, laughing, correcting herself. "*My dad's gold medal* hangs above the fireplace. It's been there our whole life. It's almost like something we've looked up to."

During the holidays, Gable sits in front of his television and watches *White Christmas*. He's seen it hundreds of times, sometimes alone, sometimes with his kids piled around. It's about General Waverly, who is relieved of his command and struggles to build a new life. At the end, General Waverly puts on his old uniform and is greeted by the soldiers who loved him during the war, who sing "The Old Man." This is the Gable family's favorite part, because it echoes their own lives: a general and his troops, happy to be finished with the battle but missing the fight. At the end, Dan always falls silent, tears in his eyes, no longer thinking about an old movie but about his wife and his girls.

"We'll follow the old man wherever he wants to go," the song goes. "Because we love him."

Gable spends his days trying to be useful. There's a wrestling-sized hole in his life, and he is always trying to fill it. His struggle is never clearer than when he stops by the Iowa wrestling office, to pick up mail that still arrives there addressed to him or to sign autographs. One afternoon, Gable comes into the reception area, making small talk. He asks the secretary, "You need me?"

She smiles and pulls out a stack of posters for him to sign.

"Don't I always need you, Dan?"

"I hope so," he says.

She gives directions, telling him to just sign his name or to add a personal note to a specific fan. After finishing, he walks up a narrow stairwell, toward the lobby of Carver-Hawkeye Arena. People nod when he passes, and he zips his Iowa wrestling coat. It's freezing outside. A bitter laugh escapes his lips, and he looks tired and uncertain.

"I don't know where I'm at when it comes to this Olympic wrestling," he says. "I almost feel—not useless, but . . ."

The IOC's decision is based on internal politics, he explains. The international wrestling governing body's leader and lieutenants weren't respected in the Olympic community and were told repeatedly to make changes to the sport, to fix many of the confusing rules that had been added over the years. They refused. After the IOC decision—its ruling can be cemented or reversed in a September meeting, during which wrestling, squash, or baseball and softball will be chosen—the president of FILA, the international wrestling body, was pushed out by his own board. Gable has used his fame to bring awareness and to lobby behind the scenes, constantly working the phones or getting on planes. He's on fire these days, energized. Gable is on the newly formed Committee for the Preservation of Olympic Wrestling. Dan calls it "C'Pow," like the sound a fist makes on someone's jaw. This battle has, as Kathy Gable says, awakened a sleeping giant. He is fully himself again, filling up the leatherbound calendar he takes everywhere. "Dan is a man of purpose," his friend Doughty says. "This is a new purpose."

Part of his role with CPOW is helping redesign the rules, an important request from the IOC. But Gable fears that the old FILA politics will keep the rules from changing. He fears he is powerless to create that change.

"I don't know," he says now. "I'd like a little more ability to have my fingers on it."

Outside Carver-Hawkeye, he takes small, sliding steps toward his truck, past the statue of him put up a year ago. The bronze Gable isn't lifting his fists in victory, or wagging a finger, but raising his arms in what wrestling fans recognize as a stalling call. It's as if the statue of Lombardi outside Lambeau Field were forever calling delay of game, demanding his teams keep pressing. It's perfect, really. There was no greater sin for a Gable wrestler than to be caught stalling—backing up, eating clock, not attacking and destroying—and once Gable even screamed at a ref to call it on his own guy. The statue is addressing everyone who passes, demanding that they keep fighting. Even before the IOC decision, Gable worried about the future of his sport and hoped to inspire people to save it. On the plaque, he wanted the inscription to read STALLING, as if the bronze Gable were screaming at people. School administrators worried people wouldn't get it, so after weeks of fighting, they settled on a compromise: (NO) STALLING. The statue is also there for his girls and for his grandchildren, so that if they ever need advice when he's dead and gone—he figures he's got 15 years—there will be a piece of him left, forever, reminding them to get off their asses and fight.

A student walks past and doesn't recognize him. Gable looks up at himself and down at the plaque, which is covered in snow, his carefully chosen message obscured. His face is chapped from the cold. Leaning over, he carefully wipes the snow off with his hand.

The five-mile drive from the arena back to Gable's house takes him from the heart of campus into gentle rural hills with clapboard farmhouses and grain silos. It's just him and Kathy now. All four girls have moved out, started lives of their own. In five years, he'll have been retired for as long as he was a head coach.

It's a Sunday afternoon, and he heads down to the basement, which is covered with trinkets from his travels. He loves the two cats, which like to crawl on his legs. Rudy is outside, playing in the woods, but Peekers is by the couch, hacking and dry heaving. The noise stops Gable, and he looks down, his face stern.

"Don't puke," he orders.

The cat hacks a few more times, bobbing her head, then vomits all over the carpet. Dan takes a step back, then rushes toward the door.

"Oh, she puked," he says. "Oh god."

He looks up the stairs.

"Kathy!

"Kathy!

"Hey, Kath!"

"What?" she calls.

"Kath! She just puked. It wasn't good puke either."

In the kitchen, Kathy starts laughing, imagining the scene.

"It looks gray," he says.

He is helpless in the face of the sick cat. Fierce showdowns with Peekers seem like a comical use of the authority he built by demanding everything from himself and from athletes who wanted to be like him. Even 16 years after losing the opiate of competition, he's still grasping for something to replace it. One of his girls says he lost confidence in himself when he turned over the program he built, too burned out to continue, his identity too tied to wrestling to ever let it go. "I've had some unbelievable conversations with Kathy Gable that Dan Gable doesn't know about in that fucking closet right there," says current Iowa coach Tom Brands, sitting in the Iowa wrestling room. He later elaborates: "She just . . . it just pains her that he's not content. He needs something to do. He needs to be relevant."

That's why Gable never fully pulled away, even after he left coaching in 1997, making good money on the lecture circuit, keeping an administrative job in the athletic department. From the beginning, he worked to stop the death of wrestling, many programs cut because Title IX required that schools add women's sports, and the scholarship-hogging football teams paid everyone's bills and were untouchable. The fight gave him focus. When asked by Al Gore to appear with him at an Iowa rally, Gable had a single question for the vice president: What is your position on Title IX? (He did not appear at the rally.)

When Gable started lobbying, colleges were losing more wrestling programs each year, down from 146 in 1981–82 to 77 in 2011–12. His work paid off. After years of a slow reduction in the annual losses, the number of D-1 programs held steady last season. Every state but one now has high school wrestling, and every state but three has college wrestling. "Saving the sport" became his mantra. Still, most afternoons he found himself drawn to the Iowa wrestling practices, sitting in the bleachers like a fan, offering tips. Year after year, when the room cleared, Gable would change into his gear—he kept locker No. 1—and practice moves on the Takedown Machine, trying to keep intact a world he'd first built as a seventh-grade boy.

His time in the wrestling room, and his quest to make sure the sport survived, helped control the storms he felt inside. Gable's life is governed by justification and guilt, as if he's forever paying off some unseen debt. He doesn't like to eat, for instance, without working out, constantly balancing a ledger in his mind. One day in March, he stared at a bowl of pasta, hungry and stubbornly trying not to eat. He'd skipped the gym and now looked longingly at the noodles.

"I don't deserve it," he said quietly.

MAY 31, 1964, WATERLOO, IOWA

Dan and his parents went to Harpers Ferry, Iowa, on the Mississippi River, to fish. They left his older sister, Diane, at home. She was 19. That night, a local boy raped her and stabbed her to death with one of the Gables' kitchen knives. A neighbor found the body. The family threw away all its knives, not knowing which one had been used. Dan's parents fought, torn apart by the murder. They wanted to sell the house and move, but Dan begged them to stay. Nobody touched Diane's room. Her ghost lived there. At night, Dan heard the fights, the words burrowing into his memory, where they'd remain forever. The drinking escalated. He'd lost his sister, and now his deepest fear was coming true. The family was dying with her, and he would be left alone. One evening, his mother screamed, "I wish I'd raised her a whore!" and that was all Dan could stand. Enough! he thought. He got out of his bed, crossed the hall, and climbed into Diane's bed, turning to face the wall. Half an hour later, his parents opened the door, humbled by the courage of their son. He felt the bar of light shining on the bed but stayed still. That night, he didn't sleep a wink. In the morning, he moved his things into Diane's room. The arguments slowed, then stopped, and his parents focused their attention on Dan, who started his junior wrestling season on a tear. He never lost, and his parents never missed a match. Dan loved the look on their faces when he won. He wrestled with a fury his opponents did not understand.

Diane remains a daily presence in the Gable home.

Around the corner from Dan's favorite chair, an overstuffed brown recliner, is the big family room. Above the fireplace is Dan's medal. Kathy has already put out Easter decorations, including stuffed bunnies and an Easter tree. But the first thing you see when you walk in, in a prominent place by the door, is an 8-by-10 picture of Diane, smiling and happy, forever a teenager.

"That's my sister," he says.

He's always been a protective parent, never letting his girls stay home alone overnight, even when they were in college, no matter how much they complained. He put hammers in their cars in case they ran off the road into a body of water. Diane's death is a psychic phantom limb, a complicated pain he talks about more each year, even if he still can't articulate how it makes him feel. One afternoon, he shows his collection of oversize black scrapbooks, which live in the same room as his used crutches and a pile of rifles and shotguns.

His mother made the books, collecting mementos from his journey, starting with local papers, rising up to *Sports Illustrated* profiles. Katie and Mack Gable kept everything. His parents saved his weights from high school, which he still uses in the barn. When his mom died in 1994, he found hundreds of letters he'd written in college. The Gables invested so much in their only remaining child that everything touched by Dan took on a talismanic meaning. Later, over beers at a local bar, he tries to remember when the collecting began.

"They were doing it before I died," he says, then catches himself. He's quiet for a moment.

"Before my sister died," he says, and he changes the subject.

MARCH 28, 1970, EVANSTON, ILLINOIS

After moving into Diane's room, Gable kept winning. He graduated from high school 64–0, a three-time state champion. He didn't lose as a sophomore at Iowa State, or as a junior. He won 118 times in college, entering his final match undefeated. An unknown opponent from Washington named Larry Owings waited. ABC's Wide World of Sports showed up. Gable lost. The pain of his sister's death had been waiting on a moment of weakness, an opening, and in defeat, he couldn't find the strength that had gotten his family through her passing. He thought he'd let Diane down. He'd let his mom and dad down. When he got home, he avoided his parents. When his mom would get him on the phone, he couldn't talk. His throat closed, and the words refused to come out. Everything unraveled. Katie Gable drove to Ames. She confronted her son and slapped him, hard. Dan turned his focus to the Olympics. He got better, more dangerous. Every day for two years, he tortured himself, refusing surgery for torn cartilage in his knee, scared he would miss out on the Olympics. All else he shoved aside or pushed back down. Nobody scored on him in Munich, and when he won, he tossed the medal in the bottom of his gym bag. For a brief period, his panicked parents thought it was lost. They didn't understand. For him, the reward wasn't a medal but seeing how winning it made them feel. A family was his reward. Years later, sitting in a Des Moines hotel hot tub, Gable would bring

up the Owings loss, which he does about once a day. He tried to de-
scribe what it did to him and to his mom and dad. Finally, choosing
his words carefully, he said, "It was like a death in the family."

When the Gables finally arrive in Des Moines for the NCAA tournament, 37 days have passed since the IOC decision. "I'm coming
here with one thing in mind," Dan says after checking into his
suite on the 10th floor of the Savery Hotel, reaching into the closet
and thumbing past two Iowa jackets before pulling out one that
reads USA. In the days ahead, he'll talk to the Iowa state legisla-
ture, to groups of fans, to dozens of reporters, using his fame and
influence to protect Olympic wrestling. Everyone expects him to
lead the fight against the IOC. All his life, Gable has been able to
sense other people's hopes, just as he feels other people's pain as if
it were his own.

Taking on other people's pain is why he left the sport. The *Des
Moines Register*'s wrestling beat writer, Andy Hamilton, said that
Gable quit coaching, in large part, because he could no longer stomach seeing wrestlers he cared about lose. It sounds like coachspeak
and only makes sense once you've watched Gable watch wrestling.
In Des Moines, as the tournament gets under way, he starts making
noises that sound like an animal's death rattle, a moan that starts
somewhere very deep inside.

"Why do I do this to myself?" he says.

He sets his feet far apart and leans down toward the mat. His
hands twitch. The Hawkeyes lose match after match. They're not
wrestling aggressively, not attacking until the end of the third period, and after yet another defeat, Annie rushes back to Dan and
says, "Dad, you gotta start coaching again," an idea that is repeated
not much later by a former college wrestler in the suite. "You want
me to be dead in about two years?" Gable says. "I got out of it to save
my life."

All of his angst coalesces into one brief window of agony, on Day 2, during Matt McDonough's quarterfinal match. A year ago, McDonough dominated people, and now, for some reason, he is wrestling without anger or energy. Upset at the Big Ten tournament, he'd thrown his second-place medal in a trash can and stormed off. Now he is losing again.

"Dad coached McDonough's dad," one of the girls explains.

Generations now have come and gone, and Gable remembers the losers more than the winners. He can rattle off the wrestlers who suffered with him but never got the brief redemption of a championship. He never cheered after one of his own matches, but he'd leap into the air after theirs, and he'd mourn with them after defeats and sit in a sauna wearing a coat and tie to help them make weight. He lived and died with his wrestlers. One of them, Chad Zaputil, still haunts him. Zaputil wrestled at 118 and lost three times in the national finals. After the first defeat, he got the Herky the Hawk mascot tattooed on his thigh. After the second, he got another tattoo, over his heart: an angry golden hawk, wings out, talons sharp and ready. Then he got beat a third time, ending his career. Zaputil disappeared. Gable heard the whispers and searched for him, hanging at his house until he saw him go inside. Gable knocked. Zaputil wouldn't answer, so Gable broke down the door.

"Let me see that tattoo," he demanded.

"No," Zaputil said.

Gable ripped Zaputil's shirt off, and what he saw staggered him. The tattoo had been expanded, to show the hawk clawing out a human heart, with blood splattered all down Zaputil's torso.

"It just killed me," Gable says. "I couldn't handle it."

He thought quitting would spare him the pain, but he was wrong. In Des Moines, McDonough is losing, and Dan is in a panic. His family panics with him. Mackie brings her knees up to cover her face, wraps her arms around her knees. Jenni screams. Dan is screaming now, too, spittle flying out of his mouth.

"What's he doing?" he yells. "McDonough, get up! What's he doing!?"

"McDONOUGH! GET OUT OF THERE! No, he ain't. No, he

ain't. That's bullshit. Ohhhhhh. McDonough got beat! NICE JOB, McDONOUGH!"

The arena falls quiet.

"I'm gonna throw up," Mackie says.

Gable can't sleep that night, haunted by McDonough's loss and the losses of every wrestler he's seen in the past few days, even ones from other schools, kids he's never met. It all combines in his chest, a consuming ache.

"I know the pain," he says.

His daughters have been watching. Not just the past month, or the previous few days, but their whole lives. They've seen the peaks of arrogance and the valleys of self-doubt. They've learned a lot about him by having their own kids. If they don't fully understand what pushes him, they know which clues are important. Lately he's been taking the time to understand new things, like the straps and buckles on his grandkids' car seats. He's been more emotional, calling old wrestlers on the phone to tell stories about how it used to be.

These things must mean something. During a lull in the wrestling, the girls and their husbands sit in the suite, trying to connect the stories, explaining how losing the Olympics feels like the beginning of the end to Dan. "If they drop wrestling," son-in-law Danny Olszta says, "he'll feel he failed."

"I feel bad for my dad," Mackie says. "I don't even know how to explain it. This is . . . his life. Having that taken away, I don't want to say it's killing him. . . . You gotta understand, wrestling is what he went to when he recovered from his sister passing away."

Oldest grandson Gable sits in his chair, never taking his eyes off the mats. His patience astounds them, and they're starting to wonder what his future might hold. He's 9, but he can lock into a sporting event for hours and is so disciplined, he cries if he thinks he might be late for school. While he watches, his mom and his aunts crowd around one another.

"I feel like none of us would be here were it not for wrestling," Jenni explains. "After what wrestling did for my dad and his family, after their tragedy. Wrestling saved them from going down a path of destruction."

Jenni thinks the IOC members would change their mind if they came to Iowa. Drive them through the cornfields to this suite in a deafening, packed arena. Meet her family. See what wrestling means out in the middle of the country and in places like it all over the world, where the thin line between survival and extinction is guarded by toughness. Make them understand what Olympic wrestling has meant to her family, to her father and to her sisters, and what it will mean if it is taken from her sons.

"I have these kids," Annie says. "I have this son. I have this new baby son. How can I possibly look at them and tell them they can never become an Olympic champion? It's part of their blood."

"Like their grandpa," Mackie says.

Gable has been watching himself, too, looking inward, changing, thinking about his family. This year, for the first time since seventh grade, he hasn't spent at least three or four days a week in a wrestling room. One day, as he walks from the hotel to the arena, he tries to explain why. There's a long pause as he thinks.

"Time to move on," he says.

"Why?"

"I had never seen a sunset," he says, and he's laughing at himself, at how he sounds. The wrestling rooms of his life come back to him, bunkers, dark and hot, without windows or natural light, a lot like a poet's vision of hell. Dan loved them. The Iowa wrestling room was perfect, carefully constructed over decades as a confessional, a place where pain could be traded for absolution. Even when he went on long speaking trips, it remained there, a spiritual home. The idea of the room kept him tethered to something, and he remained its alpha. Then he stopped coming.

"This year," he says, "I was getting pulled in one direction toward the wrestling room, but"—he sighs—"I think my wife, the love for my wife . . ."

There's a yawn of silence. Ten seconds pass.

"I got hurt in July," he says.

He hesitates, considering how much to reveal. "Starting a chain saw," he says.

His rotator cuff, long abused, snapped. He felt it immediately, a burn, and when he says "burn," his voice changes, like he's feeling it anew. He couldn't use his arm for two weeks, couldn't crank a boat, couldn't chop wood. Then he reinjured the shoulder—someone tapped him and he swung around, his own motion doing the damage—and doctors told him he couldn't go into the wrestling room. During the heat of summer, when a team is formed, Gable stayed at home, not connected to the Hawkeyes. He liked his time alone, looking out on all he'd built. That surprised him.

The rotator cuff injuries, and an earlier painful fall while hauling in the Christmas tree, had left him hobbled, feeling his age, thinking about the future. He couldn't wrestle, not even on the Takedown Machine. Piece by piece, he'd been stripped of the things that had kept his demons in check since seventh grade, in the gray cinder-block dungeon at West High School. First he lost his sister and his perfect record. Then he lost his wrestling career, then his coaching career, then he lost wrestling itself, seeing former opponents fall victim to Title IX and shrinking budgets. He lost his relevance. His girls grew up. He endured eight knee operations and four hip replacements in exchange for whatever relief wrestling brought. Then doctors told him he couldn't wrestle people any longer, and the Christmas tree and the chain saw nearly took away the Takedown Machine, and that is just about that. Some essential part of Gable is gone forever. He'll likely never wrestle again, stripped of the most important part of himself, his ability to keep his pain buried inside.

Now the IOC wants to take away the Olympics.

Gable walks four or five blocks during this conversation, winding above the sidewalks and streets of Des Moines on the skywalk. A guard checks his ticket and waves him into the suite level. Making the turn down the hall to join his family, he thinks about his useless gear gathering dust in the Iowa wrestling room.

"Maybe it's time to turn my locker in," he says. "It might be."

His words carry many different emotions: surprise, relief, resignation, and, just maybe, acceptance.

"They might need it," he says. "I don't want to hold back any progress."

A few hours before Iowa's final round of the tournament, Gable and two friends find a sauna in a private gym, accessible by an unmarked door and a metal staircase. The temperature rises toward 200. Gable scoops his hand into the water bucket to splash his face. He's been vulnerable, raw after the Olympics fight and the Hawkeyes' collapse. Maybe that's why it hits him now. The memory of his sister comes to him, vividly. He is being pulled backward, toward her death and his complicity in it.

He brings it up on his own, and the story trickles out. Every now and again, he splashes water on his face. His friends look at the floor in silence. The It was a Sunday.

They'd driven the block from a rented fishing cabin to a nearby pay phone. He sat in the back seat. Nobody answered at the house in Waterloo. Dan remembers his parents feeling antsy. They got a neighbor to go check. He said the door was locked but the television or radio was playing. Mack Gable told the guy to get in the house and call back.

They waited.

Dan remembers the noise the phone made, the metallic, guttural rattle.

"Rrrrrrring," he says now. "Rrrrrring."

It's hard to breathe in the sauna.

Mack answered and listened as the neighbor described Diane's half-naked body dead on the living room carpet, in the same room where Dan once sat in the window. Katie kept bumping her husband, asking over and over what he was hearing. She studied his face for clues. Mack dropped the phone. It swung back and forth, slowly, back and forth. Back and forth.

Dan sees the phone again. He pictures it now: a swaying receiver connected by a creaking metal cord to a box.

"She's been hurt," Mack said.

"How bad?" Katie asked.

"She's not alive," Mack said.

Dan hears the words again. *She's not alive.* The sweat rolls down his arms.

Katie tore off toward the cabin, with Dan sprinting after her, Mack chasing in the car. When Dan reached the cabin, he found his mother pounding her head on the floor, over and over again.

"Blood on the floor of the four-dollar-a-night cabin" is what he says in the sauna, and his friends don't say a word.

"It's hot," Gable says suddenly. "I'm gonna step outside."

Mike Duroe and Doughty watch him compose himself. Gable returns, ready to continue. His family had started the endless drive across small Iowa highways when Dan said he might know something. Mack swerved off the road, pulling his son from the car. Dan explained that a neighborhood boy named Tom Kyle had been saying aggressive, sexual things about Diane, but Dan thought it was just normal guy talk. He never said anything to anyone. He didn't know. He was just a boy. Mack slapped Dan, hard, across the face, then hugged him. Pain and relief, even then.

"Helped him," Dan says now. "Helped me."

They drove home, and Dan moved into her room, winning 182 straight matches before losing. Some part of Gable never stopped blaming himself for her death.

His story isn't finished.

Tom Kyle went to prison for life. Then two years ago, on the ride home from a fishing trip, Dan's cell phone rang. It was the prison. Kyle, they explained, was dead. Dan looked out his window as he listened and shuddered. He was passing the parking lot where they found out about Diane, where his dad dropped a pay phone that swung slowly on its cord. Kyle's death brought back the sorrow and grief, the anger and guilt, and Gable walked around his 45 acres when he got home, yelling and screaming at the tall pines. He needed to purge these feelings.

"I didn't get it all," he tells his friends, standing outside of the sauna, leaning in, "but I got a lot. Like the Owings loss."

He closes the door and sinks into a chair. *Like the Owings loss.* Something is very close to the surface, and he tries to force it back down. The pain about his sister is combining with all the other pain he's felt in his life, with Larry Owings, with the Olympics, even with McDonough. He struggles with it. This is the price of trying to bury a lifetime of hurt. At some point, each loss stopped being a separate thing, blurring into the ones that came before, until there isn't even such a thing as individual losses, just loss. Every new pain feels like all his pain. Gable is hunched over. His friends wait for him to move. He rises to his feet and raps the sauna door goodbye.

Four hours later, the emotions that started in the sauna force their way out, released by his joy over Derek St. John's national title. Mackie rushes to find Kathy, who comforts him. "I had to get it out of me," he says, still sniffling, wiping away his tears. "A lot of pain. I had to have a win, just to get it out of me."

They're back in Iowa City. It took all morning to pack the hotel room and load grandkids into the proper vehicles. There'd been drama with Annie, who didn't want to stop and eat together on the way back. It turned into a big fight, tempers flaring, everyone sensitive and exhausted. It's an enormous pain for moms with young children to relocate to a different city every March for a wrestling tournament.

Dan walks through a foot of snow toward the barn, cranking the ATV, the powder blowing over the tires as he accelerates through a clearing in the woods. He pulls up to a small barn with a low ceiling and steps inside to gather wood. The logs are still wet, and the air smells like oak and elm. He's thinking about the recent drama, not sure if he'll be able to get everyone to do it again next year.

"I don't know how long we'll keep up this wrestling stuff," he says.

He steers the vehicle onto a hill where he used to run, pressing the pedal to the floor, kicking up a wake of snow. When he comes to a trail blocked by a fallen tree, he turns around, making a note to come back later with a chain saw. This land is a lot of work, and he's getting older. He's got to be careful. Another fall might be more than he can handle. They're thinking about downsizing. Building a small house and selling the big one to Jenni. Next year, for the first time in their lives, Dan and Kathy are spending January and March in Florida, returning to Iowa in February for wrestling events. They've rented a place. The sun will be a relief, easing Dan's aching joints. Here, surrounded by his forest, he has found the strength to finally surrender, which is its own kind of victory. To his left, five deer move through the trees. Snow piles on the branches, two inches at least.

Up ahead in the driveway, he sees his daughter's car running, coughing exhaust smoke. Mackie and Justin are about to leave, making the drive to Dubuque, where she teaches kindergarten and he coaches soccer. The reverse lights are on by the time Gable reaches the car. He leans in and gently kisses her on the forehead. Mackie's car disappears around the bend, leaving behind a red glow and then not even that. Everything is still. The house is empty. He'll know the fate of Olympic wrestling soon enough. His fighting days are nearly finished. Gable goes back inside. All he can do is wait for headlights to shine through the windows, letting him know one of his girls has come back home.

AUGUST 2013

Beyond the Breach

A summer in search of saints, sinners, and lost souls
in the New Orleans that Katrina left behind.

I. THE 10-YEAR FLOOD

With the air conditioner off for filming, the only noise in Steve Glea-son's home is the breathing machine that keeps him alive. That's as good a place as any to start a Katrina story, with the wires and plugs and tubes strapped to the back of his wheelchair, a life-support apparatus doing the heavy lifting for one of the most fervently alive people the city has ever known. The city has known its share. New Orleans treasures hyperlocal folk heroes: Soulja Slim, the king of the street rappers before the storm, shot at least three times in the face and once in the chest, dead in his black Reeboks; Trombone Shorty, who closed out this year's Jazz Fest instead of Elton John or Lenny Kravitz; Chris Rose, the Pulitzer Prize–winning newspaper columnist who wrote the best stories about the storm until his life unraveled and he found himself waiting tables. Gleason is that kind of hero. In the team's first night back in the Superdome after the storm, he stretched out his arms and blocked a punt in the opening series of a Monday Night Football game. There is a nine-foot statue of him outside the Dome now, but the actual Steve Gleason is para-lyzed, four years into an ALS diagnosis. Most people don't make it past five.

"OK, I'm rolling," the camerawoman says.

Gleason uses his eyes and an interactive tablet to highlight the first sentence of the text, one of a series of love letters to the city that a local nonprofit asked influential citizens to write on the 10th anniversary of the storm. Since he can no longer use the muscles in his mouth, he speaks through a computerized voice, his humanity blunted by a droning, syllable-centric machine. Nothing works but his eyes.

"Dear New Orleans," he begins, and when he finishes reading the letter, one of his assistants, Lauren, wipes Gleason's eyes and nose with a towel.

"I cry every time I read it," he says.

Lauren stays strong in front of Steve, but when she gets around the corner into the kitchen, she falls apart, slipping into a bedroom to be alone. It's an ugly thing to watch someone fight a battle he cannot win. Living, then, is in the fighting. "No White Flags," it reads on the Team Gleason foundation's T-shirts and wristbands.

Dear New Orleans.

No white flags.

Rebirth has been the standing field order of the past 10 years in New Orleans, a powerful force shaping the city in ways big and small. Everything is governed by this spirit of renewal, and everything is viewed through its lens, from the fervent love of brass bands to the New Orleans Saints, the standard-bearers of a city struggling back to its feet. But within this hopeful word an idea hides in plain sight: For something to be reborn, it must have first died.

One afternoon in August, the mayor of New Orleans, Mitch Landrieu, meets me at an old seafood market reimagined after the storm as a high-end culinary destination. He tries to explain how 10 years passes like a day.

"For those of us who were here, it was a deeply emotional, deeply personal, painful experience," he says. "I mean, it was hard. But we were in a near-death environment, so we didn't really have time to process it. We literally had to get out of harm's way so that we could stay alive. Then we immediately had to start rebuilding. And I'm not sure that a lot of us have had a chance to process it."

"Have *you* grieved?"

The question catches him off guard, and for just a moment he drops his smooth politician's front, closing his eyes, looking away.

"I really don't know the answer to that question," he says. "Probably not fully. You know, I find myself really getting choked up."

The hurricane lives in a complicated place. Everyone's experience is both communal and personal, obvious and hidden. The memory of the death is everywhere, buried in shallow and temporary graves.

Each summer in New Orleans has a soundtrack.

In the blistering, rainy summer of 2015, that soundtrack is provided by Boosie BadAzz, formerly Lil Boosie, formerly prisoner No. 560699, home from a three-and-a-half-year stay in the plantation fields of Angola for a marijuana charge. New Orleans has the highest incarceration rate in Louisiana, which has the highest incarceration rate per capita in America, which has the highest incarceration rate in the developed world. Eighty-five percent of the inmates at Angola never get out. They take a one-way bus ride to an eastward bend in the river near the Louisiana-Mississippi line. Boosie is one of the lucky ones—he made the trip back south—and now this summer his anthems of Louisiana street life throb out the windows of speeding cars, the floating hint of a hook giving away the track, drowning in cardboard subwoofer fuzz, trunks, and rearview mirrors.

You hear the songs over and over again, like now in Shack Brown's pickup truck, headed out of town on Interstate 10. Brown is a youth football coach, driving to Jackson, Mississippi, to do a stand-up comedy gig, one of the many jobs that allow him to spend most of his time working with kids. He talks quietly with music in the background, until a remix of Boosie's "Show da World" comes on. Brown turns up the stereo and sings. *God keep blessing me 'cause I'm a good father . . . diabetes steady working on my kidneys, man . . . hoping kids learn from my mistakes and take a different route.* Brown got his nickname because he grew before the other boys, then quit growing just after his friends started calling him Shack. He's about 6-foot-1—and was as a seventh-grader. He's got a barrel chest and the gut of a man who never let his changing metabolism alter his love for fried food. His New Orleans East neighborhood smells like bread and coffee, from nearby factories. In the summer, the streets smell like crawfish.

Over and over, he listens to "Show da World," cuing it up when he needs a dose of self-confidence: "Lemme hit that Boosie," he'll say, and one line always makes him rise out of his seat and rap hard with the track, hitting an imaginary drum on each word.

"I'M A PROJECT NIGGA!" he shouts into the steering wheel.

Shack, who gets his name, if not its spelling, from the LSU basketball star, grew up in the Iberville projects. It is his armor and his weapon. Everything in the city rises on the ashes of something else, whether Shack Brown himself or the neighborhood where he was born. Before it was the Iberville, the streets between the French Quarter and what's now I-10 were the most famous red-light district in the country, Storyville, which the navy insisted be closed in 1917. (At some point, big iron wrecking balls are cheaper than years of penicillin.) Only one or two of the buildings that were whorehouses and saloons still stand; an old jazz club is now Iberville's corner store, the New Image Supermarket. The older men drink beer on the sidewalk a block away at Basin Super Market Seafood and Grill. Sometimes Shack visits old friends, but mostly he stays far away from the Iberville, or what's left of it.

People in the projects respect Shack Brown because he survived the early '90s, when Iberville was at its worst. The cops in the nearby French Quarter ride horses, and Shack can still hear the pounding of hooves on concrete, like something from a dystopian Wild West movie. They followed purse snatchers back into the projects—cops in shiny helmets brandishing sticks and guns, flying through the Iberville courtyards, the horses breathing heavy in the thick, wet air.

"I've watched older dudes steal Greyhound buses," he says, laughing.

The kids trust Brown because he was them. He sold drugs and tasted that life—$10,000 a week, he claims—which he realized would lead either to Angola or to a cemetery at the end of Canal Street. Mostly, he couldn't deal with the damage he saw himself causing, making a bad place worse instead of trying to make it better. He was a lousy drug dealer, letting people slide on credit, not cracking down on the addicts who couldn't pay. When he searched his past for men who'd done something positive, the only ones he remembered were coaches. They were respected, the lone alternative to the dealers. In New Orleans, especially, they are the front line in a fight to save just a few of the brightest young men in every generation. Shack started coaching, wanting to help kids but also hoping to feel good about his life, to wash clean the hurt he'd caused. So in the mid-1990s, he devoted himself full time to helping kids, trading the drug cash for $234 a month, working a straight job for Blair Boutte, another former Iberville resident, who today runs the most successful bail bonds company in town. Now 38, Brown works as many jobs as he can find, all while funding his youth teams.

He lives on the margins; until the price of oysters went up, he set up his cooker rig and chargrilled them at parades all over town. Now a croker sack costs $45 and he can't sell them for more than $60, which he says doesn't pay his expenses. During big events, like the Super Bowl, he drives a limo. He volunteers time and money for kids, spending his own cash on ice and water and mouthpieces. On game day, he cooks a meal for his players, who often arrive hungry. A po'boy here, a plate lunch there, feeding 9-year-olds, it adds up.

For a year after Katrina he sat in Houston, going through the motions of a new life, his thoughts never far from the kids in the projects he used to coach. They got so close, the boys latching on to any male influence they could find, and now that he was displaced, he found that he needed them too. He came back to New Orleans in August 2006, shortly before the Superdome reopened, coaching in Mid-City, working on setting up at a place closer to the Iberville.

Three years later, on July 18, 2009, he opened a football program in Lemann Playground, the only public green space between the Iberville and the Lafitte projects, both occupying the gray blocks northwest of the French Quarter. On the day the league officially began, a drill team of neighborhood kids he'd trained led a procession through the gates into Lemann. The adults released balloons. Across four age groups, 125 boys played football, Brown says. That was six years ago. Now the Lafitte projects have been torn down, replaced by mixed-income housing. The Iberville is almost gone, the last of the city's projects. He remembers the hope of opening Lemann Playground. On that sunny day in 2009, with a newspaper reporter taking notes and pictures, he didn't suspect that his football league would be killed by the very spirit of rebirth that rose from Katrina's receding waters.

The next morning, Shack drives back toward New Orleans. His comedy gig went well.

Halfway home, he passes the exit to Gillsburg, Mississippi, right on the state line, where the plane chartered by Lynyrd Skynyrd crashed in 1977. I start to tell the story, but after getting a blank look, I ask Shack if he's ever heard of the band.

"No," he says.

He asks about their famous songs, and I tell him "Freebird" and "Sweet Home Alabama." Nope, he says, those don't sound familiar. We laugh, because there are only four miles between the mostly wealthy, mostly white Uptown neighborhood where I rented a house, where everyone has heard of Skynyrd, and the mostly poor, mostly black neighborhood where he grew up.

Those four miles might as well be an ocean.

He's flipping through the radio stations. A fellow comedian named Blowfish is crashed out in the back, wheezing and snoring. The highway is a drone, and 103 miles from the city, Shack gets quiet.

"My life can't go nowhere but up," he says at last, "living in the Superdome . . . ," trailing off, pulled back in time.

Shack rode out the hurricane with 17 family members in the Iberville. The old projects stood strong. The storm didn't knock out the water or the gas, so his mom cooked Monday night as Katrina hit Louisiana. She made turkey necks and gravy, rice and peas. That's what they ate through Tuesday, watching the water rise, first above the parked cars, then above the street signs.

On Wednesday, the project's running water went off and Shack's mom told everyone it was time to leave. The streets were flooded, and all 17 of them linked arms and tried to walk to high ground. The sun hammered down, more than 100 degrees, dead bodies floating in the muck. Shack found the mules of Mid-City Carriages still tied to a fence. That's how they tried to get people through the water at first, riding on top of the stolen mules. The mules hated the water, and mules don't do anything they don't want to do, so Shack tied them back up. His family walked to the Orleans Avenue exit, rising steeply up to I-10.

They walked a mile and a half the wrong way down the interstate, his grandmother stopping often to catch her breath. The inside of the Superdome smelled like feces, and he held his 4-year-old daughter in his arms so she could go to the bathroom. The free water and blankets got stolen by local gangsters, who then sold them. Tweaking drug addicts wandered the stadium. Brown kept his family in a small corner on the plaza level. They took turns sleeping, someone always standing watch.

Two days later, he loaded his family onto a bus, getting the women on first, then making sure the boys made it, then working to help the police keep loading those still inside the Dome. Because people respect coaches so much in New Orleans, most everyone in the projects had at least heard of Shack Brown. As the sun set, a cop came to him.

"I held the bus with your family," the officer told Shack. "It's time to go."

That's how Shack Brown left New Orleans, riding down the

empty interstate, passing small groups of people still walking to safety, like something from *The Grapes of Wrath*. He doesn't think about it much, at least not on purpose. His memories aren't a cancer, slowly eating away, but a bomb that goes off from time to time without warning. Sometimes he'll be driving alone in his car and look into the mirror and see himself silently weeping.

He doesn't tell anyone about it.

All New Orleanians can describe three moments from the past 10 years in cinematic detail: their escape from the storm, where they were when Gleason blocked that punt, and where they were when the Saints won the Super Bowl. These are the tentpoles of biography since Katrina, and in telling them, people reveal their most unguarded selves. Like a love of the Saints, this is one of the few things in the city to bridge all the deep race and class divides: Everyone suffered through the storm; everyone cried when Gleason blocked the punt; and everyone still struggles to express the emotions they felt when the Saints won in Miami.

Shack Brown went to the Monday night game against the Falcons and saw Steve Gleason block the punt in person, and he doesn't talk much about that either, except to say that during the game he found the spot in the plaza where he'd huddled with his family.

Three years later, in February 2010, he sat with his grandmother in her nursing home as the Saints took the field in Miami. He'd promised her they'd watch the Super Bowl together if the Saints ever made it, the team's historic awfulness becoming a running joke about her mortality. On that Sunday, they sat side by side in front of the television. The game ended, and the Saints won, and his grandmother exhaled: a deep, resonant sigh.

"Now I can get some rest," she said.

He made a joke about sleeping, and she just looked at him, and then he understood.

"I saw it all," she said.

Her health started failing not long after, and she never really got well again. Near the end, Shack had a fourth son, Lorenzo, and he took his boy to meet his grandmom. The baby rested in her arms, and she rested in white sheets, her head on a white pillow. Two days later, she died. That night, Brown slept with Lorenzo on his chest, and around 3 a.m., the baby woke up gasping for air. The next morning Shack got the news about his grandmother, who'd passed away between 3 and 4 in the morning.

"That was them exchanging breaths," he says now, as he looks out the windshield at the long, blurred yellow line of the highway. He's gone from rocking Boosie to silence, the truck somewhere between Jackson and New Orleans, nothing but trees and swamp on either side of the road. His friend is asleep in the back, or at least pretending to sleep out of respect. A plastic butterfly pin hangs on a lanyard looped around his rearview mirror; they wore these pins at his grandmother's funeral. The wings are made from small pink-and-black feathers, and when he's stressed, he'll pluck a feather and say a prayer: "Grandmama, I need you to use your wings over me."

He plucked one a day or two ago.

His oldest son is now repeating the life Shack worked so hard to leave behind, the young man who carries his name, Leander Brown Jr., facing two aggravated assault charges in Georgia, to go with a long and violent rap sheet, the résumé of a habitual offender. Shack doesn't have any money or connections to find a decent lawyer.

"I don't want my child sitting in jail for the rest of his life," he says softly.

He's spent the past two decades trying to save kids, and he can't do a thing for his own. A few years ago, it all got to be too much, fighting the battle for his park, still dealing with the trauma of the storm. He told his wife he wanted to die, let this pain wash away.

"I have my moments," he says, "when I feel like I can't hold it no more."

———————

The night Steve Gleason blocked the punt, Chris Rose was in the stands at the Superdome. It was his job to take the madness around him and somehow put it into words for *The Times-Picayune*. Nobody did it better. He was part of a team that won a Pulitzer Prize for its Katrina coverage, and he was nominated individually for a second, the poet laureate of New Orleans. Two days later, Rose's column about the game appeared, which was subsequently included in his best-seller *1 Dead in Attic*, a collection of his work in the aftermath of Katrina. Two years ago, when the Super Bowl came to New Orleans for the first time since the storm, a local organization got Gleason to read that column on video. The link is still on the Internet. In it, Gleason's voice is slurred, the camera tight, the weight in his body already stealing his ability to talk. . . . *It is superficial and meaningless and a sign of total loss of perspective, but I stand before you and I declare: It is good to feel like a winner . . .*

Gleason's eyes are red and watery, as if he just finished crying or is about to start. A three-day stubble covers his face. This is not the future he'd imagined when he retired in 2008 from football and started pursuing an MBA from Tulane, hoping to read books and debate their ideas, working in his free time to rebuild neighborhoods destroyed by Katrina. Those dreams died with his ALS diagnosis. With whatever time he had left, whether years or decades, he decided he'd fight to not let his disease define him and to help others who didn't have the resources afforded to someone who once blocked a punt in prime time. He started a foundation, which did the usual things like raise money but also something uniquely Steve Gleason. It encouraged people to get out and live. A group of people, including his former Saints teammate Scott Fujita, carried Steve and another ALS patient to the top of Machu Picchu.

On the video, he continues to read Rose's column. . . . *And out my window today as I write this—my open window, oh, glorious day—I*

*hear the same sounds I hear every day—chain saws and hammers
and drills—and it would be foolish to suggest that the workers have
more pep in their step today and that everything is going to be easier
now because, well . . . because it's not . . .*

Gleason's T-shirt reads "No White Flags." When he swallows, the
microphone picks up the noise. His voice is loose and childlike, sharp
vowel sounds the first to go, his tongue heavy in his mouth. The
book is held firm in his hands, the spine bent over. The man who
lives forever in bronze at the Superdome—the statue is named
Rebirth—remains inside him. Gleason's voice grows in strength for
Rose's last line.

Only a game, you say? Like hell it was.

Steve Gleason stares into the camera until the shot fades to
black.

"Shit, between him and the archbishop," Chris Rose is saying,
standing outside an Uptown corner bar, waiting for it to open.
"'What's the archbishop say and what's Gleason say?' I mean, those
are the two guys who people look to when we're confused about
something. I mean, he's the—literally he's the moral epicenter of
this city."

Rose loves how Gleason weighs in on the important issues of the
day, from the cuts at *The Times-Picayune* (against) to gay marriage
(for), and how people look to him as the best of what the human animal does under duress—almost the exact opposite of how people
see Rose.

"The people of this city didn't turn on me," Rose says, sounding
deeply grateful. "I feel the love every day when I walk around."

His voice sounds like tires crunching through an oyster-shell
parking lot, and he moves with a herky-jerky walk, all arms and
legs, like Keith Richards playing himself in a Tim Burton movie. His
hair is curly, gray, and wild, and his T-shirt has a quote from one of
his old stories. It's a few minutes before 4. We check the door to St.

Joe's Bar on the corner of Magazine and Joseph, but it's still dead-bolted. We can see people moving inside. The Roman candy man, a dollar a stick, click-clacks in his donkey-drawn cart. Wooden wheels on uneven streets. There's music coming from somewhere. One of those summer New Orleans storms hit a few minutes ago. Wide rivers of water rush through the gutters, the streets already starting to flood. Rose huddles beneath a vestibule awning, trying to stay dry.

At a little past 4, they let us inside.

"What everybody lost," he says, "was the stuff in the back of their closets, and shoe boxes full of photographs. You know, your letters from your uncle who served in Vietnam, or the awards you won when you were a child. There are people in this town who don't have photographs of their grandparents. It wasn't about couches and TVs and automobiles and Sheetrock. It was about your history being taken away from you. You don't have photographs, the images, the words, the awards, report cards, letters, mostly letters. Diaries. Imagine how much unpublished music was destroyed in that storm."

He lights a cigarette.

When people see him, they instinctively remember Katrina. Many feel compelled to share their own personal horrors. Afterward, they feel better and he feels worse. He doesn't go out much.

"I make a lot of people cry," he says.

The hours slip away, sitting among the red Chinese lanterns on the bar's covered outdoor patio. Most of his troubles made the paper: depression, then drug addiction, $800 of Oxy a day. He took three trips to rehab and the third one stuck, but not before he lost everything. He lost his wife, then got arrested after stalking his new girlfriend. He lost his house; his ex-wife lives there with a new man. He lost his career. He left *The Times-Picayune*, taking a buyout from the place where he'd done his best work, then wrote for the alt weekly until that fell apart. He did television essays for Fox 8, until it sent him packing. He wrote the seminal work on Katrina, a *New York Times* best-seller, then spent all that money on opiates. He's broke.

"Destitute," he says.

That's why he started waiting tables a year and a half ago at a French Quarter fish restaurant. "I strapped that fucking apron on," he says. "There was no time to be proud."

New Orleans was being reborn, rebuilt, and the voice of the city's destruction had been left in the past. Many diners recognized him.

"Are you doing a story?" people would ask.

He shook his head.

"What are you writing these days?"

"I'm writing your order, that's what I'm writing."

The rain picks up now outside the patio, pouring hard and loud. He's quit his job at the restaurant and is looking for writing work again, hoping to find himself in the shadow of the anniversary. His biggest client is a magazine run by a local grocery store. He's still trying to get a local media company to take a chance.

He's making changes. Three days before Christmas, tired of living in the French Quarter, he rented a house in Bayou St. John, a quiet neighborhood north of his old one. The next day, he got a nice check from the grocery store. The day after that, Christmas Eve, he went and bought four bicycles, one for each of his three kids, ages 16, 14, and 12, along with one for himself. He put them under the tree, a father's promise that the future would be better. "The kids are why I'm alive," he says. "God knows what lessons I'm teaching them. I don't know, but I know I'm giving them hard shells."

The heavy raindrops look like a broken rainbow, falling through the prism of the late-afternoon sun. It is sunny and pouring at the same time.

Rose laughs. His laugh is a treble machine gun.

"It's sunshine!" he says.

He's quiet, just listening, watching, sun and water and noise and light.

"That great Tennessee Williams line," he says finally. "'Every raindrop is a piece of time in your hands.' He got it dead-on. It's the only place I know that rains big drops like that when the sun is shining."

He's leaning against the bar, a curl of hair on his forehead. Because he used to be a newspaper reporter, a very, very good one, he's totally aware of what's happening, what I'm writing down about him and why. The beam of yellow light shining through the lattice to his left hits him on the arms, moving up to his chest, glittering off the gold letters on the T-shirt, bright on his face. Ten years come and gone.

"Almost everything's better," he says. "It feels like it happened a million years ago. On the other hand it feels like it happened yesterday. Its manifestations in the city are very few. Its manifestations in my life are complete and total."

During the summer of the anniversary, Rose works on his latest writing assignment: a follow-up of perhaps his most famous piece, an odd experience given the way his life has changed in between. Ten years ago, just eight days after the storm hit, he wrote an open letter introducing the fleeing citizens of New Orleans to the communities around the nation taking them in. The same local nonprofit that got Gleason to write and record his letter reached out to Rose for a new version of his column. The group is called Evacuteer, and it created a website to collect the love letters and offer readers a way to donate. Rose plans to read his piece at an event near the end of May.

On the appointed night, an hour or so before his reading, a crowd starts to gather at a community center on O. C. Haley Boulevard, once a Central City no-go zone between the Magnolia projects, birthplace of the Cash Money record label, and the Calliope projects, where No Limit rapper and founder Master P grew up. The city tore down both, and now the neighborhood is a few months, maybe a year, from being acceptable to suburban white people. There is still violence. This summer, a hit man walked up to the St. John the Baptist Church and shot someone once in the chest; meanwhile, half a mile away, chef Adolfo Garcia, a culinary star in a city that treats a chef's coat like a low-slung guitar, just opened his latest place. It's across the street from Rose's reading, which folks are talking about at the bar. Chris is one of Katrina's many ghosts.

"They became whispers of themselves," says Caroline Fayard, a local attorney waiting on the event to begin.

"Hopefully this Katrina 10," Garcia says, making his rounds, "he can parlay that into something better."

Across the street, as the crowd files in, a woman on the stage plays a mournful tune on a cello. People sit quietly in the uncomfortable chairs. This is one of the first Katrina 10 events of the summer. Many more will follow, academic conferences and TED Talks and a Hot Boys reunion outside the Superdome. Economists and education specialists will gather all summer, quoting facts and figures, looking to the future.

The letter project also serves as a memorial to those who died in the storm, so their deaths will not have been in vain. Even 10 years later, nobody knows how many were lost. The best guess is 1,833, but that's just a guess. At the end of Canal Street, in a pauper's cemetery, there is a memorial to the dead. Six sleek marble mausoleums hold the remains nobody ever identified or claimed.

"Some have been forgotten," the marker reads. "Some remain unknown."

The cello on the stage makes the saddest sound, the people here occupying both cities, the one of the dead and the one of the living, trapped in between. That's what the anniversary is doing, one last time: forcing people to go to a place they've tried to avoid. Behind the stage hangs an enormous photograph of Louis Armstrong Park, named for the patron saint of the city, who made New Orleans music so popular that it remains so. Everyone who comes to town arrives at the airport bearing his name, but Armstrong didn't live in that New Orleans. He grew up in a violently segregated city—his first cornet was given to him at a detention facility named the Colored Waifs' Home—and while his deepest feelings about his childhood died with him, this fact is true: When Armstrong became famous, he moved to New York City and almost never returned. His body is buried in Queens. He sang "What a Wonderful World" as a prayer, a song about a place that didn't really exist. The only New Orleans he wanted to visit was the one he imagined with his trumpet, a vision of what the city still tries to be.

The event begins. There's a strange feeling in the air, people avoiding eye contact, quiet and alone with their memories. Rose has been mingling, slouched at a James Dean slant, joints cocked, sleeves rolled up on his T-shirt. He looks every bit "the avenging angel of the 504," as a writer once described him. Ten years ago he wrote about New Orleans for the world, and now he's writing for 50 people in a room.

David Morris, from the nonprofit hosting tonight's benefit, welcomes the crowd and explains that five years ago people didn't have time for extravagances like public remembrance, focused as they were on rotting Chinese drywall and getting all their family members back in New Orleans. Ten years from now, the seniors in high school won't have even been alive during Katrina, and it will all fade away, like Hurricane Betsy in 1965, the flood of 1927, something studied by coming generations but not felt. "So on the 10th anniversary," Morris says, "we have this incredibly special moment where not too much time has passed, but just enough has, so we can pause and reflect for a second. I think in a lot of ways this is going to be the first and quite possibly the last collective and cathartic experience that New Orleans experiences together."

The first speaker, a local radio DJ named Fresh Johnson, reads Chris Rose's original story.

Dear America . . .

Her voice is supercharged with the thrumming energy of the young. She's a can of Red Bull with dimples. Standing near the back of the room, Rose looks haunted. He jams his hands down in his pockets and rocks. Nobody bothers him. His body language repels people, and every now and then, as he listens to this dispatch from his former life, he blinks.

> *When you meet us now and you look into our eyes, you will see the saddest story ever told. Our hearts are broken into a thousand pieces.*
>
> *But don't pity us. We're gonna make it. We're resilient. After all, we've been rooting for the Saints for thirty-five years. That's got to count for something.*

He laughs when Fresh mentions the Saints, and then, as she finishes reading his old words, Rose inches farther and farther from the stage, until he's alone and against the wall. There isn't anyone behind him. He closes his eyes. When the next speaker starts reliving her memories and pain, Chris quietly slips out and stands by the curb. He holds the script of his new letter in his hand, reading it again: "It's hard to believe it's been 10 years," he's written. "We may be haunted by our past, but we are not bound to it."

A cloud of cigarette smoke rises above his head, and he leans against one of the poles holding up a balcony. A little tremor runs through his body, and his shoulders rise and fall. From behind, it looks like he's either coughing or crying. Inside, a deaf and blind woman talks about how she's found her own kind of vision and music in New Orleans, and outside, he's got neither.

He smokes and waits.

"It opens up a lot of old vulnerabilities," he says, shaking his head. Then his time arrives, and the crowd stands and cheers. He whispers to the musician onstage that he'd like her to keep playing while he reads. What he's got on the page isn't a letter so much as a ballad, a prayer like the ones written by Louis Armstrong. Rose, a native of Maryland, came here to work, and like many transplants, he cannot imagine a life anywhere else. The place has swallowed him, and on the stage, he finds his pace and rhythm. "The most important four-letter word in the English language is not 'love.' It is 'home.' Home, where the senses are filled with the comforting. Where the streets, the accents, and the church bells are familiar. Where the air smells like coffee, sweet olive, fish fry, mule piss, and sex."

Everyone in the crowd laughs.

He smiles, hoping this is the start of a future, not a nostalgia trip to a past forever gone. His letter is poignant, funny, and sweet, and a common idea flows through every line. The hurricane isn't something that happened a decade ago. It's something that is still happening, good and bad. The anniversary isn't a commemoration of the past but a civic prayer that the city's longest day might finally come to an end.

II. THE PROBLEM WITH NEW GODS

In the courtyard behind the St. Louis Cathedral, which rises above Jackson Square, there's a statue of Jesus missing its thumb and forefinger. Katrina broke them off, and people here joke about Jesus using those missing digits to flick the storm away. At night, if you're walking down Royal Street, past the antique shops that sell Liberace's sterling serving pieces, a spotlight throws a silhouette of Jesus against the back wall of the cathedral. It towers above everything else, heaven and hell so close together. That's New Orleans. After Katrina, the church said it would leave the statue broken, out of solidarity, until the city had recovered. This year, on the anniversary, the archdiocese is reattaching Jesus's fingers.

With the recovery coming to an end, at least in the public dialogue, people are remembering how much the city invested in its football team, which is itself so closely aligned with the Catholic Church, from the name of the club to the Masses the Benson family holds in the Superdome before games. This summer, on the last day of a run of practices, Drew Brees takes off his helmet and signs autographs along a rope line of fans. One of the items waving at him from an outstretched hand is a copy of the Monday, February 8,

2010, edition of *The Times-Picayune*, the day after the Super Bowl. The headline reads "AMEN!"

The day after that game, when staff members got to the newsroom, they found readers stretched around the corner, waiting. The paper sold 687,000 copies, more than double its typical circulation, people of all ages and races buying them by the bundle. The presses printed into the next night. People wanted to save these papers, pass them down to their children. That front page is now hanging in every imaginable establishment, from the inside of a food truck that sets up at Second Line parades on Sunday afternoons to the corner of the stand-up bar at Tujague's, whose interior always seems filled with a beautiful, strange yellow light. The framed cover is an anthropological document of sorts, capturing a specific madness that swallowed New Orleans in the years after the hurricane.

The city in that time suffered through Ray Nagin's two terms as mayor—like many Louisiana politicians before him, he is now in federal prison for a litany of crimes, including bribery, conspiracy, and money laundering. Nagin declined comment for this story, but when he left office in 2010, the city had a $97 million budget deficit. The police department was being investigated by the Department of Justice, and the FBI had set up an office inside the Orleans Parish School Board, so deep was the corruption (2,000 employees had health insurance for which they weren't eligible, according to Tulane researcher Doug Harris). New Orleans was a place struggling to stand up. And so it was that the people tied their personal and civic self-esteem to the play of a football team, as if 53 men and their coaches predicted whether the city would get off its knees.

People call New Orleans a Catholic city, but that's not really true, not anymore. With every census, the percentage of practicing Roman Catholics declines. The religious iconography laid over the rise of a football team would have been considered blasphemous a generation ago, and maybe even for this generation, had the people in New Orleans not needed to believe in something so desperately. The public institution that has replaced the church's ubiquity is the Saints, and so, "Amen," the headline writers decided—the most beautiful and surprising gift for a city stripped of its faith: an answered prayer.

If the most visible day in the past 10 years was the day the Saints won the Super Bowl, the most impactful might have been the one before, a Saturday, when people went to the polls and overwhelmingly elected Mitch Landrieu as mayor. To many, his election is the moment when the city began its rebirth, dividing the past decade into two distinct halves: from the storm to the Super Bowl, and from Mitch's election until the anniversary. Landrieu's media advisers understood this, placing billboards around the city that tied his victory with the victory of the Saints. They read ONE TEAM. ONE FIGHT. ONE VOICE. ONE CITY.

Landrieu took over where the Saints left off, and near the end of this past May, he walks toward the microphone to give his fifth State of the City speech to a packed room, where a gospel choir sings him onstage. The event takes place at a renovated theater across from what used to be the Lafitte projects and is now part of a major construction plan for the city, the Lafitte Greenway, a long public park and bike path connecting City Park and the French Quarter. In Landrieu's speech, he describes the summer's Katrina 10 events and celebrations, and the recovery the city has made. "When we took office in 2010, we inherited a mess," he says. "Simply put, five years after the storm we were struggling to make it."

Two weeks later, he's back in his office at City Hall, which is built on the plot of land where Louis Armstrong's childhood home once stood. He loosens his blue necktie, taking a short break between meetings. He was born and raised in New Orleans, the brother of former U.S. Senator Mary Landrieu and the son of a former mayor, Maurice "Moon" Landrieu, who integrated city government in the 1970s, hiring dozens of young black staffers, and was called "Moon the Coon" by angry whites. On Mitch's office wall, there's a framed newspaper editorial about his father, with the headline "CAN AN

HONEST MAN WIN?" There's a book on his coffee table called *How to Rebuild a City*.

"We're going to build it the way it should have been if we would have gotten it right the first time," he says, for the third time in 20 minutes. "We're doing great. We're an ascendant city."

He sits on the ratty couches he inherited, along with a nearly bankrupt city, hit by a hurricane and then the criminal tenure of Nagin. "The governance wasn't good," Landrieu says. "Nobody was working well together. The recovery wasn't going well. Finally it started to jell the year before I got elected. And just that weekend, us winning the Super Bowl and then the new election."

Today, he carries precincts in the projects and on tree-lined old-money streets. Landrieu is the first white mayor in three decades—the last was his father—and he has the trust of most of the city's black population; in his last election, he defeated two African American candidates. Saints coach Sean Payton, who is politically conservative, believes in the mayor too. "Both Landrieu and [Governor Bobby] Jindal, agree or disagree with their politics, they're not going to be arrested someday for it," he says. "They're trustworthy."

Landrieu has a vision for what New Orleans might be by the time his children inherit the city. He points to the nearly completed Lafitte Greenway, almost three miles of public space, with energy-efficient lighting, fully compliant with the Americans with Disabilities Act. There's a crushed-stone walking path and more than 500 trees providing shade on those hot summer days. It'll be a beautiful, modern centerpiece of the city, running through a place that was blighted and dangerous before the storm. Landrieu's interest is complicated. He is trying to drive an economic rebirth while rebuilding the city itself, but when you hear him talk about things like the greenway, his excitement seems to be about something simpler: He remembers a New Orleans that looked and felt like a city on the rise, and he wants to leave that city behind when his time as mayor is up.

The new University Medical Center and VA hospital, the biggest medical construction project in the country, are positioned near the Lafitte Corridor, and the hospitals fit into the modern design, with no parking visible from the street. This summer, a developer bought nearby land to convert into restaurants and shops. A Whole Foods recently opened near the path of the greenway, right on the edge of Treme, the corner of Bienville and Broad. The neighborhood is already filling with tourists. Pedestrians walking from either direction will be able to step off the greenway into Dooky Chase's Restaurant and Willie Mae's Scotch House, two of the most famous soul food places in the city.

This is one of the oldest and most important African American neighborhoods in the country. Free blacks lived here during slavery, and in its clubs, jazz was born. Some call it Treme, and others call it Lafitte, after the former project. Its original name best expresses its place in the minds of the white citizens who named things back then: "Back of Town."

Now it's the front yard of the New New Orleans.

Mitch Landrieu was in New Orleans during Katrina, the lieutenant governor then, walking through the crowds in the Superdome while Ray Nagin locked himself in a hotel suite and literally wept, as his aides looked at him in shock. When Steve Gleason blocked that punt, Mitch was there too. To him, it felt cathartic and cleansing, like the team had taken the Superdome back from Katrina. Three and a half years later, the day after he won his election, he went to church and then to his brother's house in Lakeview to watch the Super Bowl. The whole family was there, and when the game ended, and the Saints had won, his 80-year-old mother led the family out of the house, dozens of Landrieus running around the block in rapture.

Katrina brought the two central players of the Saints' journey together.

Sean Payton took the job five months after the hurricane, after the Green Bay Packers turned him down. He instinctively understood how the flood might unify the team; the Friday night before the first game back in the city, he gathered the Saints at midfield and played a video showing the devastation of Katrina. The Dome felt like a church. Payton said that the same people suffering in those images would be back in the stadium the next evening and that the Saints needed to remember these pictures when they played because those were the people in the stands cheering.

Payton signed a quarterback nobody but the Dolphins wanted, Drew Brees, who was coming off potentially career-ending shoulder surgery and still unable to throw. The team flew in Drew and his wife in March 2006, and after pitching them on the Saints, Payton drove them around, only he got lost, and the carefully curated tour of New Orleans turned quickly into a war zone. They passed houses ripped off foundations, with boats and cars at odd angles. They passed houses with the fluorescent orange X's painted on them, the utilitarian National Guard system for keeping track of what got searched and when.

Ten years later, the X's mean different things in different neighborhoods. On Magazine Street, they are something from the past, almost ironic now, or at least a way for survivors to nod at one another in solidarity and silence. Across town, driving into the 7th or 9th Ward, dozens of abandoned houses still have X's painted on them, one more divide in a city separated by money and opportunity, as well as time and race. Life in white New Orleans is much different from life in black New Orleans, no matter what Landrieu's billboard says.

Near Carver High School, Marshall Faulk's alma mater, an abandoned lot of graffitied cop cars looks like a scene from *Mad Max*, a square of official government land, left in the panic of full retreat. Trees grow out of windowless houses. Carver still isn't finished, even 10 years later, the students attending class in white trailers. Near the old Desire projects, the Savemore Supermarket is boarded up, with a graffitied warning: "Do not make this mistake again." Near

Humanity Street, a rooster walks and clucks through the neutral ground. An X says a house was searched on 9/6, another on 9/15. The street names remain: Abundance, Benefit, Pleasure. The nearby Press Park complex is abandoned, just shells and skeletons, each collapsed in its own way, snowflakes of blight.

This is the kind of destruction Drew and Brittany Brees saw on their drive through the city, and instead of feeling repelled, they felt called. They didn't move to the suburbs like most players and coaches, instead rehabbing a big white house in Uptown, near St. Charles. And when Drew wasn't practicing or playing football, he was donating or raising money, much of it aimed at the 9th Ward. He wrote a $100,000 check for the new field at Carver.

When the team started winning, kids would write signs and tape them to the iron fence at his property line, like something that might happen to the high school quarterback. After the Super Bowl, Brees arrived home to find a few six-packs of beer on his front walk. He took them inside. Hidden among the big poster-board and butcher-paper banners, there hung a note signed by the Argus and DiPaola families, written on printer paper torn in half: "My family lost everything in August 2005. Last night you and our beloved boys gave us everything back."

The Saints matter deeply to the people of New Orleans, but in the year after the storm, the man who owned the team did not. Tom Benson became public enemy No. 1 because people saw him threatening to move the team to San Antonio. Fans booed him when the Saints played at LSU's Tiger Stadium, and he threw a temper tantrum over the abuse. With the city filled with rancid refrigerators, a meme emerged: People spray-painted them with the words DO NOT OPEN: TOM BENSON INSIDE.

Former NFL commissioner Paul Tagliabue said that Benson wanted the team based in San Antonio for the 2006 season and that team officials were telling employees to prepare to move. The mayor of San Antonio pushed for the relocation. One of President Bill Clinton's Cabinet secretaries—HUD director and former mayor of San Antonio Henry Cisneros—reached out to the commissioner, arguing on behalf of moving the franchise. The Saints fiercely deny the team tried to move. "It was the priority of Tom Benson to get the Saints back to New Orleans as soon as feasibly possible," Saints spokesman Greg Bensel says. "His only public statement back in 2005 was that we were returning home and that we would lead the charge to rebuild. In fact, many other businesses did not and have not returned. But following Katrina, we can proudly argue that Tom Benson has led a renaissance in our city."

Citizens worried because Benson kept a ranch in Texas and spent much of the time there. He is not, however, a Texan. He grew up poor in New Orleans' 7th Ward, near the corner of North Johnson and Elysian Fields—on the wrong side of a divided community, in one of many blue-collar families who made the rich elite of St. Charles Avenue richer and more elite. Anyone who expected him to be civic-minded in the immediate aftermath of the hurricane does not know Tom Benson. The city exists in his memory as a place he escaped. He fought his way out. Call it greed or focus or drive. The ancestors of the blue bloods who curry his favor today would have looked right through his father, who worked as a clerk in a department store and would give Tom 7 cents to ride the streetcar to school.

Tom walked and saved the money.

Much of Benson's past remains hidden, and only a 2001 profile in *The Times-Picayune* managed to partially reveal him. He served in the navy, a yeoman on a battleship in the months after Japan surrendered, and when he returned home, he started work as an accountant at a local Chevrolet dealership. He moved up, managing the office, then the sales staff, and soon his own dealership. He turned one into more than 30, the start of a sprawling financial empire. He hired his three best friends from the 7th Ward and fired two of them—ultimately cutting ties with all three. Nobody would stop his rise to success. Eventually, he'd spend much of his time on a ranch in Texas, the open space as far from the cramped streets of a New Orleans slum as a little boy could travel. The Saints coaches and executives of the past decade are a reflection of Tom Benson's bruising approach to business and life—the Bountygate scandal, and the team subsequently shrugging off the NFL's inquiries, a perfect Bensonian moment.

In Tom Benson's mind, Tom Benson is a winner, and he doesn't care whether people like him, which is lucky because after Katrina nobody did. Even before the storm, he'd been publicly pushing for a new lease, saying he needed millions in concessions from the state to stay competitive in the New Orleans market. His offensive burned bridges, and after Katrina, the business community believed he was using the disaster as the final piece of leverage. Tagliabue decided to meet businessmen from New Orleans to hear directly from them. He'd heard the Saints complaining that the storm had made the tough economic climate in the city even more difficult. Another NFL owner, Robert McNair of the Texans, set up the meeting. They gathered at the river camp owned by shipping magnate Thomas Coleman, at one of a dozen exclusive shacks built on the thin, fragile strip of land, called the *batture*, running between the levee and the river. Generations of New Orleanians have used these shacks, just a couple of miles from Audubon Park and the mansions on St. Charles, for whiskey drinking and holding meetings too secret for the public exposure of an office.

Everyone ate dinner and admired the Louisiana folk art on the walls. No politicians were invited, just businessmen and bankers. Tagliabue listened to the men's belief in New Orleans and their frustration with the Saints. Their hope for the city underscored what he already thought and what he'd told Benson. In a recent phone interview, Tagliabue recounted the conversation.

"There is no way this team is going to be in San Antonio for the 2006 season," Tagliabue said.

"How can you say that?" Benson responded.

"It takes three-fourths of the owners to move a team," he replied, "and there's no owner out there who is prepared to abandon New Orleans."

Two women helped change the way New Orleans felt about Tom Benson after the Saints returned. The first, his granddaughter Rita Benson LeBlanc, made him finally seem in tune with the city. Rita's rise to power in the organization was primarily about repairing relationships between the family and New Orleans.

She grew up in Texas, spending summers running around the Saints' practices, until she went to college and spent her summers interning at the NFL office in New York. Tom Benson, whom she called Paw-Paw, adored her and saw in her his best chance to turn the Saints into a family dynasty. With each year, he gave her more responsibility and the titles to go with it. Between 2006 and 2010, when the Saints were still building toward something, the now 38-year-old Rita became the public face of a youthful, modern corporation, fully in tune with the city it represented. Actors and celebrities watched the games in her suite, everyone's place arranged according to a seating chart she closely managed. The art museum wanted her for its board, and she found herself at the nerve center of the city, drinking whiskey and talking politics in James Carville's living room.

Better than anyone else at the Saints' facility on Airline Drive, Rita saw the connections between the town and the team in the years after Katrina, and she talked about them in ways that weren't ham-fisted and trite. At a meeting as the team prepared for its first season back in the Superdome, she listened as marketing people pitched pop-culture slogans and themes that ignored the drowning elephant in the room. She said the team's slogan needed to be something that reflected the goals of a football team and, subtly, of New Orleans itself. They hung a banner on the Superdome that read OUR HOME. OUR TEAM. BE A SAINT.

Over the years, in the news stories leaked to local reporters by the Saints, a counter-narrative has emerged. Rita has been described as a tyrant, burning through dozens of personal assistants. Even in the run toward the Super Bowl, she showed signs of the strain that would come out in later years; after one big victory in 2009, she got agitated when a guest in her suite, a famous painter from New York, opened the bottle of Perrier-Jouet Fleur de Champagne that had been icing down during the game. The bottle was hers to open.

The night of the Super Bowl, she reveled in her glory, holding court at the team's victory party inside Miami's InterContinental Hotel, dancing with her friends by the stage to New Orleans frat-rock band Better Than Ezra. She'd protected and resurrected her family's name in the community, especially with Uptown business-men who never trusted her 7th Ward grandfather. The party raged all night. Jimmy Buffett laughed with Carville out in the hall, and Sean Payton cradled the silver Vince Lombardi Trophy, now covered with smudges and fingerprints. He took a picture with anyone who wanted one.

That victory party was the end of the Saints as the standing army of the Rebirth of New Orleans, less a pro sports franchise and more the 1980 Olympic hockey team, a vessel for hopes and dreams. The team had served as a life-support system, nearly as essential as the one strapped to Steve Gleason's wheelchair, keeping the city breathing until it could breathe on its own. Rita danced and Payton raised a glass, and in the city of New Orleans, and everywhere its sons and daughters had been scattered, people remembered their journey away from the flood.

Tom Benson met the other woman who's shaped his past 10 years, his third wife, Gayle, at Mass. They married a year before the storm, and in the decade since, she's made him into one of New Orleans' most generous philanthropists, giving away the millions he worked so hard to make. The couple gave $5 million to Team Gleason. Tens of millions have gone to hospitals, churches, high schools, and universities. He cried when the team unveiled a statue of him outside the Dome, and in all the photos, Gayle was by his side, wiping away the tears. The years between spray-painted refrigerators and a big bronze statue of Tom Benson were dominated by Gayle.

She herself is a character in a supermarket novel; married twice before, nearing financial peril and without prospects, and suddenly pulled into a world of privilege and luxury. She shares with Tom a deep Catholic faith; both clearly nurse the wounds and insecurities all poor kids carry with them through life.

She grew up in Old Algiers, directly across the river from the French Quarter, her father a janitor at a local store. They lived in a small shotgun house in a working-class neighborhood, where generation after generation tried to inch out of the mosquito bogs and sugarcane plantations. The money spent on the big Uptown mansions is made down here. The air smells like sugar or sulfur, depending on the wind and the century, and the flare stacks of the refineries throw shadows onto the fields and levees. You can always see the skyline of the French Quarter, and in the other direction you can see the cities of pipe and smoke out in the marsh, stretching mile after mile, bracketed by where you're going and where you've been.

Brenda LaJaunie says her sister always wanted a better life than the one they had growing up. Gayle barely appears in her high school yearbook, one of those nowhere girls who doesn't find a place with any group. "Sometimes people are sufficiently motivated to change their lives so thoroughly that they abandon any trace of their previous existence," says Dave McBane, who graduated in the Class of '66.

Gayle Benson says, through a Saints spokesman: "Mrs. Benson has provided for her family for years and now she continues to give and offer her time and focus to charities throughout our city. She has no comment about what others may say about her. Her focus remains taking care of her husband and doing what she can to help our city grow and prosper."

Rita Benson LeBlanc and Gayle Benson, it is fair to say, have never gotten along—Rita, by many reports, was convinced that Gayle was using her grandfather for his money. Last December, during a Saints game versus Atlanta, the contentious relationship finally reached the public. Rita had learned that, for the first time in her life, she would not see Tom Benson on Christmas. Rita and her mother, Renee Benson, blamed Gayle for splitting the family apart. In the suite this past December, witnesses say Rita shook Gayle and screamed at her. Rita denies this, calling it a fabrication of the Saints' spin machine. She says she merely begged Gayle to let them see Tom during the holidays. Six days after that game, Tom Benson sent a memo to his daughter and grandchildren saying he never wanted to see them again because of, among other things, their disrespectful behavior toward Gayle. He also said he wanted to take the shares of the team out of the trust he'd set up for them and give the Saints to Gayle.

Before the memo, Gayle stood to inherit a few million dollars upon his death.

Now she stands to receive assets worth almost $2 billion.

On the first of June, the Benson family feud hits Louisiana district court—the family tearing itself apart, in New Orleans and in Texas, through a series of lawsuits challenging Benson's competency and right to disown his daughter and grandchildren. Benson has placed shares in the Saints in an irrevocable trust, which means he'll need to replace them with assets or cash of an equal value. And before fighting over that amount, his granddaughter is taking him to court, challenging his mental capacity to make such a draconian decision. The battle, when whittled to its essence, pits Gayle Benson against Rita Benson LeBlanc, fighting over money, over love, and out of spite.

"Psycho," an insider on Gayle's side says about Rita.

"Not sane," an insider on Rita's side says about Gayle.

It's the first day of hurricane season, and in another courtroom in the same building, a lawsuit over the 22 Katrina-related deaths at the Lafon nursing home begins. Family members of the dead believe the nuns and nurses who ran the facility effectively killed their patients by refusing to evacuate ahead of the hurricane. Nurses had stood in the streets and tried to flag down the passing National Guard. No one had stopped. A nun still wearing her habit had found a New Orleans police officer who'd promised to help but never actually did. Now, in the courthouse, nuns and priests walk through the lobby, some quietly waiting by the vending machines for their turn to testify. They carry rosaries.

The crowd of television cameras and newspaper photographers isn't there, though, for the nuns—the 22 awful deaths holding none of the fascination of an intrafamily battle over billions, the whole scene feeling like a piece of performance art about the state of America. Reporters wait on the first day to finish, everyone turning to the elevators at the far end of the long hall whenever they open, waiting to hurl questions at a Benson. A black Mercedes pulls into the sally port and parks by the curb, and Tom Benson's driver, Jay, comes inside to wait on his boss. Upstairs, family members face one another, the first time they've all been in a room together since everything collapsed in January. Renee Benson, Tom's last living child and Rita's mom, clutches religious medals and photographs of their family, before money and time tore it apart.

Outside, people smoke on the steps of Loyola Avenue, two blocks from the corner where an 11-year-old Louis Armstrong fired a pistol and got arrested, learning to play the horn while incarcerated. He first performed in jazz clubs that were torn down to build this courthouse. Perdido Street was flooded during Katrina, and if you'd been here 10 years ago, you'd have ducked and covered from the noise and toxic spray of fan boats cutting through the water.

Their turbines threw a mix of human waste and chemicals into the air. The survivors from Charity Hospital a few blocks away were headed toward safety, finally. The staff had been abandoned for three days after the storm, watching helicopters land at every nearby medical facility where the patients paid for their care, the rescuers leaving behind those at the hospital where care was free. Among the last to leave Charity was NOPD officer Daryle Holloway, who'd weathered the storm with his mother, one of the head nurses at the hospital.

Holly, as his friends called him, worked the Desire and Florida projects. The people in the community respected him and thought he was fair. His fellow officers still talk in hushed tones about the morning, years ago, when they responded to a shootout in the Florida project. They arrived to find total chaos, people bleeding and screaming. One of the gunmen's young sons had been hit in the crossfire and died. The boy's mother wailed over his body as the cops tried to figure out what had happened. They sent Holloway into the apartment of the dead boy to see whether anyone else was armed. Holloway saw four or five kids inside, looked around at the empty cupboards and fridge. He walked back outside, and everyone stopped for a moment to see him go into a corner store; buy cereal, eggs, and milk; then walk back through the active crime scene to feed the hungry kids stuck in an apartment with no food.

That's Holloway.

In the days after Katrina, he and Charity staffers went out in a boat to find survivors. They passed a man sitting on his porch with his dog, drinking a bottle of Jack Daniel's. The man refused to get into the boat. They found girls on the roof of a house and brought them in the boat to the Superdome. On one trip, the prop hit a floating body, and the body, filled with gases brought on by decomposition, exploded—the foulest smell and sight any of them ever saw, and on the emergency room loading dock afterward, someone snapped a photo of Holloway, staring out at the city, his eyes empty and hollow.

The bonds of community, and even civilization, frayed and broke during those long days, but the bonds of family held strong. Holloway refused to leave his mother, even though he'd later be suspended

by the police department for abandoning his post. On Day 3 in Charity, a nurse named Jewel Willis worked in what had turned into a
sort of Civil War triage hospital: no power, little medicine, the big
brick building an oven during the day and not much cooler at night.
One day, a man with a thick Cajun accent showed up in his fishing
boat. He'd somehow navigated his way through the disaster, pulling
right up to the emergency room doors.

"I came to get my daughter," he said.

Willis came outside, and there he was. Her dad had come to
save her.

"Get in the boat," he said. "We're going home."

She started crying and hugged his neck; then she whispered in
his ear.

"I can't leave," she told him, and he understood, so they started
running rescue missions, and he called a friend in the Louisiana
Department of Wildlife and Fisheries, who brought the fan boats to
take the patients to higher ground. That all happened a few blocks
from the courtroom where the Benson family tried to figure out how
$2 billion might make five people happy enough to get along.

Out at the Saints' facility on Airline Drive, there's a sense of remembering prompted by the approaching anniversary, along with the
humbling experience of last season's 7–9 record. Each passing year in
the NFL is a reminder that everyone and everything has an expira-
tion date. It's been almost six years since Sean Payton coached the
best team in the league. Payton watched the Warriors win the NBA
championship and the Blackhawks win the Stanley Cup, and he focused on the flash of joy in the seconds after the deciding games
ended. He wants to feel that again, which becomes more and more
unlikely every year. Drew Brees must also be considering the end of
the most important relationship in his professional life, the undim-
ming love affair between his family and the city that took them in.
Both of them exist around town as pop-culture deities: T-shirts for

sale that read "Free Sean Payton" or "The Krewe du Drew," or the signs pledging faith to "Breesus." These days of hero worship are numbered. One day, someone else will own the team, and Brees will live in San Diego, and Payton will be replaced by a new coach with the energy and hunger he used to have. He'll be content living on the coast of Florida, remembering when they were all young and invincible.

The hearing ends and, when the elevator doors open, Tom Benson passes security guards and takes a left, stooped and slow, an octogenarian helped into his car by his attorney. No less a moral arbiter than the archbishop said Benson's mind remains sharp, and Tom jokes with reporters. He carries a black-and-gold walking cane.

"I can't talk about nothing," he says before leaving. "I just feel good."

Renee, Rita, and Rita's brother, Ryan LeBlanc, come down next, their attorney, Randy Smith, answering a few questions. Rita has a thousand-yard stare, audibly scoffing when one of the Saints beat reporters asks a question. She looks exhausted.

"We want the best for Tom Benson," Smith says.

The three of them walk down the steps, across Loyola Avenue, disappearing into the Central Business District. Watching the two sides go in opposite directions, as if the photo of them on the field in Miami were being ripped in half, feels like the end of something. Only five players from the Super Bowl remain. The Saints' front office has the highest amount of cap space taken by players no longer on the team, the barometer of a front office's ability to spend money smartly. It's all coming undone. The third day of the trial occurs on the 30th anniversary of Tom Benson buying the team, and now he's an 88-year-old man who will never see his daughter and grandchildren again, at least outside a courtroom. In a few weeks, Renee will try to call Tom on Father's Day and instead will get a letter from his attorneys, telling her to stay away.

III. THE DOWNSIDE OF BUILDING BACK UP

New Orleans has never been one static thing. The city has both died and been reborn with every agent of change that lands on its shores, immigrants and floods alike. Its people fled revolutions and dictators and famine, arriving in waves from Haiti and Ireland, Italy and Vietnam. The immigrants re-created the city, as did the levee breach of 1849, the flood of 1927, and Hurricane Betsy in 1965. That's how it's always been. New Orleans is a port city, a slave market, a river town, and, since an assistant engineer of Sieur de Bienville's laid out the French Quarter's grid almost 300 years ago, a place that has never been sentimental about what it was. Ten years after the flood of '27, the local papers did not run a single anniversary story. Anniversaries are a modern invention, as is the idea of holding on to one New Orleans instead of just embracing whatever rises in its place. Katrina lives, and so does the New New Orleans, until another agent of change comes to erase them both.

The only television show to ever really get the city, David Simon's *Treme*, revolved around a theme common to Simon's work, that people in urban America aren't Shakespearean characters with free will but actors in a Greek tragedy, all subject to the whims of postmodern gods: cops, mayors, schools, newspapers, oil company CEOs—and in New Orleans two more, Rebirth and Recovery, the most powerful local gods of all. They bless some lives, curse many others, controlling the future of people who are rebuilding what was taken away.

One morning, a rapper and producer named Nesby Phips says there's something he wants to show me. He's from Hollygrove, a poor 17th Ward neighborhood stretching between Uptown and the Jefferson Parish line. He has a Mayan amulet on his necklace and the word PATIENCE tattooed on his arm. He says he can reduce the entire ecosystem of New Orleans to one street corner. Academics quote statistics about the inequality of the city, the extreme prosperity so close to extreme poverty; a study last year puts New Orleans' wealth gap on par with Zambia's. Katrina didn't create this problem, but it did make it worse.

Phips can do better than calculating the Gini coefficient.

"I want to show you how much it changes within a turn," he says. He starts to laugh.

"Because right behind this neighborhood is a fucking country club."

He points at a chain-link fence on Hamilton Street covered in some green cloth or nylon so nobody can see inside the New Orleans Country Club. There are three lines of barbed wire on top. "This here's the golf course," he says. "Them covering the fence like that, it's basically out of sight, out of mind. We don't cross that line. They don't cross that line."

Driving west, past the corner of Mistletoe and Peach, he winds around toward the clubhouse. Grass grows up around abandoned houses. There's an empty foundation, all facing the golf-course fence. The entrance to the club is at the intersection of Quince and Last Streets. The security guard eyes Phips as he drives through the gate into the parking lot to turn around.

"Once you go past the golf course," he says, "they're selling drugs. Welcome to New Orleans, man. Everything is right up on each other. Same zip codes. Same street names. Country club right here."

He points back toward the neighborhood and the people who live there. "I guarantee you," he says, "these kids over here have never seen a golf tee, let alone the ninth hole."

From the club's parking lot, he sees some young white kids in polo shirts and khaki shorts, waiting between the clubhouse and the putting tee. Phips is sure they know every lyric on *Tha Carter* but have no idea Lil Wayne grew up in the neighborhood on the other side of the fence, the green shade blocking the poor kids from seeing in and the rich kids from seeing out.

Since Katrina, life on the wealthy side of that fence has improved. The New New Orleans really is a safer, wealthier place with more responsible institutions. "Almost everything's better," Chris Rose says. "You know, it's the one thing that no one can speak. Nobody dares write it . . . but how many people said, 'It's the best thing that ever happened to New Orleans.' Now, here's the problem: It was rich white people who were saying that when we weren't even finished burying our dead. We still hadn't even *found* our dead and people were saying that. Now, you look back and you gotta think about what it was like in 2005, our crime, our corruption, our police, our education. They're all better now. Would they have improved had we not had this intense, overwhelming catastrophe, which forced us to not only rebuild and recover and repopulate but also reimagine ourselves? Would that have happened? I think it's safe to say no."

To drive through back-of-town neighborhoods to the intersection of St. Claude and St. Roch is to cut through the heart of pre-Katrina black New Orleans—thriving decades ago, now battered—only to find, at the corner on the Lake Pontchartrain side of the street, a new market that's gleaming and white inside, high, tall windows reflecting light on the tile floor.

This is the St. Roch Market, one of the places Mayor Landrieu likes to use as an example of what the city might be. As a kid, he remembers coming to the back to get crawfish for his mom from the Italian family who ran the place. He grew up, and the market fell into disrepair, eventually abandoned.

Now it's home to more than a dozen small businesses. The market sells things rich people like—expensive balsamic vinegar, Negronis, fusion Korean food—and for someone who lived in the city before Katrina, the sheer number of white people walking around this stretch of St. Claude is disorienting. One night, at a rap/funk show at a bar a few blocks away, a political, black-nationalist rapper performs for a mostly white crowd in a place that sells "artisanal popsicles." Later a jam band noodles and solos over a sampled Malcolm X speech. It's just a whiter city than before. You see white people in places they never used to go, which the people who live in those places notice too.

The white population has grown, while the overall population has shrunk by more than 100,000 people, almost all of them black. More than half of the black males in the city don't have work. More than half of black male ninth-graders fail to graduate from high school on time. There are few jobs and fewer places to live—none of the city's housing projects was seriously damaged in the storm, but all of them have since been torn down, which opened up the valuable real estate trapped beneath them. One study says there are now 3,221 fewer low-income units than before the storm. In 2005, a two-bedroom apartment averaged $676 a month. Now it averages $950. The city didn't replace the public housing units one-for-one, so poor citizens are being pushed toward the outskirts of town. The crime in suburban neighborhoods, like New Orleans East, is exploding. There are shootings and stabbings night after night.

With the lack of affordable housing, activists tried to save some of the projects, among them the Iberville, the last project to come down. One group came a few years ago to meet with Blair Boutte, Shack Brown's friend and former boss. They wanted his help in stopping the demolition. Boutte not only runs a prominent bail bonds company but also has built significant real estate holdings and a political and business consulting firm. He knows the streets better than anyone else, and politicians pay for that knowledge and influence. During the activist group's meeting, everyone sat around Blair's conference room table, in his office across from the Orleans Parish Prison in Mid-City. He recognized only one or two people. Everyone else was from out of town. He listened and, when they finished, he asked one question.

"Why?"

A hush came over the room.

One person he didn't recognize answered, "That's our home, and we can't let them just come in and take it."

"Ma'am," Blair said. "Can I ask you a question? Where are you from?"

"I live here now," she said.

"Well," Blair replied, "where are you from?"

"I'm from Boston."

"How long have you been here?"

"A year."

Boutte took a breath, and before ushering everyone out of his office, he told the group his only regret about the Iberville was that he couldn't tear it down himself. "I discount everything you said," he told them, "because I realize you weren't here when the Iberville project was a death trap to many people. The poorest of the poor, the most uneducated, were all boxed into one geographic location. And we suffered through that. And for anyone to come in and suggest somehow that that is a great thing, that we should preserve it, they did not live through it."

Gentrification is a weaponized word, swung around New Orleans by all manner of people with all manner of agendas. There are no easy answers and no readily assignable villains or heroes. The Iberville should come down, and whatever rises in its place will not be designed to help the people who used to live there. Battling to save the projects is really a proxy fight against the helplessness that poor citizens feel. The decisions about their future will be made by unseen people in unseen rooms, then handed down like tablets, their tomorrows already carved in stone.

Throughout the summer, the state continues debating how to use the vacant Charity Hospital building on Tulane Avenue, even as its replacement hospital prepares to open just before the anniversary of the storm. The state fought FEMA in the halls of Washington and eventually secured around $475 million to build new hospital complexes for University Medical Center and the VA about a mile away. Although UMC's complex will continue to serve as the gunshot emergency room for the city, the spirit of serving the poor mostly died with the nuns whose ranks at Charity began to dwindle in the 1990s. Katrina merely destroyed what little of that mission remained. Charity stands empty now, while the new hospital stretches over three blocks in upper Treme, on the Mid-City line, which will soon be home to the Lafitte Greenway. The plan is working. Real estate prices in nearby Treme are the fastest growing in the city. This was a dangerous, blighted neighborhood before Katrina. In just 21 days this summer, from June 10 to July 1, the average price of a Treme listing rose a stunning $126,913, from $220,000 a house to nearly $347,000 a house. These prices will only continue to climb. In two generations, nobody will remember the dangerous back-of-town streets between Orleans and Esplanade—or the people who died defending tiny pieces of forgotten turf—and nobody who grew up in the shadow of Willie Mae's Scotch House and Dooky Chase's will be able to afford to live there again.

A mile and a half up Broad from Dooky Chase's, there's a music club on the narrow wedge of land where North Broad and Hope Street intersect.

Blair Boutte is waiting at a table in the back.

There's little he's not connected to in New Orleans. His bounty hunters can find bail jumpers who remain invisible to the police. The famous Rebirth Brass Band started in his house, he says, with Blair on the saxophone, and when he left the projects for college, the band re-formed without him—was reborn, you might say, hence the name. In his office on South Broad Street, two photographs hang on the conference room wall. The first is Boutte with Nelson Mandela, taken when the South African leader visited Louisiana. The second is a close-up of the street signs at the intersection of Crozat and

Iberville, so he can look up at that wall and remember how far he's come.

Boutte has brought me here because he has a story to tell.

"A tale of two parks," he says.

He leans toward the middle of the table and begins to talk. The parks in the city, he says, are the knife's edge. In a place where the most disenfranchised group is young black males, a good park is sometimes the only thing holding someone upright. "Let's not say *making* it," Boutte says. "Let's say *surviving*. It's about surviving in my neighborhood. It's about . . . 'Who's gonna get the right break? Who's gonna be able to avoid the land mines?' There are many in the neighborhoods of New Orleans. Having a coach, having a team, having something to do after school can minimize the risk."

He points to the first park, Harrell, in Hollygrove, where the rapper Lil Wayne grew up. Coaches got together and raised money, building a thriving youth league, drawing kids from the neighborhoods in the 17th Ward: Hollygrove, Pigeontown, and Gert Town, the last a shortened version of the racial slur that gave the place its name. They got a concession stand up and running, which allowed the park to become self-sufficient, and when the Super Bowl came to the city, the NFL installed a field. That's a success.

Then there's his friend Shack Brown.

In 2009, Brown came to Boutte asking for help. The men from the neighborhood wanted to start some organized sports at Lemann Playground near the Iberville projects where Blair and Shack grew up. "These are guys of very humble means," Boutte says. "Let's just talk candidly. When you're dead broke, now you're gonna try to figure out how to finance a playground? Helmets and shoulder pads and jerseys and mouthpieces, the whole deal from scratch. I admire these guys. They came to me: 'Blair, how do we get the money?'"

He gave them the first donation.

Shack Brown took on this impossible task, and damned if he didn't get the park running. They had four to five age groups playing football by 2013, more than a hundred kids running around.

Then Shack and Blair began dreaming bigger.

They figured the boys and girls needed restrooms. First they tried a port-a-potty, but it got filled with junkies and drug needles. Blair decided to build a cinder-block concession stand, which would provide restrooms and a way for the park to make enough money to survive. He got an architect involved while Shack found bleachers to set up by the field. Boutte wanted the kids in the Iberville to have the same opportunities available to the boys and girls growing up around Blair's new neighborhood, Uptown. He says the biggest threat to a child's future is the two hours after school and before practice. Empty warehouses sat useless across the street from the field, and Blair made plans to buy or lease them. He wrangled retired teachers and started thinking of tutoring programs to go with the field. By the overpass, in between the old Iberville and Lafitte projects, he says, a little organic miracle was flourishing.

Then it all fell apart.

"We're gonna run the Lafitte Greenway through that park," the city told Brown and Boutte. The parks department tore down the makeshift concession stand and forbade them from building a permanent one, according to Brown. Without a way to support itself, Shack's football program died. The people who'd spent their own money on the league felt powerless and impotent, as if they weren't residents of a neighborhood but a problem to be solved so the neighborhood could reach its potential. They felt in the way, which they were.

Now the program that Shack built is gone. By the time the greenway is completed, Boutte and Brown won't be able to find all the scattered kids.

Sitting in the jazz club, Boutte sighs.

"What they are calling 'a better New Orleans,'" he practically sneers, before regaining his composure. "You know," he says, smiling, "we got all these new people who moved to town, with their fancy little hats. They want to ride bicycles everywhere. Journalists and artists. All the *ists* are in town. These people need a green space to walk and ride their bikes on."

He stops for a moment. There is a point he wants to make clear. The choices are tough, and he understands. Even inside himself, he's torn, happy to see Iberville come down and nice, mixed-income housing built in its place, even as he mourns the same rush of progress crippling Lemann Playground. For Blair, two contradictory ideas are true at the same time; there aren't good guys and bad guys, but there are certainly winners and losers. A public green space is part of a modernizing city. Boutte knows that. He also knows that park could have saved a lot of kids.

He imagines the boys he saw flying around the field, disciplined in their gap assignments. Parents filled the bleachers during games. Now that's all gone. Only the best two or three athletes get taken to a different park, since coaches can fit only a few in a car. The best kids find a new team, and the rest fade away.

"You know where they land?" he says. "On the stoop out front. You know the story. These guys are in an uphill battle with cement shoes on, and it's slippery. We send them right back to the jungle. And we tell them, in our most authoritative voice, 'Be good. Do well.'"

Shack Brown stands in the empty Lemann Playground.

It's an early afternoon in June. The field is a narrow patch of green near the interstate. When he closes his eyes, he can see how it was before. The kids playing ball ranged in age from 5 to 14. Every year, he says, at least one had a parent murdered, and Shack watched helplessly as the boys slipped through his fingers. One of his player's dads threw his body over his children during a shootout. He died, and they survived. Shack tried to fill the hole in their lives. The playground served as a safe haven, which it will undoubtedly be again. An official with the city's recreation department insisted that there'd be youth football in Lemann in 2015, although parents and coaches in the neighborhood don't seem to know anything about it. Everything in New Orleans happens over and over, so this is perfect, really, the idea of something new trying to find a foothold in the same place where something beautiful has been destroyed.

Trees line the edges, one taller than the rest, on the right if you're facing the old projects. Brown heads over to the Iberville, parking on the side street between the two corner stores. Some guys hang outside the New Image Supermarket. One of them, a kid named Spencer, rushes over.

He played for Shack at the Lemann, even went out of town with the team. The boys on those trips still talk about the foreign experience of staying in the host families' houses. They'd never heard of a breakfast casserole or seen big backyards with swings and pools.

"I'm an alumni of that park," Spencer says. "Went to Nashville, everywhere."

He played offensive line and linebacker, decent but not good enough to find a new place to play. Many more like him suffered the same fate when the park shut down, collateral damage of the city's new urban corridor. Now he's just on the corner, and soon enough, we find out why. Shack heads into the store and buys two Big Shot sodas, and when he swings the door back open and steps outside, he walks right into what looks like a drug deal in progress. Spencer is making some sort of transaction with an old junkie. The older guys hanging by a truck a few feet away look embarrassed and try to shoo the junkie away, at least until Shack leaves. The whole time, Spencer's mother is standing a few feet away, stone-faced, looking at him and then at Shack. She doesn't smile, the only one who doesn't seem happy to see her son's old coach.

The parts of the city falling further behind were in trouble long before Hurricane Katrina formed over the Bahamas. New Orleans is one of many American cities that rely on tourism and sales tax to support themselves. To survive, New Orleans needs mega-events and massive entertainment districts and an aggressive police presence in places where consumers gather. Sociologists describe this as

post-Fordism, the economy of a place after the death of manufacturing jobs. The new focus divides a community into consumers and
criminals. Most post-Fordism economies see a rise in zero-tolerance
policing and incarceration rates.

That's exactly what has happened in New Orleans since 1970.

During roughly that time frame, half the city's white population
moved to the suburbs while the murder rate grew by 329 percent.
Between 1981 and Katrina, the incarceration rate increased by 173
percent. The city lost 13,500 manufacturing jobs between 1970 and
2000, and the low-paying service industry grew by 136 percent. All
the while, the city's most famous institutions were born. The Saints
started playing in 1967. The Jazz & Heritage Festival began in 1970.
The New Orleans Jazz NBA franchise formed in 1974. The Superdome opened in 1975, created as part of the city's new vision of itself.
New Orleans as a carnal playground famous the world over didn't
happen on its own; it was a calculated and sophisticated marketing
campaign. Mardi Gras made the city $4.3 million in 1986 and $21.6
million in 2000. In 2014, direct spending for Mardi Gras totaled
$164 million. The city closing those housing projects closest to boom-
ing entertainment districts isn't an accident.

The rich stayed rich in this new economy, but the poor trapped in
the housing projects were almost exclusively a financial engine for
tourism. The jobs available didn't pay to build a middle-class life. The
city needed its black people to shuck oysters and pour drinks but
chased them back to the Iberville on horseback at the slightest
provocation.

Boutte drives down Basin toward Iberville Street, where a few
blocks away, the sign from the Hotel Monteleone dominates the sky.
If you lived in the Iberville, you saw that sign every day of your life
and never once went inside unless you carried bags or cleaned
rooms. The glowing sign is always there, a reminder that four blocks
is a nearly impossible distance to travel in this life.

Boutte rounds a corner and sees the first flash of red brick.

"There she is," he says, the Iberville coming into view.

He stops in the New Image and talks to some guys hanging outside. Being back here reminds him of his own rebirth, of death too. One afternoon we sit in his office, in the room with the photo of him and Mandela. He describes the project as "quicksand," then says, in a voice quieter than before, "I ended up in all of that."

He's deciding how far to go.

"My story is a bit different," he says. "We can touch on that if you'd like. I very seldom talk about it."

The only sounds are the air-conditioning compressors and the rain outside.

"I went to prison," he says. "I had a very . . . I don't like to go back here."

He's talking slowly, considering every word. "I had a really bad night after I graduated from college," he says. "Like I said, this was a very bad place."

He settles in to tell the story. Blair Boutte's mother raised him and his three siblings by herself in the '80s and '90s in a New Orleans housing project. She never drank or did drugs, never bought herself new clothes. Everything Blair wanted to do, she supported. "If you understand a single mother living in the housing projects of New Orleans," he says, "bringing up four boys alone. Sometimes working two jobs, sometimes not being able to work at all. It's a pretty rough ride. And my brothers and I, we weren't singing in the church choir, all right? We were typical New Orleans boys growing up in the housing projects in every sense of the word. And she fought and she fought and she fought, and she scratched, and she toiled, and she basically became the anchor to whatever good we had. She never wavered. She never abandoned ship. She never gave up."

Blair got out of the Iberville, made his way to Grambling State University. His mom came up for his graduation. They had a party at a local restaurant, and while everyone celebrated, he looked over and saw her in tears. He didn't understand. After graduation, he got a full ride to Tulane Law School, and before classes began, he went back to the projects. "It's not like I had a credit card to go buy an apartment Uptown," he says. "So I came back from school like any other kid. What do you do? You go back and you live with your parents, right?"

The first thing he did was buy a gun. The city was a dangerous place, around 250 murders a year. He went and registered the firearm, wanting to both protect himself and be legal. On April 10, 1988, Blair walked through the Lafitte projects and a drug dealer nicknamed Two Pistols drew both guns and tried to rob him. Blair pulled his gun and fired, and the man fired back.

In his office, a universe away from that night, he looks haunted. He's almost whispering now.

"I had to make a very tough decision," he says, "and it didn't end well. At the end of the day, I ended up pleading guilty to manslaughter. An innocent bystander was actually the one who died."

He looks down, thinking about Charles Martin, the 14-year-old boy he shot. Tulane took away Boutte's scholarship, and he did three years, nine months in jail. When he came out, he started his business. It grew into an empire, with real estate holdings and his B3 Consulting firm. Few people in New Orleans understand more about the goings-on in the shadow city.

"I know the streets," he says. "They talk to me."

The most exclusive street in New Orleans tells the same story as the intersection of Iberville and Crozat—the history of a city where some people pull the strings and other people move at the end of an invisible wire—just from a different point of view. The fortunes might come and go, but the houses on Audubon Place remain. They are monuments to the way things have always worked and the way they always will.

At No. 16, with six white columns and a fleur-de-lis above the front door, Gayle and Tom Benson live a life impossibly far away from the one they knew growing up poor in New Orleans. He'd never wanted to live Uptown, but she wanted a home on Audubon.

The houses there all tell similar stories too. The sugar-and-coffee baron who built No. 16 left home just past his 15th birthday, moving to Indianapolis and building a fortune from nothing. The man who lived at No. 2 left his farming family in Russia at 14, taking a boat to America and changing his name to Samuel Zemurray. He built an empire, as well, United Fruit, overthrowing governments in Central America, commanding a private standing army of mercenaries and cutthroats. His soldiers terrorized a village where a young novelist grew up; the book based on the massacre is *One Hundred Years of Solitude*.

Gabriel García Márquez's novel shined a light on United Fruit, which later changed its name to Chiquita. Zemurray died in 1961 and gave his house to Tulane University, and the school's president now lives there, talking about social justice while walking the same halls as the man who gave the world banana republics. The architect who drew the United Fruit house also designed the Bensons' home, as well as the Hotel Monteleone, the one whose glowing sign dominates the sky in the Iberville projects.

A hidden world plays out behind the stone-and-wrought-iron entrance to the street, where a guard approves everyone in or out. Last year, parents threw a debutante party for their teenage daughter that required building a structure on an empty lot near their family's mansion. The guests, the sons and daughters of dynasties, made their way through a so-called Gallery of Stags. Through another set of doors, the ballroom waited, where the girl's family had flown in Maroon 5. They were the opening act, because the family also flew in Wiz Khalifa, who rapped and smoked joints in the bathroom with future Wall Street titans. The party cost millions of dollars and lasted one night.

James W. Hearn built the Bensons' home in 1902, his reward for the coffee-and-sugar empire he'd created. His money came from the same plantation parish where Gayle LaJaunie's father lived. There's nobody from Hearn's family left in New Orleans, an empire built and lost. The house changed hands four more times before Tom Benson bought it, the history of the city's financial health told through the transfer of deeds: a bank president to a railroad man to a real estate developer to an oil-field equipment supplier to the owner of a football team. A tech billionaire will surely buy it next.

Gayle oversaw the interior decoration of the house, no expense spared. A golden stained-glass window in the stairwell, with deep greens and airy lavenders, accents the gold walls and the heavy valances. A painting by Miró hangs over a table with a statue by Remington. There's a Salvador Dalí and photos of Popes Benedict and Francis above the umbrella stand. It looks like a pre-revolution French aristocrat's dollhouse brought to life. Her china pattern is Spode Stafford White, the same table settings used on the television show *Downton Abbey*. It's everything a girl from Old Algiers could have wished for and more. On a table, there's a photograph of Tom holding the Lombardi Trophy, and over a marble fireplace, Gayle hung an enormous oil portrait of herself.

Dreams do come true. At the end of May, Boutte and 25 family members fly to see his daughter graduate from Brown University. He's got a hat that reads "Brown Dad," and he keeps it in his office, the same room as the Crozat and Iberville photo, a reminder of the distance a family can cover in a generation.

"A looong way," he says. "Longer than you could ever imagine."

"How does a family go from Iberville to Brown?"

Boutte tries to speak, sitting at a table at a bar near his office, but the words don't come. Suddenly, he stands up and excuses himself, and the other people at the table, who know him well, look at one another, stunned. They've never seen him like this, Boutte crying alone in the bathroom. He returns to the table when he has composed himself, makes a joke about the onions from the red beans cooking in the back, and continues.

"That's a tough question," he says. "It's something I've asked myself a lot, as you can see. It's an emotional thing for me because, you know, I feel like . . ."

He pauses again and thinks about his mother crying at his own college graduation and how he was too young to understand what she felt. All this past year, she asked Blair over and over about their plans to attend the Brown graduation, worrying, calling to make sure he'd booked tickets and made the reservations. His phone would ring, and she'd be on the other line.

"When is the graduation? I don't want to miss it."

"Mom, you're gonna be there," he'd say, which made her relax until she decided to check again.

They traveled north together, his mom telling every person she encountered where she was going and why. In the hotel the night before, he couldn't sleep. His mother joined him in the lobby.

"I want you to know something," she said. "I'm very proud of you."

Blair just looked at her.

"What did I do?" he asked.

"You got her this far," she said.

Sitting in that lobby, he understood finally what his mother had felt all those years before.

"You know what," Blair said. "I'm proud of you."

His mom looked at him.

"I got her this far because you got me this far," he said.

Both of them cried then, feeling the weight of their past and also feeling somehow free from it. His mother raised four boys in the worst kind of hell America can throw at a family, and Blair has mirrored her devotion and belief. His children grew up in the city's affluent Carrollton neighborhood. His daughter graduated from the city's most elite private prep school, the alma mater of Peyton and Eli Manning. In one generation, the Bouttes had made it to this hotel in Rhode Island. The next morning, Boutte wore white pants with a pink shirt and a pink pocket square, bucks on his feet—"looking like a Southern gentleman," he says, smiling—and the whole family waited on the college green as the seniors marched through the old stone-and-iron gates. Red and white balloons floated everywhere. The graduates came on campus in procession, and Blair looked to find his daughter first in line, holding the sign that read "Brown University."

He felt everything slow down. It was a perfect day, 82 degrees, blue skies. Most of the time, he just watched his mom take it all in.

"She was in her glory," he says.

The old stone buildings, some of the oldest in an old-money world, rose around them. You couldn't get farther from the Iberville, and that's what Blair thought about and couldn't articulate: He was watching a family change its arc. No Boutte would ever live in a housing project again. And when the ceremony ended, the degrees awarded and the hats thrown, the Bouttes, from the corner of Iberville and Crozat, took out an iPad and cranked up the Rebirth Brass Band. They made their own Second Line that day, dancing through the crowd, waving hankies embroidered with Elaina Boutte's name.

"Where are you guys from?" one lady asked.

"New Orleans," Blair Boutte said proudly.

IV. THE CYCLES OF THE CITY

There's a map on the Internet of the city's worst flood before Katrina, in 1849, when a levee ruptured on a sugarcane plantation west of town. Water rushed in, and if you look at the map of that flood and a map of the areas flooded by Katrina, they are almost the same. The United States invested millions of dollars, following plans drawn by the best scientific minds of the day, the construction coming at a great cost, both financial and human, and in the end, it didn't matter. Katrina flooded the same areas, almost down to the block. The high ground along the banks of the river, raised by a thousand years of floodwaters depositing silt, stayed dry in 1849. The land farther back, what is now Lakeview, New Orleans East,

Chalmette, and the Lower 9th Ward—all that was then empty marshland. That's how it would have stayed, except that in the 1890s humans created the ability to drain swamps so that more people could build homes and lives. By 1915, the first phase of the draining project was complete, and new neighborhoods grew unchecked until Katrina turned them back into brackish swamps. But the drainage had an unintended side effect. As the pipes and pumps drained the water table, the land compacted, and the city began to sink. Today, almost everyone knows that New Orleans resides below sea level, but very few know that it didn't start that way. The city and its people, trying to survive and expand, literally sank themselves. In New Orleans, a place of self-inflicted wounds and unalterable cycles, the past repeats itself over and over, whether in the city's struggles against the water or against the hundreds of murders year after year, all immune to police action and prayer vigils and nonprofit intervention, as constant a threat as the water that surrounds it.

The mayor keeps a stack of red three-ring binders on the floor by his desk.

"Those books are all the people who've been killed in my city," Mitch Landrieu says.

Every murder while he's been in office is in there, with a photograph of the deceased. One victim, a 5-year-old girl named Briana Allen, lives in a frame on a table in his office. She had pigtails.

To understand the city's violence, go now to a different map. This one shows the location of each murder in 2015. The heart of Uptown is a big rectangle, bracketed by Napoleon Avenue and South Carrollton Avenue, Freret and Tchoupitoulas. Inside this enormous swath of bungalows, shotgun shacks, and mansions, there have been zero murders. In the Central Business District, from the Superdome down to the casino, there have been zero murders. In the French Quarter, there have been two.

Now go to the other New Orleans.

The 5th Police District, which includes parts of the 7th and 9th Wards, has long been the toughest assignment for cops. Daryle Holloway, who rode out Katrina at Charity Hospital with his mother, is stationed there. The 5th District was home to arguably the worst housing project, Desire, and to the Florida projects, where Holloway bought cereal, milk, and eggs for the hungry kids whose brother had been shot. Clusters of red markers appear on the district's map, each identifying a murder, and here they come in bunches—in time and in geography. Four shootings over the course of one night, then 11 in 11 days. Four murders within a block or two of Elysian Fields and Claiborne and nearly a dozen in the corridor between St. Claude and Claiborne. Four in the small square formed by St. Bernard, Claiborne, Elysian Fields and St. Claude. Two dozen and counting in New Orleans East.

This summer, a man got shot two blocks from the New Orleans Country Club in Hollygrove, the second murder in the city within an hour. The shooting happened around 5 p.m. The dead man was the 93rd murder of the year. His name was Bradley De'Penis, so obviously he got teased in school. He was born on a Thursday in 1980. He died on a Thursday too. He was 34. When Steve Gleason blocked that punt, De'Penis was back in the city rebuilding, and three years later, he went to Miami for the Super Bowl.

He left behind a mother and a son.

Three hours later, a 22-year-old named Jermal Jarrell was shot in front of A. L. Davis Park off 4th Street in Central City; he died at the hospital. Some people die in New Orleans without fanfare or public mourning, just names and addresses in a news story, the dead come and gone on B6 in the Metro section, a paragraph, two if they're lucky.

2100 block of Governor Nicholls. Dominique Cosey. He was 27.

6000 block of Boeing. Gerald Morgan. He was 17.

1400 block of Desire. Margaret Ambrose. She was 72.

1600 block of Elysian Fields. Daryle Holloway. He was 45.

On the morning he died, Officer Holloway arrived for his shift in the 5th District. A divorced father of three, he'd had a big bowl of Rice Krispies for breakfast. His first task of the day was transporting a suspect from the precinct to central lockup on South Broad Street.

The suspect, Travis Boys, had somehow hidden a .40-caliber semi-automatic pistol from the arresting officers on the scene, one of whom recovered a box of .40 cartridges and still didn't do a full pat-down to look for the gun. Holloway then loaded Boys into the back of a car. They drove down North Claiborne Avenue. Nearing the inter-section of Elysian Fields, Boys reached the gun through the parti-tion between the front and back seat and fired a single shot that entered on the right side of Holloway's chest and exited the left. The bullet pierced his heart and lungs.

With Holloway bleeding and the car still moving down North Claiborne, Boys climbed into the front seat through the opening in the partition. He reached for the passenger door. Holloway, pumping blood from his wound, grabbed the escaping Boys and held firm with one hand while driving with the other.

"Let me go before you kill yourself!" Boys yelled three times.

Holloway refused to let go, fighting and wrestling with the pris-oner in the last moments of his life, bleeding out in the front seat of an NOPD cruiser. He held tight until he lost consciousness. Then his fingers went limp and Boys slipped out of the moving vehicle, head-ing into the 8th Ward on North Claiborne Avenue. Holloway's body camera recorded the out-of-control transport vehicle crashing into a utility pole outside a Shell station at the corner of Elysian Fields and North Claiborne. Holloway died a short time later at the hospital.

The morning after the shooting, a Sunday in late June, Hollo-way's cousin drove down there. She went to the utility pole outside the Shell station where his patrol car came to rest. She tied two My-lar balloons to the pole. Both read "Happy Father's Day." The rain from the night before kept falling. Cops found Boys; uniformed officers saw him in a gas station in the Lower 9th Ward buying a hot sausage po'boy. The monument grew at the Shell station, people writing messages in marker on the pole or leaving flowers, stuffed animals, or balloons.

At an Uptown fried-fish and crawfish joint named Frankie & Johnny's, oyster shucker Juan Pujol put down his knife and focused on the television, broadcasting news of Holloway's death. The stereo played a sad, funky tune, a perfect and mournful eulogy. The rain fell hard. The downpour outside sounded like part of the song, accenting the white spaces. Juan couldn't turn away, living right around the corner from where Holloway died. He talked about wanting to move, even a few blocks, above Esplanade, find some breathing room. Get his kids out of the goddamn shooting gallery. So many dead in the city, so many dead. A 1-year-old shot and killed in the arms of her babysitter. A 5-year-old girl shot at her 10-year-old cousin's birthday party. So much rain, washing away nothing.

Some traces of what came before cannot be scrubbed away. They're layered beneath the current iteration of New Orleans, one sprawling metaphysical capital built from the overlapping maps of the past three centuries. Crackpot locals once devised a plan to rescue Napoleon from exile and bring him to live in the French Quarter; the house they'd planned to give him is now a restaurant. The house of New Orleans founder Bienville is an insect museum between a Marriott and a Morton's steakhouse. Mitch Landrieu works on the spot where Louis Armstrong lived as a child, and four blocks from the Shell station where Daryle Holloway lost consciousness is the house where Tom Benson grew up. The small shotgun at 2127 North Johnson is still standing, although thieves stole all the wiring and pipes not long ago. An old man, Antonio Anderson, lives next door. He is a Mardi Gras Indian chief.

The Indians started appearing during Mardi Gras in the 1880s, led by Chief Becate of the Creole Wild West tribe. Their roots lie in

Congo Square, across Rampart Street from the French Quarter, where owners allowed their slaves to dance on Sundays. These dances were the few moments of freedom in a life of bondage, and every Mardi Gras Indian carries the spirit of those enslaved ancestors. In the brightly colored suits made of shiny stones and feathers, these Indians are not subject to earthly constraints like time. Elaborate rituals and customs have developed, the spy boys and flag boys, tribes battling one another, often beset by the police.

Inside Anderson's house, the walls are red and the heat is stifling. He sits in his chair most days and sews, not far from a framed photo of Barack and Michelle Obama. After his stroke, he struggles to talk. He's a chief in a small tribe in the 7th Ward. Last year's suit is hanging from a wooden stand, green, white, and pink feathers, with elaborate beaded grasshoppers and alligators on the headpiece. Next year's suit is coming together, and he's doing small detail work, running his needle and thread through a cardboard mold he made. Eventually, the suit will become a peacock.

There's something magical and rare about spotting a Mardi Gras Indian in full regalia, as if the soul of the city has somehow taken on a physical form, the man in the suit a vessel for something old and mysterious.

Parades are not scheduled or announced. The dancers just appear, mirages almost, envoys from a long-ago city. When they turn a street corner, shaking pastel feathers and bright flashing beadwork, dancing to a frenetic beat of a brass band, the rhythm that produced horn players and bounce rappers comes alive. Benson came from the same street as a Mardi Gras Indian, and although he looks frail now, the frenetic energy that drives the Big Chiefs also lives in him, the very same passion that once pulled him out of poverty, giving him the strength and callousness to crush anyone who tried to stop his rise. Friends and enemies alike agree: *Don't fuck with Tom Benson.* The judge in New Orleans this summer ruled he was of sound mind, which isn't a surprise, really. Disowning family he no longer likes is completely in character. This latest legal action is exactly something he would have done as a young man, risking the destruction of all he built in pursuit of what he wants. His final court battle is the fitting end to a life of combat and to a decade that has seen many things rise and just as many fall.

A relic from Steve Gleason's own fading past is parked outside his house: a 1965 Ford Mustang, black with gold racing stripes, a Saints logo in place of the blue oval on the grille. You should hear it in the driveway, a 302 bored up to 311, Holley four-barrel carburetor, Edelbrock intake manifold, shifter kit, roller rockers, 300 horsepower. His grandfather bought it off the San Jose line 50 years ago, January 12, 1965, metallic pea green, and when he died, he left the car to Steve in his will. After his diagnosis, Steve had it turned into a Saints-themed Mustang and sold it to raise money. Not long ago, the buyer fell on hard times and called the Gleasons, asking if they wanted to buy it back.

Steve told his wife, "I want to buy it and give it to Rivers," their 3-year-old son.

They'll get it all fixed, and then it will sit there and wait for the boy to turn 16. Rivers will climb inside and bring the engine to life. The rumbling block will be a father's whisper from the beyond— the car a way for Steve to stay in his son's life, one more reminder of the ugly truth that hovers over Gleason's resilience: His health is fragile, and he's aware of his impending extinction. Not long ago, he talked with a child psychologist about the right time to explain everything to Rivers.

"It doesn't seem to be something a 3-year-old should need to learn," Gleason says.

Already he's approaching the edge of an ALS patient's usual life expectancy. With his access to the greatest care in the world, and the sense of purpose his foundation provides him, he might live a long time. Stephen Hawking is still alive 52 years after his diagnosis. Gleason and his caregivers monitor every vital sign carefully, and Steve can tell when something inside his body isn't right.

One of Steve's oldest friends from high school, J. D. Ward, picked up the '65 Mustang in Pensacola a day or two ago and drove it back to New Orleans. They grew up together in Spokane, Washington, hitting the 4000 Holes record shop, spending hours discussing the relative merits of Pearl Jam's Atlanta show in 1994 or the Bridge School Benefit later that year. They're making a playlist for the band's XM channel, and the thing has taken on the scope and seriousness of an invasion plan. J.D. wants to work on it now, but Steve says he needs to go into his room and write a speech. He seems anxious. His wife, Michel, puts up a good front but is clearly overwhelmed, visibly stressed.

"What's he writing speeches for?" J.D. asks when Steve leaves the room.

"Money," one of the caretakers says.

While Steve works, J.D. takes the car for a spin, turning onto Carrollton with the windows down, past the working-class Parkview Tavern. He's emotional, grappling with watching his friend cry earlier. Before ALS, he saw Steve cry exactly twice. Once when they lost a high school football playoff game in double overtime to Eisenhower, and the second time during a baseball game when Steve's father screamed at him while he sat in the dugout. Now he's watching his friend lose the fight. Death by ALS is an ugly thing, and people who've seen it kill a family member will inevitably struggle to block out the memory of someone they love begging to die.

After a stop for a beer, J.D. cranks the car and heads back toward Steve's house. The Pearl Jam show that happened just after the levees broke plays on the car's stereo.

He points to his arm.

"Chill bumps," he says. "Are you kidding me?"

He smiles.

"I'm driving Steve's Mustang with an open container," he says, then nods at the thumping speakers. "Hurricane Katrina was going on through this whole concert."

The show happened at an amphitheater built above a deep gorge in the Columbia River, in Washington State, looking down at the canyon carved by the water. It was green and blue and magnificent. J.D. was there, and a few hundred miles south, Steve stood on a sideline in San Jose during a moment of silence. They were both young and invincible then, blind to how much could be taken away.

Chris Rose is going out tonight.

A group of old friends invited him. Walt Handelsman, the Pulitzer-winning cartoonist who worked at the *Picayune*, wrote a song about the newspaper staff during the hurricane. Some other friends were playing—Paul Sanchez, formerly of the local rock band Cowboy Mouth, and a singer-songwriter named Lynn Drury—and they'd asked Walt to sing his song.

Standing on the sidewalk outside the club, as traffic passes on Canal Street, Rose postpones the awkward hellos with a cigarette. He's excited about the show; Drury wrote his favorite Katrina song, "City Life," and he's hoping she'll play it. Inside, the band covers Bruce Springsteen's "Atlantic City": *Everything dies, baby, that's a fact. But maybe everything that dies someday comes back.*

He's wearing a white T-shirt and a black vest, cool in black, leather Skechers. A bunch of reporters hang out at a table next to the wall. They all wrap him up in hugs and ask where he's been hiding.

"A Rose sighting!" Handelsman says.

The bar is dark, but people start to notice.

"I think I see Chris Rose standing out there," Sanchez says from the stage, and the crowd cheers.

Sanchez tells the story of a hurricane party for Andrew, in 1992, when they all played cards and drank whiskey as the storm blasted the city. He's got that blue-collar New Orleans accent, the Irish

Channel thick on his tongue. That night, Paul passed out in the pantry and woke up cradling a can of creamed corn and a bottle of scotch. Outside, he found Rose and some other folks wrestling in the mud. They were all on mushrooms. Rose drove a 1963 convertible with the top down through the torrential, sideways, Exodus-style downpour, tripping his face off, passing cops who just waved. They all laughed at hurricanes then.

"I wasn't there," Rose calls from the darkness of the audience.

Walt gets onstage to perform his song, about the *Times-Picayune* staff coming back to report from the wounded city. He sings about Rose's columns, about "the rage, the fear, the tribes, the tears."

"Oh, God," a voice in the crowd says softly.

By the stage, Rose asks Drury to play his song, but she says she opened with it. He steps outside, smoking cigarettes and holding court. The newspaper reporters start telling Katrina war stories, about cops at a looted Walmart. One cop stepped up as people were smashing a jewelry case. "Free bracelets!" a man had screamed, holding the fake diamonds above his head. The officer stepped in front of the case. A reporter taking notes thought, *Finally, some order.* Instead, the officer wrapped his hand in a bandanna and just cleared out the jagged pieces of glass so people could loot safely and efficiently.

"Protect and serve," the reporters joked.

Rose is happy, everything about him looser and softer, even his voice and the lines on his face. He looks like he swallowed one of the lightbulbs hanging over the sidewalk outside the bar. He'd told his kids he'd be home by 9:30, but 10 has come and gone and 11 is hanging out there, tempting. They're rolling now, jokes about photographers never leaving the office without a broken doll and a tattered American flag in the trunk, in case a picture needed punching up. Nostalgia is as addictive as opiates, and almost as dangerous.

Standing outside the bar, a nervous, middle-aged woman named Cathy McRae approaches Rose.

"I just want to say how much you meant to New Orleans," she says.

She gives him a big hug. He seems fragile in her arms.

"Ten years later," he says.

She starts to cry, a little at first, telling him how often she's failed to tell people in her life what they meant to her; then she completely breaks down.

"From all of us," she says, almost gasping. "You really made a difference. When we were in exile, you really kept us connected."

"Ten years later," Rose says. "You're gonna get me crying."

"Don't," she says.

"I cry every day," he says.

His friends pay their tabs and come outside, happy to have seen him. They pose for pictures with Rose, leaning into one another with the ease of people who've done battle together. They ask him how his search for work is going and whether he's quit waiting tables. They talk about minivans and leave with heartfelt goodbyes. As they walk down the sidewalk, it's clear they've moved on and lived an entire decade since the hurricane, and Chris, standing back on the sidewalk outside an emptying bar, has been living the same day over and over. Their hurricane ended, and they moved on. His did not. Somehow he got stuck.

"You look great," Sanchez says when they're alone.

"It's dark," Rose says.

Sanchez's guitar is in its battered case on the sidewalk. Drury comes out, and Rose looks at her, then at the guitar, then back at her. He asks if she'd mind playing the Katrina song he loves so much. She takes out Paul's guitar.

"Got a pick?" Lynn asks.

She strums, bobs her head, and sings.

I love this city life, and the dust, and the dust-covered trees.

Sanchez sits and shakes his head slowly, from side to side, while Rose stands and sways. He gently touches the back of Paul's head.

They glitter like diamonds from somebody's broken windowpane.

Somebody keeps time on a beer bottle. Lynn plays muted chords then full strums. The streetlights are yellow balls of fire. Cars speed by, tires on wet pavement.

I guess, I guess I'd rather be . . . , she sings.

. . . messed up than pretty, the table sings back.

I guess, I guess, I guess . . . I'd rather be messed up than pretty . . . , she sings.

. . . just like this city, everyone sings together.

Rose sways and dances and turns. The bottom edges of his black vest flare when he spins. Cigarettes look like stage props wedged between his fingers, the avenging angel of the 504. The song washes over him, and a streetcar rattles past. There is no pain as long as Lynn keeps singing. Paul closes his eyes. Chris looks around him in rapture and says, "God, I love this town."

They sing the line, *Messed up is better than pretty.*

The last chord lingers. Chris and Paul toast Louis Armstrong; then they toast each other. At some tables, the conversation always slides back to the storm, to a time when their pain made sense or was at least shared by everyone around them. The people who loved the city the most got hurt the worst.

Sanchez looks right at me, with soulful eyes and a wide fighter's nose.

"The despair was deep enough," he says, "guys like me and Chris, we're never gonna recover. It was an amputation. It's a scar that's never gonna heal. I still think that leg is there. It's not, you dig?"

They sing a few more songs, and the bar moves the table inside. Paul Sanchez packs up his guitar again and walks to the parking lot in the back. In the dark, he quotes Shakespeare—*to sleep, perchance to dream*—and nods toward his friend out front. He remembers the Chris Rose tripping on mushrooms, driving a muscle-car convertible through a hurricane, the cockiest motherfucker you ever met in your life, lean and dangerous like a switchblade. That man is gone, and a weathered, humbled, loving father of three remains, making beef stroganoff out of a box, still trying to put back together what his poor choices and a hurricane broke apart. No media company in the city will hire him. He writes for a grocery store. Perchance to dream, indeed, for in that sleep of death what dreams may come.

"That's a shell of a man," Sanchez says, "hanging on by a thread. My heart breaks."

V. THE MORNING AFTER THE LONGEST DAY

The U.S. federal government has spent billions on new hurricane barriers in the past decade, doubling down on the belief that a city can be protected from the forces surrounding it. While this might seem like common sense on the surface, the plan ultimately will be as successful in eliminating the threat of nature as mixing a garbage can of rum and fruit juice and watching the clouds roll in. Building elaborate levees and defenses is the folly, while a hurricane party is a fairly sensible response. At least the party acknowledges the unavoidable truth of both life itself and of the city of New Orleans: It is fragile, hanging on to existence in a violent world, and although the people who live there cannot control the water around them, they can control how they respond to it. The citizens in New Orleans, generation after generation, have chosen hope and joy in the face of disaster and oppression. Everything unique about the city is a reflection of that choice. They choose to spend a year making a suit of brightly colored feathers to dance for one glorious day. They choose strong coffee and fried fish. They choose Mardi Gras and Jazz Fest. They choose to eat gumbo in white linen suits because fuck it. They choose music.

In the summer of the 10th anniversary, they come to mourn Officer Daryle Holloway, but something amazing happens instead. His family asks the community to stop by their house in the 7th Ward for a candlelight vigil. They publish the address in the paper, and people start to arrive late that afternoon.

A patrol car parks out front. The department rotates shifts

standing watch on the family home, 24 hours a day since Daryle died, a show of respect. One of his daughters needs to fly in from New York, and when she arrives at the airport, a police officer meets her there. The cops get her luggage and put her in the front seat of a cruiser and bring her home. Now Daryle's 19- and 16-year-old daughters and 13-year-old son greet visitors on the porch, generations coming together. This block has been the center of this family for generations; Eunice Belfield moved here in the 1940s. She sewed costumes for the all-white Mardi Gras Krewe of Proteus. Her son grew up to be the King of Zulu, the prestigious and mostly black krewe.

Holloway's cousin Eric Belfield sits on a stoop next door. After Daryle's divorce, the cousins moved in together to save money. Eric is a chef at a hotel in the Quarter. Someone brings him a plate of food and a bottle of water. The day Daryle died, Eric found the empty bowl of Rice Krispies by Daryle's bed, next to the previous night's supper, a fish plate. Reminders are everywhere. When he cut on the television this morning, it was on the last channel Daryle watched: the Cartoon Network. Daryle was a big kid. He loved Legos and cartoons, and the DVR light keeps switching on, recording shows that won't ever be watched. The family sent Eric to get a clean uniform for the funeral. Sitting on the neighbor's stoop, he starts to cry. He picks at a chicken thigh on a disposable plate.

Uniformed officers bring loads of balloons into the house. Staff members from the Walgreens on Elysian Fields and St. Claude, where he worked security, arrive and are fed. The family feeds anyone who's hungry, friends in the backyard dipping chicken into cornmeal and dropping batches into a pot bubbling on a propane burner. This is why they moved back after Katrina, Belfield says, pointing at the crowd gathering outside the house.

The most powerful four-letter word is home.

"Nobody celebrates the life and the death of our people like we do," Belfield says. The neighbors across the street put out big speakers, and a radio station sends a DJ. Music pours onto the street. Eric dances with his sister and twirls her on the brick sidewalk. A young girl plays a plastic trumpet.

A man, James Wilson, walks up to the house with his bike. Leaning against a trash can, he looks broken. He worked at the Superdome with Holloway. James did concessions, and Daryle did security, and last Saturday, when Holloway didn't show up for his shift at 1:45 p.m., James knew something was wrong. He rode here from City Park, and he looks up at the front porch of the house, where Eunice sits in a chair and sees how many people loved her grandson.

"This is so sad," Wilson says.

Daryle's mother, a nurse at the old Charity Hospital, sits on the porch too. Women fan her with the plastic plates. A crowd from the 9th Ward arrives, and people from the old Desire and Florida housing projects. Every off-duty cop in the city walks onto the street, which is almost full. They're white and black, in combat fatigues and dress blues, names like LeBoeuf, DeSalvo, and Jones. The detectives wear suits out of central casting, with loosened ties, big guns, and cigarettes dangling from their lips. On the sidewalk, a group of teenage girls Nae Nae. Police officers stand side by side with people from the projects, locking arms, and if they can come together for a day, then anything is possible in New Orleans.

The chief of police, Michael Harrison, looks out at the sea of citizens.

"I have never seen a community do something like this for a police officer," he says.

Olander Holloway asks to speak, and a hush comes over the crowd.

"That was my baby boy," she says. Hundreds of people pack the street, shoulder to shoulder. Mourners gasp and sob. "I cannot believe this is for my son."

Those gathered light candles and sing "Amazing Grace." The sun hasn't set, and it all blurs together, noise and laughter and singing and tears. A brass band comes down Kerlerec Street in full swagger, the tuba bobbing above the crowd. Belfield, who plays drums, bangs on a cymbal with a screwdriver. Motorcycle engines rumble. Olander Holloway is on the porch, watching, holding it together. A police cruiser rides slowly down the street. In front of the house, the officer hits his siren.

She starts to cry.

The band marches and the motorcycles rev and then it happens.

Mardi Gras Indians, two Big Chiefs, one in pink and the other in red, round the corner onto Kerlerec. A spy boy dances and yells in front of them. One chief comes from Creole Wild West, one of the oldest tribes in the city. The other comes from the 9th Ward, marching in someone else's territory for a day, a repayment of respect for a police officer who showed it to them when he walked their streets. No turf wars today.

It's madness on the block, brass and stereo speakers and revving engines. Balloons float into the sky over Esplanade Avenue. Smoke rises from motorcycle burnouts. People hold up T-shirts with Holloway's picture on them. Police officers hit their sirens. The Big Chiefs move slowly, to the rhythm of the brass band playing Bob Marley, the trill roll of a snare drum, the deep bass of the tuba. They march to the house and salute the family on the porch, two Mardi Gras Indians dancing in the light of a setting sun.

In July, a local radio station hires Chris Rose.

He says getting the job feels like the first day of the rest of his life. Work is starting to find him. *New Orleans Magazine* gives him a column called Me Again. He guides people on tours of the city for big paydays, sharing his hard-earned knowledge. One book, a biography of fried-chicken king Al Copeland, is nearly finished, and Rose is thinking of writing a memoir of the past 10 years. At least one high-powered New York agent is excited at the prospect of taking it to market. He's grinding, pushed by deadlines for the first time in a while. Rose writes on his front porch in Bayou St. John, sitting in a chair with a towel around his neck.

He wrote an obit for Copeland when he died. That's how the book came about. The family loved it and sought Rose out during his darkest time. Sitting on the porch, he finds the obit online. It ran two-plus years after the storm, and in it, he ends up back in Katrina, talking about the first Christmas after. In addition to founding Popeyes, Copeland strung up the most Griswoldian Christmas lights display at his house, and traffic backed up on Folse Drive, people riding by slowly to gawk. Rose wrote:

> My kids and I were driving around town to see what Christmas lights we could find. Naturally, we ended up at Copeland's house. It was as it always was. A fairy tale. Over the top. The Great Escape.
>
> There was a sign in front of the house that year. It was signed by Copeland and it had an inscription about how it was more important than ever before that he put on a show for the children of the community. It had words like 'sacrifice' and 'spirit' and 'gratitude' and all the right notes.
>
> I cried when I read it. I cried a lot back then.

Rereading the column, Rose gets quiet, remembering his children 10 years ago, young and still believing he was the strongest man alive. That little girl is a teenager now, inside the house wearing headphones, smiling and rolling her eyes at her dad when he does things like pour coins into a jukebox.

Earlier today, he listened to the radio station where he'll soon work, and it ran a program about preparing for this summer's hurricane season. When his next freelance check comes in, he says he needs to go load up on water, candles, batteries, everything he'll need. One day, another hurricane will arrive.

"We'll never rebuild," he says. "We can't. We've rebuilt the city. Just like before: Do the levees work now? Who knows? Nobody knew before. They were never tested, and there's no way to test them. You can only put 4 million metric tons of water against them and see what happens. And the first time they were tested . . . it turns out they didn't work. Now they say, 'We got it now; we're all good.' What you see around this entire city is blind faith."

He's laced through with that faith, some left over, some found anew. A beat-up, black-and-white United cab is parked across the street with a broken trunk, beneath the spaghetti tangle of wires running overhead. You can't worry about a hurricane, he's learned the hard way. It will hit New Orleans or it will turn, but until then, the new city created by Katrina lives.

"Now we wait," he says.

He's got a shopping list, carrying with him the lessons of the past.

"We go to Home Depot and we get our candles and duct tape," he says.

On the edge of his porch, little clay pots show the first sprouts of life. "I grow flowers," he says. The colors are pastel, bright, going well with the sunflower he brought home. A thunderstorm passed through earlier, and around the city plants look green and healthy.

"They look so much happier today."

Sitting in his office preparing for the upcoming season, Sean Payton feels a glow. The Saints' facility smells like cinnamon potpourri as players stop by to talk about the off-season weight program. Payton asked an assistant earlier today to make a list of everyone who'd been part of the Saints for all of the past nine seasons, the players and coaches who arrived just after the storm, when nobody knew whether there'd even be a city of New Orleans. There are four of each.

"We'll walk together forever," he says.

As a thank-you for the past nine years, Payton is buying each of them a Rolex and hosting a dinner. He's not telling them why he's called them together, excited to see how long it takes the room to figure out what it is they all have in common, especially the players:

Drew Brees, Marques Colston, Zach Strief, Jahri Evans. The anniversary of Katrina is making even the most type A strivers take a minute to consider their lives.

Just yesterday, it seems, he left the stadium in Miami after the Super Bowl, climbing onto bus No. 1. Traffic snarled around them, and the buses headed back to the team hotel, and he remembers so clearly sitting in the front seat, wishing the drive would take forever.

Two years later, he got suspended for his role in Bountygate. In private, he raged about a year being taken away from him in his prime; he and his son watched the NFL draft like any fan, sitting in a suburban Fuddruckers, helpless. But something else happened that fall. He coached his son's sixth-grade football team in Texas, the offensive coordinator and playcaller.

Payton cut oranges, mixed Gatorade, and signaled in plays, using simplified versions of the same calls he made for the Saints, the sixth-graders running Right 34 Bob, or Fake Right 35 Bob Poly. His deep anger faded on the sideline of the Liberty Christian Warriors, who dominated opponents until running into a team from Springtown called the Orange Porcupines, country boys from about an hour outside Dallas. "Listen," Payton says, laughing. "They had a real good coach. It was one of those single-wing guys. You know it's like a little clique."

His team couldn't stop Springtown's single-wing attack. Convinced they'd meet the Porcupines again in the playoffs, Payton reviewed the film that one of the dads recorded, then got Bill Parcells on the telephone. Together, they broke down a sixth-grade team's offense.

"Penetration kills the single wing," Parcells said, and they worked out a plan. Liberty Christian did meet Springtown again in the Super Bowl for the sixth-grade football league. Payton's team played better, and much harder, and he remembers being on the sideline watching his players make the right reads—following Parcells's advice—spilling the guard and making the tackle for a loss. He felt proud of his team's effort, not bitter over the eventual defeat.

Payton told his young players that he needed them more than they needed him, and he meant it. The essence of football, that's what he felt connected to, and in his office on Airline Drive, back in New Orleans, he pulls out a scrapbook someone made for him, pictures from that season. Even back in the grind of the NFL, he gets that glow describing his favorite moment. A kid named Paulie, who was in the band, wanted to be on the team. "We put a play in for Paulie," Payton says. "Fake Right 34 Bob O, and the fullback, the O, pulled around and we handed it to the Z around left. And he scored a 15-yard touchdown walk-in and his mom was in tears on the sidelines and Paulie just threw the ball up and it was like when Lucas scored. And I'm telling you, it was one of the best memories ever. I had a play designed, they executed, and Paulie walked in."

Something else has happened since Katrina.

When Payton arrived in New Orleans, he lived in the suburbs, where things are scrubbed, orderly, and boring. Then his marriage failed in public, and he lost his team for a year, and along the way, he fell in love with the city, as the city has fallen in love with him. A year ago, he bought a condo in Uptown, eight blocks from Clancy's Restaurant and six blocks from St. Charles Avenue. Now he's got a goldendoodle named Murphy, and he likes to walk Murphy up Webster to St. Charles, turning left through the park. A long row of houses fronts the park, with the tall oak trees and walking paths as a lawn, and he and his dog enjoy the shade and air. People leave him alone. Sometimes he stops for a sno-ball. At night he loves Clancy's, the clubhouse for the neighborhood. The women who answer the phones have a list of customers who are always to be given a table, regardless of how packed the reservation book might be. Payton, like any sensible person, orders the panned veal atop the pasta—Veal Annunciation, it's named—and looks forward to dessert. "I want the frozen peppermint ice cream that sat in the back of the freezer," he says.

Ten years ago, Sean Payton arrived in New Orleans young and hungry, willing to do anything to reach his dreams. Some of those dreams have come true, and some of them have not. Whatever happens now, a strange thought occurred to him not long ago: He will never sell that condo.

Some part of him will always consider New Orleans home.

Steve Gleason is 38. Rivers Gleason is 3. They're both kids.

Every Tuesday, they do something fun together. They call it Dude's Day. The plan today is a big warehouse filled with trampolines named Sector6. They've been before, and Rivers refused to go off the trapeze. That's the goal for today.

"Awesome ain't easy," a painting in Steve's living room declares. Rivers is at his swimming lesson up the street. Gleason is getting his trach hole swabbed with hydrogen peroxide. It hurts, but he doesn't complain. The light in the big windows makes his house open and airy, the bookshelves a window into the broad and diverse life being crushed by his disease: *The Goldfinch*, *Catch-22*, *The Lords of Discipline*, *The Road*, *One Hundred Years of Solitude*, the book about the town brutalized by United Fruit. Blair Casey, a former college athlete who works for Steve, mixes coffee with coconut water and injects it into the feeding tube.

Casey loads Steve into the front seat of the big black custom van—black rims and tinted windows—and locks him in place. They pick up Rivers, who bounds across the lawn and into the back seat.

"You wanna go to Sector6?" Steve asks.

"Trapeeeeeeze!" Rivers yells. "I be a good boy!"

Casey straps Steve's head in place for the bumpy ride, and Rivers gets quiet in the back seat. He pays close attention whenever his dad needs help; even at 3, he is aware that something is different. The graphs and gauges on the back of Gleason's chair give constant readings, and Rivers watches them too: H_2O, 19.7, Peak Flow, 41.5.

"Rivers, what's our rule on Dude's Day?" Steve asks.

"No crying!" Rivers says.

"No crying or we have to go home," Steve says.

Casey drives up a ramp, onto the interstate, rain pelting the windshield. Steve uses his eyes to call up a playlist called Rivers' Sing Along Songs, and he hits play.

"Put me in, Coach, I'm ready to play!" Rivers sings.

Three-year-olds sound like they're drunk when they're singing. It's hilarious and impossibly cute. A *Lion King* song comes on.

"I just can't wait to be king!" Rivers sings.

The third song is "Release," by Steve's favorite band, Pearl Jam.

"Rivers, who's singing?" Steve asks.

"Eddie Vedder!" Rivers says, a grinning stick of 3-year-old dynamite, vibrating with an energy that every one of Steve's former teammates would recognize. Today, Rivers will try to confront his fear. He wants to jump off the trapeze, flying through the air toward a pool of foam blocks, looking oddly like a grown man laying out for a punt.

Rivers Gleason wasn't alive during Hurricane Katrina. He wasn't alive when his dad blocked a punt on Monday Night Football, and he wasn't alive when the Saints won the Super Bowl. Those things are just words to him, stories he'll hear as he gets older. He doesn't understand them, just as he doesn't understand that his father has a fatal disease. There are other things he needs to learn that his father might not be around to teach. That bothers Steve, who has solved the problem as best as he can. On a hard drive at the house, there is a series of five-minute videos, hundreds of them, for when Steve dies and Rivers needs a daddy. Little tutorials, things like how to whistle, or change a flat tire, big things like drugs and alcohol, or what to do when your heart is broken—things a son should learn from his father. Things that need to be passed along, in stories and code, when one generation takes over where the previous one left off. Rivers Gleason, like his hometown, must learn from the past and remain unafraid.

Sector6 is a personal injury attorney's chicken dinner. Kids fly through the air, doing flips and landing akimbo, slinging dodgeballs at one another's faces. Rivers gets inside and tears off through the trampolines.

"Rivers, are you gonna do the trapeze?" Steve asks. "Are you ready?"

Rivers nods.

"Me, too," Steve types.

Rivers does backflips into pits of foam blocks, and he dances to the music. Saints fans ask Steve for photos, and he takes the time to type out hellos to them. One young boy comes over and says, "No white flags."

Gleason suddenly struggles to breathe.

"You need to cough?" a friend asks, calling to Casey to come help. As Casey gets the electronic machine to help Steve cough, the friend rubs Steve's arm, talking softly, reassuring him. Steve is shaking.

"Coming right now," his friend says.

Casey hooks up the coughing apparatus, and Steve returns to normal.

"Rivers," he says, "I want to watch you on the trapeze."

He's been pushing him, encouraging. Last time, Rivers made it as far as the platform in the air, looking down at the pit before refusing to jump. Today Rivers heads up and stands in line.

"He's going up the steps," Casey says.

Steve motors his wheelchair so he can get a clear view. He is laughing with his eyes, and Rivers grabs the rope and jumps off into space, flying through the air. He did it. Climbing out of the foam, he runs straight to his dad, slapping his right hand.

"Did you see me?!" Rivers asks.

"Nice job, Rivers," Steve types. "The trapeze isn't scary anymore. I'm so proud of you."

The car ride back is quiet. Rivers is exhausted, falling asleep, while Steve watches him with his tablet's camera. One day Rivers will understand. People will tell him stories about his father, a brave man who did so many things. Big things, like changing the way people with ALS live their lives, and small things, like blocking a punt. Rivers's eyes flutter and close.

"Done," Steve says.

The van rumbles over the awful New Orleans roads, passing the bayou and the levee wall. Mardi Gras music plays on the stereo. At the house, Casey carries Rivers to bed, the boy's sleeping head resting on his shoulder. Then he goes back outside to unload Steve. Rivers wakes up and tiptoes around the corner, slipping back to the van to get his blanket, which he can't sleep without. Steve sits in the space between the foyer and the kitchen. Casey is mixing the shake for lunch. Now it's Steve's turn to sleep, his eyelids heavy. Rivers sees that his dad's head has fallen forward, hanging limp. And after looking around and seeing Casey at the counter, he decides to handle this all by himself. Rivers puts his tiny palm on his father's forehead and gently pushes him back into place.

AUGUST 2015

The Greatest Hitter Who Ever Lived On

Ted Williams's ambitions shaped his legacy but wrecked his relationships. If his lone surviving child has her wish, the family's cycle of suffering might at last be broken.

Claudia Williams found comfort wearing her dad's favorite red flannel shirt. It smelled like him. Time frayed the threads, pulled apart seams, and years ago the shirt went into a safe. She keeps many things locked away. In a closet next to her garage, her father's Orvis 8.3-foot, 7-weight graphite fly rod leans on a wall. His flies are safe, too, and she can see his hands in the bend of the knots. She feels closest to him fishing but has been only once or twice since he died. Nearby, pocketknives rust at their hinges. His old leather suitcase is there, too, in its final resting place after years of trains, ballparks, and hotel rooms.

Her husband, Eric Abel, comes home from running errands. He'd been through the safes and the storage unit they keep filled to its 10-foot ceiling, hunting for the flannel shirt. She is laughing in the kitchen, a lazy Sunday morning. Eric takes a breath and enters the room. "First of all, Claudia," he says slowly, "let me apologize; I don't know what we've done with that shirt."

Suddenly quiet and hiding now, she says, "I don't wanna think about it," as one more piece of her father slips away.

She is hiding from loss and from regret, hiding from her family's past, which is always operating the strings of her daily life. Whenever she lets herself go back, she ends up at the same place: the beginning.

Ted Williams's mother gave him nothing but a name, and as soon as he grew old enough, he gave it back, changing Teddy on his birth certificate to the more respectable Theodore. He longed to rewrite the facts of his life. His father drifted on the edge of it. His mother, May, was obsessed with her work at the Salvation Army, abandoning her own kids, and the descriptions of his lonely life exist in many accounts, most notably biographies by Ben Bradlee Jr. and Leigh Montville. San Diego neighbors would watch Ted and his younger brother, Danny, 8 and 6, sitting alone on the front porch late into the night. The anger that dominated both their lives started there, on those lonely evenings outside 4121 Utah Street, waiting for their mom to come home. May Williams never saw her son play a major league game, even though she lived through his entire career. When she died, 11 months after he hit a home run in his final at-bat, he went through her things and gathered up family photographs. He tore them into pieces and threw the pieces away.

That was 1961, and he never wanted family to hurt him again. He lived most of the next 41 years as a kind of island. He died in 2002 and is frozen at 7895 East Acoma Drive in Scottsdale, Arizona. Claudia and her brother, John-Henry, supported cryonics; older half sister Bobby-Jo wanted her father cremated and sued her siblings in the courts and fought them in the media. Ted Williams gave his three children the name he'd made famous, and when he died, their battle turned a solemn passing into a late-night punch line. Death exposes everyone, and it exposed Ted Williams, stripping away the armor he'd created as a boy on Utah Street, revealing what he'd tried so hard to hide: He came from damaged people, and he left damaged people behind.

Claudia Williams, now 43, rarely tells anyone about her relation to Ted Williams. Her co-workers at the Crystal River, Florida, medical center where she's a nurse are only now finding out on their own. It was two years before her best friend knew.

If people do know, she tests them constantly, to make sure they don't like her for her dad's name. She recently stopped to pick up swim fins from a workout partner, and he said he was having an office party and invited her in. Instead, she sat in her car in the parking lot, stewing, wondering whether he just wanted to show off "Ted's daughter," and finally she drove away, enraged, leaving the fins behind.

Upon occasion, she curses exactly like he did, stringing together blistering oaths, a kind of profane poetry: "that whore of a bitch fucking cunt of a bimbo," say, of a nurse who spoke to reporters about the family. Claudia is beautiful and familiar, her face a combination of her mother's *Vogue* model cheekbones and her father's all-American jaw. When she is up, laughing with a goofy smile and light in her eyes, you cannot get close enough to her, and when she is down, spiraling into a darkness only she can see, you cannot get far enough away. With no children of her own, she's destined to remain a daughter. She's young because her dad was much older than her mom—Ted, the eternal player, tossed Dolores Wettach a note across the first-class cabin of an international flight, introducing himself simply as a fisherman—starting Claudia's lifelong struggle to hold tight to something slipping between her fingers. "I hate time," she says.

She lives in a sprawling Florida community popular among retirees whose first resident and primary pitchman was her father. He's everywhere. Her country club membership number is 9. Every day, she drives on Ted Williams Memorial Parkway. She turns from West Fenway Drive onto Ted Williams Court in her black Acura, the Euro club music rattling the rearview mirror.

"You should look at the lyrics," she says as the stereo plays. The songs bleed together into a singular anthem of loneliness and loss. *This will be my monument / This will be a beacon when I'm gone / You're everywhere I go / I promise I won't let you down / It's not over, not over / Not over, not over, yet.* The lines speak to the two competing desires governing her life: She wants to be close to a father she didn't really know for much of his life, but she wants to escape his shadow too.

She left home at 16, moving to Europe to finish high school, working as a nanny, training for triathlons, living in France, then Switzerland, then Germany, any place where nobody'd ever heard of Ted Williams. In letters home, she described being adrift, telling her dad she felt "like a lost athlete looking for a sport." She cooked hot dogs in a gypsy circus. Her father offered her money, but she refused it. In this stubbornness, she found the emotional stability sought but never discovered by her brother, who died 11 years ago from leukemia. "I surpassed John-Henry quicker because I got away," she says.

She never asked for anything. Her dream was to attend Middlebury College in Vermont. When she didn't get in, Ted called the governor of New Hampshire, who pulled some strings. The reconsidered acceptance letter made her weep with rage because she knew what had happened. She told Middlebury no. Her friends at Springfield College didn't realize her father was Ted Williams until she asked some guys who played baseball to teach her to throw; the Red Sox had requested she toss out a first pitch as a surprise to her father, and she didn't want, as she told them, "to throw like a girl." Her brother lobbed one wild, but Claudia kicked her leg and delivered a strike. Ted beamed, a reward she seldom got while he lived and craves now that he's gone.

"I think I'm just looking for him to still be proud of me," she says.

She trained for a triathlon and then devoted her life to making the 2000 Olympic team, falling just short. Around 2005, she started playing tennis with some older ladies in the neighborhood. Then the Williams kicked in: She moved up the USTA ratings, 3.5 to 4.0; then, she says, she became the best 4.0 in Citrus County, then the top-ranked 4.0 player in the state. Hooked, she decided to play at the local junior college. For a season, at 37 years old, she competed against teenagers. After her father died, she received a sponsor's exemption to run the Boston Marathon in his memory; she turned it down, trained, and ran fast enough to qualify on her own. "I don't know who has to say, 'You did well,'" says Abel, who was the Williams family attorney when he met Claudia.

When she decided to be a lifeguard, she completed the most advanced open-water rescue training. After deciding to make jewelry, she took classes to become a master craftsman. She learned how to sky-dive, and after having to deploy the backup shoot on her first solo jump, she went back up again: *I'll show you, sky!* Her workout routines—miles in a pool and on a treadmill, hours daily in a gym— break the alpha dogs who try to hang with Ted's daughter. She makes them earn their story. In the past few years, she studied nursing, and even that hasn't been enough, so now she's studying biology and statistics, prerequisites for graduate school. Her top choice is Duke, and in her application essay she talked about her life as a frustrated athlete without a sport. She talked about the influence of her father, but she never mentioned that the father in question was Ted Williams.

This story began two years ago, when I reached out to Claudia about meeting at her home in Hernando. The timing never worked for her because she struggles to look past her obsessions: nursing school and a book she wrote about her father, which started as a stocking stuffer about lessons she learned and turned into a cathartic exploration of the person she's still trying to be. Finally she said yes. The first visit lasted a week in the fall of 2014, and we made paella and she told funny stories about her dad—he'd call the public phone in European hostels and boom at unsuspecting travelers, "Is CLAUDIA WILLIAMS there? This is her FATHER! OL' TED WILLIAMS!"—and she got melancholy later and said, "We need to laugh more."

She let me poke through the family's filing cabinets, its safes, her dad's hospital records, anything I wanted—she could prove, she said, that her father agreed to be frozen. We talked for hour upon hour. To her, the many accounts of Ted Williams are all fatally flawed because most people didn't understand that the two famous acts of his life—ballplayer and fisherman—occurred only because he was hiding from the third and final act of his life: fatherhood. He'd been raised by an erratic and absent mother. He had a cousin who was murdered by her husband, and a criminal brother who died young and angry.

He hid in the hyperfocus required by baseball and fishing; most nights after ballgames, he returned to the hotel where he lived—he never purchased a home in Boston—and tied fishing flies alone. He preferred to spend off-seasons in the woods or on the water. Once, he arrived late to spring training because he lost track of time while hunting wolves in a cold northern forest, and the media focused so much on the process story of the tardiness that nobody seemed to notice the window Williams had briefly opened into his truest self: He sought peace in the wilderness with wolves.

Ted Williams hated his childhood home, leaving before graduation the same as Claudia, never going back. His lifelong feud with the press began when a writer asked rhetorically in a column what kind of boy didn't go home in the winter to visit his mother. How could he be expected, then, to create a family when he despised his own so much?

"I was for shit as a father," he confided once to a cousin.

On the day his only son, John-Henry, was born, Ted was salmon fishing in Canada. He'd been retired for eight years. That night, like always, he wrote in his fishing log. Ted wrote about the water temperature (70–72 degrees), his friends who came up to fish, and details of the trout and arctic char he caught while casting for salmon. He never mentioned a pregnant Dolores, and he never mentioned the boy.

To the public, he was a success, but to himself, he was a failure, consumed with shame and regret. Bobby-Jo came into the world first, in the middle of his career. When she was young, he got so mad at her that he spit a mouthful of food in her face.

Ted drove her back to her mom's house in Miami once, and when they arrived, it transpired that Bobby-Jo had forgotten her keys, and Ted, raging, kicked her out of the car and left her standing alone there in the dark, exactly as his mother had done to him.

Instead of Bobby-Jo becoming the first Williams to graduate from college, which Ted wanted as desperately as he wanted to hit a baseball, she got pregnant. Rather than tell her father, she slit her arm from the wrist to the elbow. She entered a psych ward, which he paid for, and got an abortion, which he paid for, and when her scars taunted him—physical proof that he'd become his mother—he paid for plastic surgery too. He couldn't buy her peace. Doctors diagnosed manic depression, and she moved from booze to pills, cheating on her husband with a neighbor and giving herself another abortion with drugs and alcohol. Doctors gave her electroshock therapy. She threw plates and knives. Her voice turned childlike whenever she spoke to him, a thin "Daddy." She asked for money and begged for help. She never held a job. At the funeral for Williams's longtime girlfriend, Louise Kaufman, Claudia recognized her half sister, Bobby-Jo, whom she'd never met, simply by seeing a familiar wave of fear register on Bobby-Jo's face at the sound of Ted's voice: He boomed in the next room, sucking up all the oxygen, and two women, born 23 years apart, flinched.

"You must be Bobby-Jo," Claudia said.

"Claudia?" she replied.

Ted talked with Bobby-Jo moments later.

"Hi, Daddy," she said.

"Are you still smoking?" he asked.

"I'm down to one pack a day," she said.

"Jesus," he said, then he walked away.

By the time Eric Abel came into the Williams inner circle as the family attorney, Ted had already excommunicated Bobby-Jo. At Ted's request, Abel wrote her out of the will, and Abel said over the nine years he spent around Williams, he heard him mention Bob-by-Jo maybe three times, and every time he called her a "fucking syphilitic cunt."

He called Claudia a "cunt" too, and a "fat bitch," and told John-Henry he was the "abortion I wanted." They tried to understand his rages and why they'd even been born. "I mean, he had [me] at 53 years old," Claudia says, her voice wavering. "Right from the start, we knew we weren't gonna have much time, you know? The lessons that he had to teach us, we didn't have the time to learn. . . . We're desperately trying—I say 'we' like John-Henry's still around—but we're desperately trying to figure out what made him tick."

Their mom, Dolores, and Ted didn't last long. He got his freedom, fishing every day. She got the kids. Claudia remembers growing up with a mother increasingly bitter over her failed love affair, on a Vermont farm without a television, isolated by their environment and the fame of their absent father. The children created their own world, and only they understand what it felt like to live in it. All they had was each other, and both longed to decode their dad and maybe find themselves in the process. Whenever they'd ask questions about his childhood, or his life, he'd scowl and grumble, "Read my book."

Claudia loves dragons. She especially loves movies about dragons. On the living room cabinet, there's a ceramic statue of Toothless, the star of the animated movie *How to Train Your Dragon*. She got it as a gift. Her voice changes and her eyes and face soften when she says, "Toothless."

A few years ago, she and Eric's teenage daughters from his first marriage went to see a movie called *The Water Horse*, about a boy who raises a Loch Ness Monster—which is close enough to a dragon for Claudia—then releases the beast to save its life. It is named Crusoe, and as the movie ended, Eric's girls looked over and saw Claudia weeping, shoulders rocking up and down, distraught over the boy taking the dragon out to sea.

"You were sobbing," says Eric's daughter Emma, now 22, grinning as she tells the story. Claudia smiles.

"My heart hurt," she says.

That night, after Eric cooks steaks and Emma bakes sugar cookies, everyone piles onto the sofa for movie night. Claudia picks *How to Train Your Dragon*, bringing another round of catcalls and laughter. Everyone settles in, and the movie starts.

"Toothless!" she coos.

"He's real to you, isn't he?" Eric asks, kindly. No one is laughing now, and Claudia reaches for Eric's hand from time to time. Every now and again, she sighs. The story is about a boy trying to live in the shadow of his powerful and domineering father—about a child searching for his place in the world. Watching her watch a dragon movie makes it all make sense.

Sitting on her couch, she cries when the dragon saves the little boy.

"You won't always be there to protect him," a character in the movie tells the father, and Claudia smiles, turns to Eric, and says, "John-Henry would've loved this movie."

John-Henry Williams loved frogs.

He loved anything small and weak. During storms, driving up the hill toward their house in Vermont, he'd jump out of the car in the pouring rain, trying to get the frogs to move before they died beneath the wheels of the car. Like any damaged person, he took his protection too far. He saved a wild duck he found, and countless other birds. If they bit him, he'd tap their beaks to scold them, as if they loved him with the same intellectual fervor he loved them. Claudia still remembers Bangor the Cat. Driving back from visiting Ted's compound in Canada, Dolores and John-Henry stopped in Maine to spend the night in sleeping bags at a rest stop. In the night, he heard a kitten crying, and after searching for and finding her, he tucked the cat, fleas and all, into his bag.

At home, he brought her back to health and felt hurt when she wanted to roam outside. Always scared of being abandoned, he fit a dog harness on a long leash and tied Bangor to his bed. Claudia tried to get him to release the cat, but he refused to listen.

He protected Claudia too. The first time they visited Ted in Florida together, he made sure she knew not to annoy him, advising her to use the bathroom before leaving the airport. At Ted's place in Islamorada, in the Keys, she got a terrible sunburn. Terrified of Ted raging at them, John-Henry quietly fed her ice chips and got her ginger ale when she vomited from sun poisoning. She was about 9. He was 12. John-Henry rubbed Vaseline on her shoulders and told her not to cry.

That was three decades ago. There is only one picture of John-Henry in her house. It hurts too much. When he got leukemia a year after Ted died, she donated bone marrow, and when he needed another transplant and her blood count was too low, she begged the doctors to try anyway. She screamed at them in the blood lab. An agnostic, she stopped in a church near the Los Angeles hospital and got on her knees and begged. It was the first and only time she has prayed. She asked God to take her instead. John-Henry died on a Saturday, and as he requested, his body was suspended at Alcor, too, in the same tank as his dad.

Eleven years he's been gone.

"Grief is weird," Claudia says, riding at night through the dark neighborhoods around their house. "The first seven years, any time I would have a break, any fun, one moment—inevitably, guilt. Just horrible guilt. Like I didn't deserve to be happy."

"I'm the one who reached down to keep pulling you up," Abel says, driving. "Still do. I love you. When you laugh—"

She interrupts him. A heavy rain is falling, blurring the streetlights reflecting off the asphalt, and she looks out into the glare of the headlamps and sees something move.

"Did you see the frog?" she says suddenly. "You gotta watch for him!"

"No," he says.

"I don't know if you ran over him," she says.

"Did I hit one?" he asks.

She starts slapping his arm.

"*Stop! Stop!*" she cries.

He presses hard on the brakes, and she gets out. In the rain, in the glow of their house, she shakes her foot along the pavement, clearing a path, making sure no frogs get caught beneath the tires of the approaching car.

A mile away, a secret remains locked in one of Ted Williams's safes.

On a shelf above a Desert Eagle .44, his fishing logs tell a different story from the one he gave his fans and his children. In public, he seemed to revel in the solitary pursuit of baseball greatness, then fishing greatness, but really, his lonely existence was a self-imposed exile, not because he didn't want to know his children but because he was scared of hurting them, and of being hurt.

Something happened to Ted Williams in the years after his son came into the world. "What's incredible as an observer was to watch him in love with his kids," says Abel, now 52. "The vulnerability of having love for your children. You could see it just gnaw. It was everything against his grain to succumb to this outside influence of children. Love had control over him. He felt vulnerable. A vulnerability he never had in his life. I think he *hated* that vulnerability of feeling guilt."

In his logs, John-Henry and Claudia began to make appearances.

First, just simple mentions, when they were little: "Claudia, John Henry took canoe ride to Gray Rapids." Soon Ted gave them praise that would never reach their ears. By 1979, when they were 10 and 7, he practically gushed in his upright, loopy handwriting. On June 14, he wrote about his son: "His casting is better than I expected so he must have been practicing some. After an aching rest and a few blisters on his casting hand, he is getting a little uninterested. Finally he got his first fish. A grilse. Enthusiasm revived. 3 grilse, caught his first salmon. 10 pounds. Big day in a young fisherman's life."

Claudia and John-Henry would have given anything to know this. It might have changed their lives. Near the safe in his old house is a note Ted saved, dated December 10, 1983, when Claudia was 12. It's a contract she wrote—the Williams family loves handwritten contracts—with her mother at a Howard Johnson's somewhere: "When I grow up I will never have a child. If I do I will pay my mom 1,000 dollars."

Less than a year later, Ted sat before a stack of posters, doing one of the bulk signings familiar to all famous athletes. At some point during the session, instead of signing his name, he wrote a note to Claudia, one he knew she'd discover someday. He signed the rest, and the whole box went into storage. She found the note three years ago, 10 years after he died, going through memorabilia. Trembling as she held the poster in her hand, she finally read the words she wanted so badly to hear as a child: "To my beautiful daughter. I love you. Dad."

Ted wanted to change. Trouble is, nobody knew how to start to repair something so completely broken. It began with Claudia. About 20 years ago, she graduated from college. He asked her what she wanted as a gift, and she said she wanted time. The three of them flew together to San Diego and drove up the Pacific Coast. It was a do-over. So many firsts happened on that trip. She and her brother saw the house on Utah Street. The three of them laughed, and they asked Ted questions, and he told stories and asked them questions too. For years, she'd thought her father had stopped maturing when he became famous at 20, and now they'd both reached his emotional age, equals and running buddies for the first time. He never lost his temper or spun off in a rage. He wasn't angry, and they weren't scared.

They visited Alcatraz, and Ted used a Walkman for the first time, befuddled by the technology, and they all laughed. Something happened to Ted Williams's face when he laughed; most pictures show him stern, in concentration, but when he giggled, his jowls would hang and his eyes would squint and he looked, for just a moment, nothing like one of the most famous men in America. He looked anonymous and happy. When the boat docked back at Pier 39, they walked down the boards looking for dinner. A man at a card table was reading palms. Claudia saw him first, and she and John-Henry dragged their father over.

The fortune-teller sat on a low stool. He traced his finger over the old man's wrinkled palm. Ted laughed and made a joke about it feeling good, and the inside of his hand was soft, the calluses he cultivated during baseball long gone smooth. John-Henry snapped photos, forever documenting every moment he spent around his dad. Claudia leaned in and watched. Everything that would happen began in these moments, but none of them could see the future, not even the fortune-teller.

He looked up at the old man.

"You have heavy burdens you're still carrying," he said. "It's time to let them go."

Ted Williams tried to follow that advice. He really tried.

Nine months after that trip, he had a stroke. His health declined steadily for nearly the next nine years. John-Henry and Claudia cared for him every day, and every day they discovered new levels of understanding and knowledge. They sought out anything that might buy him more time—no matter how experimental, unorthodox, or just plain weird. They paid $30 a pill for vitamins and pumped oxygen-rich air into his room. They tried bee pollen and acupuncture and hired a therapist to work through his anger. John-Henry bought a dialysis machine so Ted could get the treatment at night. Nothing worked.

Father and son had epic fights, bad enough that the caretakers called protective services. Investigators came to the house and interviewed both men, asking whether Ted was being made to sign autographs against his will, before determining there was no abuse. John-Henry wanted to control his father—his latest Bangor—and his father rebelled. About once a year, Abel would get called to the house to mediate a bizarre dispute, usually about Ted showering to ward off infection, or taking his medicine regularly.

"You could see an internal struggle," Abel says. "'Goddamn, that's my son. He loves me, I love him. Fuck. I wanna say no so goddamn bad. Everything about me says no. But I love him.' You could just watch it rage."

Even now, Abel laughs about the scene he'd find upon entering the house.

"Dad, you have to take this medicine," John-Henry would be saying. "You have to take these pills."

"I'm not taking this shit," Ted would growl, seething. "Fuck you."

Abel would write up a contract on a napkin or a piece of scratch paper, which is what Ted liked, and negotiate a settlement: Ted agreed to take the pills every day, and John-Henry agreed to let him shower only four times a week. Both would sign it, and the crisis would be averted.

Even as he fought him, Ted knew John-Henry was struggling to find his place in the world. He worried about his son. Once, when Abel was flying to San Diego to meet with the Upper Deck baseball card company, Ted pulled him aside.

"See if you can help John-Henry get a job," Williams asked. "I know Claudia will be fine."

The guilt Ted carried slipped away when he did something to help his kids. Looking back, Claudia wishes she'd let him get her into Middlebury, because it was the only thing he knew how to do. In those last years, she taught him how to be a father to a daughter. When Claudia went through a breakup, instead of keeping her pain a secret like she'd done as a teenager, she explained how to comfort her.

"Please don't be mad," she said. "Just please listen to me. I'm hurting."

She could hear him grinding his teeth.

"What the hell do you want me to do about it!" he yelled. "I can't do a fucking thing!"

"Just tell me you love me," she said.

"JESUS CHRIST!" he yelled. "I love you more than you'll ever know."

The outside world slipped away, and the universe shrank to the three of them: a dad looking for absolution, a son who needed a dad to show him how to be a man, a daughter who'd always craved a family, which they at long last became. A strange family, to be sure, but a family nonetheless, with a patriarch who'd found escape from his guilt and his shame in the company of his children.

"He never thought he was gonna be a good father," Claudia says. "He'd given up on it. Thought he wasn't very good at it. And we actually showed him that not only was he good at it, we wanted him and we said, 'You can do this, Dad.' And once he realized 'I can be good at this, and these kids want to learn from me,' we had run out of time."

Then John-Henry read a book about cryonics.

Ted's house is full of secrets about his son, too, windows into a desperate but curious mind at work. In the long row of filing cabinets, a drawer holds a blue folder marked "Alcor." It's thick, jammed with newsletters, receipts, contracts, and John-Henry's handwritten notes taken during a visit to the cryonics facility.

He filled six yellow legal-sized pages, jotting down the price for freezing just the head ($50,000) and the price for the entire body ($120,000), making charts and decision trees plotting the potential repercussions of cryonics. On a page, he drew a horizontal graph, with a line drawn down the middle, dividing the plan into actions he'd take before convincing his father and what he'd need to do after.

In big letters, he wrote "Make Claudia co-petitioner" and circled it. She agreed. "I didn't want John-Henry to lose his father," she says. "He needed him so badly. He was still learning, he was still— he was still— What is it? Evolving? Becoming a man in his father's eyes? He needed more time."

The literature John-Henry took home from Alcor, one of the country's two major cryonics companies, worked in his imagination; he purchased every book they offered, according to credit card receipts. The most important thing he read was the origin text of cryonics, a book by science fiction writer and professor Robert Ettinger titled *The Prospect of Immortality*. Ettinger wrote that the freezer always trumped the grave, and with nothing to lose, why not take a chance? Children who buried their parents were described as murderers. Ettinger also made many other wild and foolish predictions about what science would bring to the world in his lifetime, so the book, like the Bible, is believable to those who want to believe. On page 15, Ettinger seemed to be speaking directly to John-Henry: "The tired old man, then, will close his eyes, and he can think of his impending temporary death as another period under anesthesia at the hospital. Centuries may pass, but to him there will be only a moment of sleep without dreams."

Around the long kitchen table, John-Henry began to make his case.

Ted did not want to be frozen at first. His will, which he wrote near the end of the fishing act of his life, made his wishes very clear. He should be cremated, his ashes "sprinkled at sea off the coast of Florida where the water is very deep."

Four years passed between John-Henry's purchasing the books and requesting membership documents from Alcor. Ted's health declined, more every day. John-Henry kept saying cryonics provided a chance for them all to be together again one day.

"What does Dad think?" Claudia asked.

"He thinks it's kooky," John-Henry says. "But he is interested. I can tell."

They spent hours around the dining table, and every so often John-Henry would bring it up. Sometimes Ted would curse and walk away. Other times he'd listen.

These private discussions would eventually become public, fitting into an existing narrative. John-Henry Williams, a 6-foot-5 ringer for his handsome father, had long lived in the zeitgeist as a bumbling son who took and took without ever standing on his own. In the definitive biography of Ted Williams, by Ben Bradlee Jr., John-Henry is shown as a terrible businessman and a cheat, someone who lied so often—inviting his dad to a college graduation where he didn't actually graduate, claiming to make his college baseball team when he never tried out—that he lied about Ted's wanting to be frozen too. This depiction of her brother by an author she cooperated with haunts Claudia, who believes her dad knew better, and she feels like the only one left to defend John-Henry.

After Ted died, friends told reporters that Williams disagreed with his son's obsession. The stories and biographies quote staff members and associates who say Ted continued to want his remains scattered in the Atlantic, and in the end, Bradlee seemed to conclude that Ted did not want to be frozen. Abel goes into the study and comes back with the book. He opens it on the kitchen counter, the pages full of his notes, some passages marked with a check if he feels they're accurate, other quotes highlighted and some with sharp, angry pen strokes when he's aggrieved, the margins littered with "not true" and "bullshit" and "lie." Bradlee spent a decade reporting, and while Claudia and Eric say he got many things about Ted's military and baseball careers right, they say he allowed unreliable people to give opinions couched as facts when discussing the inner workings of the Williams clan, which has forever been a complicated tribe in which truths are perceptions and history keeps repeating itself: Bobby-Jo died five years ago, of advanced liver disease, killed by the same bad habits as her mother.

The clean cryonics narrative of Bradlee's book doesn't match the messiness of that long family dispute. Claudia has spent considerable time looking for documents that would prove she was in the hospital for the signing of the informal contract. Bradlee's book strongly suggests, without ever saying so directly, that she was lying about being there. She says she visited the hospital so many times that all those trips ran together, but she remains steadfast: Ted signed a piece of paper. The argument remains frustrating for everyone: Claudia can't prove they followed her father's wishes, and Bradlee can't prove they didn't. Nobody quoted is without an agenda, whether fueled by anger, misunderstanding, jealousy, or love. Nobody is unaffected. Nobody is clean. It's a mess, all of it. Ted Williams left behind so many unanswered questions that two of his children went to the extreme edges of science to find more time for them to be answered, while his third child went to equal extremes to stop them. At the end, jealous and estranged, Bobby-Jo raged, leaving bizarre voicemails on Abel's answering machine: "This is Barbara Joyce Ferrell. I live right behind you. Prepare thyself, sir."

Bobby-Jo lashed out, and Claudia hid, and John-Henry got as close as he could. He pushed and explained his idea, working cryonics into those dinner-table evenings. One night, Ted looked at Claudia and asked, "Are you in on this too?"

"Who knows what the future will bring?" she said, and John-Henry argued some more. Ted, exhausted and struggling to keep his eyes open, sort of laughed; then his son helped him to the recliner where he slept. Months passed, and after trying every other option available to buy time, only surgery would help Ted. First, he needed a heart catheterization, and doctors worried he might not survive even that preliminary procedure. Most people his age wouldn't risk a series of operations. In her book, Claudia writes what her father told the doctor. "Doc, if you can give me any extra time with these guys, let's do it," he said. "I've had a great life, and what the hell, if I die, maybe I'll die on the table. I'd like to have some more time with my two kids."

The doctor nodded and scheduled the surgery. Claudia began to cry, and Ted's voice cracked when he tried to comfort her, as she'd taught him to do.

"I'll be all right," he said.

According to Claudia, that's when John-Henry returned to the Williams family favorite: the nonbinding, casually written contract. She says Ted sighed, agreed to go along with their wishes, and signed a piece of paper agreeing to be frozen. He knew he might not live through his procedure, and at the end of his life, he'd finally put aside his own wishes for theirs. For comedians and baseball fans and biographers, cryonics was a joke or a disgrace, but inside the Williams family, it was a profound act of love, a conscious attempt to undo the cycle of pain both felt and caused.

"If it means that much to you kids," he said, "fine."

She and Eric fell in love during the horrible siege after they froze her father, who died of cardiac arrest almost two years after signing the note. She was trapped in his house by television trucks and reporters shouting questions. Claudia, then 30 and an elite athlete, paced the halls like a wild animal. Days passed without her manic exercise routine, which she used to exhaust herself into a kind of peace. Finally Eric realized she needed to escape, so he put her in the back seat of his car, covered her with blankets, and snuck her past the cameras. They drove to a nearby park, where she could run until she felt tired enough to stop thinking.

That was 13 years ago, and while people still remember something about Ted's head being frozen, the daily onslaught is over. Claudia and Eric are moving back into Ted's old house, not wanting to sell it and not wealthy enough to maintain two homes. It's empty now, under renovation, sitting low and wide on a hill, beneath the grove of live oak trees. Claudia and Eric pull into the drive, the gate with the red No. 9 closing behind them.

Her mood founders when she stands in the towering great room, cold and unfurnished now, except for row upon row of almost empty bookshelves rising toward the ceiling. The only thing left is a frayed set of Ted's beloved *Encyclopedia Britannica*, which he bought after retiring, spending hours scouring them for the knowledge he felt ashamed not to have. When he was an old man, Harvard begged him to come and receive an honorary degree. He refused, over and over again, never feeling as if he belonged in a place with such educated people. "I don't think [Ted] at the end of his life felt like he accomplished anything," Abel says. "Ted had that constant insecurity."

The house is empty inside, dangling wires and pencil marks on the walls indicating where a range will go. Ted's white Sub-Zero fridge with the wood-paneled front is unplugged in the corner. The kitchen brings back so many memories. The wires and the hoses and the sawdust on the floor amplify how much those memories have faded. The dining table used to be there, by the window. Training for triathlons after she came home from Europe, every weekend Claudia would ride her bike here from Tampa.

"Daddy would sit right here," she says, laughing. "He would see me coming up the road. He'd be waiting for me right here. When I walked into the house, there'd be a hot dog on the table."

She didn't like hot dogs, but she loved to see her father smile, so she ate them every time.

"He thought I needed salt," she says, then switches to her flawless Ted Williams impersonation, a chin-jutting bass drum: "Yup, isn't that GOOD? That's a good hot dog, isn't it? OL' TED WILLIAMS, HUH? YOU WANNA 'NOTHER ONE?"

Her spirit lightens when she does his voice, everything lit from the inside. They spent hours at that table, talking, playing the games he never got to play as a kid—*As I was going to St. Ives, I met a man with seven wives*—and debating religion and the nature of life and death.

"Those late nights when it was clear he didn't have much time left . . . ," she says, trailing off, the light gone.

She has lost her father to old age and her brother to leukemia. Every year, she plants a tree in their memory, and leaving her dad's house one day, she sees that one of John-Henry's trees is dying. Reminders of grief surround her, and now her mother is fading too. One afternoon, she gets a frantic phone call and rushes to her mom's bedside less than a mile away. The live-in caretaker is crying. Claudia, a nurse, listens to the plodding thumps of a tired heart. She checks her mom's blood pressure: 86/60 and dropping.

"Mom, you want to go to the hospital?" Claudia asks.

"No," Dolores Williams says.

"Even if it means saving your life?"

"No."

Her mom stabilizes, and Claudia heads home. The rain pounds the roof of her car. Soon she will face herself alone, as her father faced the world stripped of the soothing focus of baseball and fishing. Tears roll down her cheeks. She sighs hard; rattling almost, jagged on the edges, a noise so full of pain that people who hear it feel compelled to protect her.

"Our time is running out," she says.

She feels lonely. She's a young woman living among retirees with only a few friends. Everyone she has ever loved except for Eric is gone or almost gone, and she's sure she'll outlive Eric.

"Who's gonna take care of me?" she sobs.

There is a possibility.

Before John-Henry died, he froze some of his sperm, and as executor, she controls it. As she parks her car and goes into the house, she's deciding whether to share an idea that has been gaining momentum and fervor.

"The legacy deserves to go on," she says finally, crying harder than before.

John-Henry had asked her to keep the family alive. "You have to have a child," he told her.

The idea is strange, yet mechanically quite simple: She'd need a surrogate mother and a name. Back at home, all of it piles up, hurt stacked upon hurt, so what started as sadness about her mom became fear and desperation over the family coming to an end with her, and she's just dissolving in her high-ceilinged kitchen, coming apart. This is the vision greeting Eric when he walks in from work: his wife, her face red and puffy, sobbing so hard she's struggling to breathe. When she sees him, she stretches out her arms. Eric rushes toward her.

"Mom's having a bad day," she tells him. "She's tired. It makes me angry, of course. She's the only thing I have left."

She asks him again about creating and raising Ted Williams's grandchild.

"That's still something, right, on the table that you and I might do?" she asks, hopeful. "We might do that?"

Normally he's not keen on the idea.

"Yes," he says.

"We might?" she says, sounding vulnerable and shaky, like she's grasping for something beyond not only her reach but even her ability to name it. She's searching, searching for a father, for a purpose, for a child, searching for the chance to complete what her dad started in the last decade of his life. That's the hope and the promise of whatever life remains in John-Henry's sperm. Doctors told her there's enough genetic material for one chance at insemination, and as long as it remains frozen, some part of her brother, and her father, remains alive with it. She also has considered using her egg and Abel's sperm to create a child, going back and forth between the ideas. She's searching for a way to break the Williams cycle—either by letting it die with her or by being the first good parent in generations—and she's searching for something much more elusive too.

She never saw her father's body, and nothing forced her to really accept his disappearance from her life. Every culture has deeply symbolic rituals for burying and mourning the dead. With Ted's remains in stasis—they didn't hold a memorial service, not even a small, private one—she hasn't moved past grief into acceptance and peace. With time, she's come to regret not having a funeral. She's searching for how to say goodbye, or maybe a way to move on, which often feels like the same thing.

Before Claudia drove me back to the airport, Abel quietly asked me to keep in touch because she didn't meet many new people and really struggled with goodbyes. I left wondering what kind of life awaited her. Maybe she'd just find ways to exhaust herself and find obsessions to occupy her mind, day after day, year after year, never breaking free of her father and never feeling as if she had honored his memory either. But something happened in the months after our first visit.

It started with her book, *Ted Williams, My Father.*

She stepped out of the shadows and did readings. The Red Sox hosted her in Boston, and a big crowd showed up, and people cried when she shared her memories, her joys, and her pain. One at a time, they said she'd shown them a side of Ted Williams they'd never known. She did an interview in the Fenway stands, sitting in the red seat marking the longest home run ever hit in the ballpark, off the bat of her dad. She got lost in thought, staring down at the tiny home plate, feeling a strange connection. She walked past the hotel where he lived, long ago turned to luxury condos. His presence seemed real. The people most affected by her book were the fans who idolized her dad, now going through the same struggles of aging and illness he had.

She got a letter from Jimmie Foxx's daughter.

"You are our voice," it said.

Seeing the joy she brought to the elderly, long her favorite group of people, reminded her of an old man she treated as a student nurse. He was difficult, so she tried talking to him about baseball.

"I love the Red Sox," he said.

"Me too," she replied.

"I was there at Fenway Park when Ted Williams hit his last home run," he said. "It was a bright, sunny day, and I was there."

"I was told it was a cold and overcast day," she said, then did something she never does. She told him she was Ted Williams's daughter. He beamed, and the next day, everything about him seemed different, and not just because he wore Red Sox gear from head to toe. He smiled and seemed lighter. It's the same look her father got when she'd care for him in the last years of his life. Those memories, and the reaction of the elderly readers, finally pointed her toward her long-sought purpose.

As part of her application and interview process at Duke—still a long shot, but her dad taught her to try to be the greatest—she said she wanted to specialize in gerontology. "It wasn't until I cared for my elderly father as his health declined," she wrote on her application, "that I discovered my true calling."

Now she just needed to get into a graduate program, do years of studying, and open her own nurse practitioner's office. Every patient who walked through the door would get treated like Ted Williams. She didn't want to waste another moment. She felt time rushing away.

The last two weeks before finding out, she swam miles in the pool and pounded out sets in the gym. Finally an email from Duke arrived, asking her to log on to its website for the school's decision.

She opened the link and started to read the letter.

"Congratulations," it began.

Claudia grinned when I walked back into her house the day after she was accepted to Duke. Standing around the kitchen, she and Eric told the story of what happened when she opened her letter. Eric rushed home and found her sitting at the computer, quiet and solemn, validated for perhaps the first time in her life. Soon she'll be studying online for a master's degree from one of the greatest universities in the world. Even in her moment of triumph, something worried her, a neurotic fear. "Do you think they accepted me because of Dad?" she asked. "Or do you think they accepted me because of me?"

Everyone who knew Ted Williams knows that his daughter's going to Duke would mean more to him than his home runs and war medals combined.

"Daddy would be so proud," she said.

"I think he knows," Eric replied.

The house felt different than before, desolation replaced by hope. A Louisville Slugger leaned in the same cabinet as Toothless the Dragon, the first bit of baseball memorabilia in the living room. The renovations on Ted's house are complete. She and Eric will move in soon. Once she gets her nurse practitioner's office open and running, she is still planning to use John-Henry's sperm or her egg to create a baby. Ted's old study would make a perfect nursery. A tire swing already hangs from a thick branch of an oak tree, plenty of room to run and play in the shade. The child could start a new future for the Williams family, built on love, or become a casualty of the cycle that shaped Claudia's life, and her father's life before that. She's hoping for a boy.

MAY 2015

The Secret History of Tiger Woods

The death of his father set a battle raging inside the
world's greatest golfer. How he waged that war—through
an obsession with the Navy SEALs—is the tale
of how Tiger lost his way.

I.

Ten years ago, Tiger Woods sat in his boyhood home across from his
father's body, waiting on the men from the funeral home to arrive
and carry Earl away. It was around 3 in the morning. Outside this
bedroom in Cypress, California, the mechanism of burial and goodbye sputtered into action, while inside, Tiger and his half sister,
Royce, floated in those gauzy first hours after a death, when a loved
one isn't there but doesn't quite seem gone either. About an hour
earlier, Earl had taken two or three final breaths that sounded different from the ones that came before. Tiger got the call and came
straight to Cypress, passing the Navy golf course where he learned
to play, turning finally onto Teakwood Street. His dad never sold the
house because he liked the easily accessible nostalgia. If Earl
wanted, he could go see the Obi-Wan Kenobi poster still hanging on
Tiger's closet door, or find an old Nintendo or Lego Star Destroyer.
Earl died three steps from his son's old room.

Royce says she sat with her father on the bed, rubbing his back,
like she'd done the last few hours as he faded.

"You're waiting for him to wake up?" Tiger asked.

"Yes," Royce said.

"I am too."

Three days later, on May 6, 2006, the family gathered at a private air terminal in Anaheim to take Earl's remains back to Manhattan, Kansas, where he grew up. Tiger's mom, Tida, and his wife, Elin, sat together in the Gulfstream IV, facing each other, according to Royce. Elin did college homework, which she often did during any free moment, in airplanes or even on fishing trips, working toward her degree in psychology. Tiger's half siblings came along; Royce and Earl Jr. sat at a table, and Kevin sat across from them on a couch. There were six passengers total, and Tiger plopped down in his usual seat, in the front left of the plane. He put the urn holding his father's remains directly across from him—Royce made a joke about "strapping Dad in"—and when the pilot pushed the throttles forward to lift off, Royce said, Tiger stretched out his legs to hold the urn in place with his feet.

The flight took 2 hours and 20 minutes. His siblings tried to talk about the old days. Kevin retold a favorite about a camping trip with a 10- or 11-year-old Tiger, in a forest of tall trees: While walking to use the bathroom, Tiger had stopped and peered high into the branches.

"What are you looking at?" Kevin had asked him.

"Ewoks," Tiger said.

Sitting in the plane, Tiger didn't say much. He and his siblings landed and drove to the Sunset Cemetery, a mile southwest of K-State's campus, past the zoo and a high school and a cannon dedicated to the memory of dead Union soldiers. Earl, a former Green Beret and Vietnam combat veteran, would have liked that. The graveyard was cool in the shade, the hills rolling from the street toward a gully. Woodpeckers hammered away in the trees. The family gathered around a hole in the ground, between Earl's parents, Miles and Maude Woods. Two cedars and five pines rose into the air. Tiger stayed strong, comforting his mother, and Earl Jr. watched him, impressed. They buried the ashes and left.

After a brief stop at the house where Earl grew up—strangers owned it, so the Woods family stood in the front yard and told a few stories, and this being rural Kansas, the neighbors didn't interrupt or ask for autographs—everyone headed back to the airport. Seventy-seven minutes after touching down in Kansas, Tiger took off again for Orange County.

Consider him in that moment, 30 years old, the greatest golfer in the world, winner of 10 major championships and counting, confident that the dreams he and his father conceived on Teakwood Street would eventually all come true. His pilot climbed above the clouds. The return trip took 40 minutes longer, exactly 3 hours, and nobody said much, feeling heavy, processing the idea that they'd left Earl behind in the Kansas dirt. Tiger Woods sat in his usual place, facing forward, the seat across from him empty now.

Almost 10 years later, on the far western end of an island in the Bahamas, Tiger Woods is where he feels most comfortable: hidden behind multiple layers of security and exclusivity, standing with two or three friends in the dark of a marina. It's early December, 28 days before his 40th birthday. His annual tournament begins at a nearby course soon. Both his boats float a few dozen yards away, in two of the first three slips: the 155-foot yacht named *Privacy*, alongside the smaller, sleeker diving boat he named *Solitude*. On the main deck of the big boat, there's a basket of sunscreen, a pile of rolled towels, and a white orchid. The marina around them couldn't be more private, without a coffee shop or store, not even showing up on the navigational charts in some maritime GPS systems. (Woods's camp declined to comment for this story.)

Docking in a luxury marina is about the only place to catch a random glimpse of Tiger, who moves through the world in a cocoon of his own creation. When he bought his plane, he blocked the tail number from tracking websites; it ends in QS, the standard code for NetJets. Many athletes, by contrast, have some sort of vanity registration, and some even have custom paint jobs; Michael Jordan's plane is detailed in North Carolina blue, and his tail number is N236MJ—the "6" is for his titles. Jack Nicklaus flies around in N1JN nicknamed Air Bear. Sitting on a tarmac, Tiger's plane looks like it belongs to an anonymous business traveler, nothing giving away its famous owner. He comes and goes quietly.

Tonight the running lights glowing just offshore belong to Steven Spielberg's *The Seven Seas*. Marina staff members come across a lot of celebrities, and when they gather away from work, they tell stories, about how Johnny Depp is down-to-earth or how Tiger isn't a diva but is just, well, he's just really weird. Once, when his dog left a tennis ball in the harbormaster's office, Tiger called down and asked someone to "secure" the ball until a crew member could retrieve it, and the staff still laugh and roll their eyes about it. They don't know that he often uses military lingo, a small window into how deep he's gotten into that world, words like "secure" and "downrange" and, even in text messages to his friend Michael Jordan, "roger that."

Standing at the southwest corner of the marina, Tiger and his group make plans for later, and then he walks off down the road. There's no entourage or Team Tiger, no agent or handlers or managers, just a middle-aged man alone, coming to terms with himself and his future, which will hold far more quiet marinas in the years ahead than packed fairways. Not long ago, he asked Jordan a simple yet heavy question: *How did you know when it was time to walk away?*

Tiger hasn't hit a golf ball in about two months. He can't really run; not long ago, he told *Time* magazine, he fell down in his backyard without a cell phone and had to just lie there until his daughter happened to find him. Tiger sent her to get help. He's had two back operations in the past three months. Yesterday at a news conference, he said for the first time in public that his golf career might be over.

A reporter asked what he did for exercise.

"I walk," he said.

And?

He smiled.

"I walk, and I walk some more."

He paused before asking himself a question. "Where is the light at the end of the tunnel?"

"I don't know. I think pretty much everything beyond this will be gravy."

His friends started hearing these admissions about a month ago. His college roommate Notah Begay texted him around Halloween. Tiger loves Halloween. He's a big kid in many ways. When he lived in Orlando, a former neighbor said, he liked to ride on a skateboard behind a golf cart in the gated country club he called home. He loves the Transformers and comic-book heroes; in the past, he's checked into hotels under the name Logan Howlett, which is Wolverine's human name in *X-Men*. When he booked his free-diving lessons in Grand Cayman, instructor Kirk Krack recalled, he reserved his spot under the name Eric Cartman. So of course he loves Halloween, and when Notah asked about his costume, Tiger wrote back.

"I'm going as a golfer known as Tiger Woods."

Sitting at a steakhouse in the Bahamas one night, Begay is quiet for a moment. He's here for the Golf Channel, forced years ago by his own bad back to make the same admissions that Tiger is making now: The dreams he dreamed as a boy are ending. They met as children—Tiger was 9 and Notah was 12—playing youth golf in California. They saw each other, perhaps the only nonwhite, nonwealthy people around, and Notah walked up to Tiger and told him, "You'll never be alone again." They've been friends ever since, passing together through each stage of life. A few weeks ago, he and Tiger were hanging out at the house in Jupiter when Woods realized they needed to make a carpool run and get his kids at school. They drove over and parked in line with the other parents, about 30 minutes early, and to kill the time, they laughed and talked about Stanford. "Tiger and I do a lot of looking back," Begay says. "He loves to talk about college."

Tiger told stories about how his daughter likes soccer and is already a prankster, and Begay said how his girl loves gymnastics and drawing, and then they both looked at each other and just started laughing: *Can you believe we are sitting in a carpool line?* Tiger is facing the reckoning that all young and powerful men face, the end of that youth and power, and a future spent figuring out how those things might be mourned and possibly replaced. This final comeback, if he ever gets healthy, will be his last.

"He knows," Begay says.

The decade separating the cemetery in Kansas and the marina in the Bahamas has seen Tiger lose many of the things most important to him, and the more time passes, the more it's clear he left some essential part of himself there in the ground between Miles and Maude Woods. How did all he'd built come undone so quickly and so completely? That's the question that will shadow him for the rest of his life. The answer is complicated and layered. He fell victim to many things, some well-known and others deeply private: grief, loneliness, desire, freedom, and his fixation with his father's profession, the military. These forces started working in Tiger's life almost as soon as his G-IV landed back in Orange County after he buried his father's ashes. The forces kept working until finally his wife found text messages from Rachel Uchitel on his phone and he ran his Cadillac Escalade into a fire hydrant (that car, incidentally, is owned by a man in rural Arkansas, who bought it used from a local dealer, neither of whom knew its own secret history).

After Thanksgiving in 2009, his life split open in the most public and embarrassing way—can you imagine having to talk about your sex life in a news conference with your mom in the front row?—but that car crash wasn't the beginning of his unraveling. In an odd way, it was the end. Everything he's endured these past seven years, including admitting that his golf career might be finished, is a consequence of decisions he made in the three years after he lost Earl. He'd been hurtling toward that fire hydrant for a long time. On some level, he even understood what was happening to him, or at least he was invested in understanding. There was a book in his car the night of the wreck, and it ended up on the floorboard, covered in shards of glass. Its title was *Get a Grip on Physics*.

The topic fascinated Woods. He'd long struggled to sleep, and when he wasn't texting or playing video games, he'd read, often military books about lone men facing impossible odds, such as *Roberts Ridge* or *Lone Survivor*, or books about theoretical physics and cosmology. The intro to *Get a Grip* laid out the basic rules of early science, from Newton and Galileo, focused on the concepts of friction and gravity. These had long interested him. Five-year-old Tiger once made a drawing that showed stickmen swinging different clubs, with the clubface sketched, as well as the flight path of the ball, including distance and apex.

That drawing is a window into something Woods himself perhaps still can't articulate; even at that age, he was curious enough to be thinking about physics. From the beginning, his golf talent has seemed to be an expression of his genius, not the genius itself. He is a remarkable person, and not because he once won 14 important golf tournaments but because he thinks about how he came to occupy his particular space in the world. "He certainly had his mind open to big questions, such as who he was or who anyone was," says a close friend who requested anonymity, "and had his mind open to the idea that sometimes the question is the answer." Six pages into *Get a Grip*, author John Gribbin sums up a truth governing both the world and the relationship between Earl and Tiger Woods: "There was a fundamental law of nature which said that, left to their own devices, things move in circles."

There's always a layer of mystery between fathers and sons, even those as close as Tiger and Earl Woods. They lived such different lives. Earl joined the Green Berets because he saw them as the only place a black man could be treated fairly, and when he retired, he played golf day after day. (Before his son, Earl had the lowest handicap at the Navy golf course near their home, despite not picking up a club until he was 42.) There were things Tiger could never know about combat, just as Earl could never really understand the cost of his son's fame.

"I know exactly how you feel," Earl said once.

"No, Dad, you don't," Tiger replied.

He grew up without siblings or many friends. Tiger and Earl did everything together, hitting balls into a net out in the garage, or spending hours at the golf course, and when they'd finish, Earl would order a rum and Diet Coke, and Tiger would get a Coke with cherries, and they'd sit and nurse their drinks like two old men. The golf pro at the Navy course, Joe Grohman, worried that Tiger didn't have friends his own age until high school. His friends were Earl and Earl's old military buddies. That's who he played golf with, retired old soldiers and sailors and marines, with the occasional active-duty guy stationed near Los Angeles. Fighter jets took off and landed at the airstrip parallel to the 17th and 18th fairways. Tiger heard the stories and saw the deep love even strangers felt for one another. His entire childhood revolved around these men and their code.

Tiger and Earl held strong opinions about how things should work and nursed deep stubborn streaks, so they often butted heads. The most serious rift between them, which festered for years, centered on Earl's love for women. Tiger hated that his dad cheated on his mom and cried to his high school girlfriend about it. His parents never divorced, but they moved into their own houses, and the only reason they still needed to communicate at all was their son's rising golf career; like many overachieving kids in a broken home, Tiger found early on that his talent could help create the family he wanted. He could mend the broken places inside all of them. It's also clear that Tiger grew up first emulating his dad and then trying to be better than Earl. All sons, whether they love or hate their fathers, or some combination of both, want to cleanse themselves of any inherited weakness, shaking free from the past. This is certainly true for Tiger, whose father seems to evoke conflicting emotions: The best and worst things that have happened in his life happened because of Earl.

As Tiger got famous, Earl traveled the world with him. The

definitive book about Tiger and Earl, Tom Callahan's *His Father's Son*, details the women in Earl's orbit. There was a "cook" at the 2001 Open Championship, and when Callahan said she must be a good cook, Earl grinned and said, "She sure knows how to keep that potato chip bowl filled up." At another event in South Africa, a stream of escorts made their way to Earl's room. Callahan reports that near the end of Earl's life, Tiger and Earl stopped talking for a while. "Tiger's mad at me," he told the author, and implied that he'd gotten into some sort of woman trouble that his son paid to make go away. Ultimately, Callahan wrote, Tida is the one who persuaded Tiger to make peace, telling her son that he'd regret it if Earl died before he made things right.

"He's going to be gone, and you're going to be sorry," she told him.

They fixed the rift, perhaps because as Tiger's circle of trust tightened to include virtually no one, he still knew he could talk to his dad about anything, even if he didn't particularly like Earl at the time. Earl never judged. They were father and son, and teacher and student, best friends and running buddies and together, one complete person.

Just after the 2004 Masters, Tiger and his dad took a trip together to Fort Bragg, where Earl had been stationed with the Green Berets. A group of Earl's old military buddies came along, while Tiger got the VIP tour, running with the 82nd Airborne and tandem-jumping with the Golden Knights, the Army's parachute team. The man assigned to take Tiger out of the plane was a soldier named Billy Van Soelen, who explained the difference between broad daylight at Fort Bragg and pitch-black combat situations. "Your dad was doing tactical jumps," he said, nodding around at the controlled environment. "This is Hollywood."

Van Soelen strapped Tiger to himself and then the two flung themselves out into space, smooth with no bobble. Tiger grinned the whole way down.

Earl was waiting in the drop zone, Van Soelen says, and he gave Tiger a big hug.

"Now you understand my world," he told his son.

Earl needed an oxygen tank during that trip. He'd been dying slowly for years and regretted that he wouldn't live to see the end of Tiger's journey. His second heart attack happened in Tulsa, Oklahoma, during Tiger's initial year on tour, and by the winter of 2005, a year and a half after Fort Bragg, it was clear to everyone that Earl didn't have much time. Now consider Tiger Woods again, in this moment the best golfer in the world, taking his first break ever—24 days without touching a club, the most since he was a boy—watching his father die. He spent a lot of that break on Teakwood Street, struggling to sleep, three days passing before he finally drifted off on the floor. On December 25, his dad woke up and threw a shoe at a sleeping Tiger.

When Tiger groggily looked up, Earl said, "Merry Christmas."

That vacation ended—they both knew Earl was dying, and Tiger made his peace with it—and Woods planned to open his season at the 2006 Buick Invitational near San Diego. But three days before his first competitive round of the year, Tiger arranged for a VIP tour of the Coronado BUD/S (Basic Underwater Demolition/SEAL training) compound, where recruits are turned into SEALs. Most classes start with about 200 students, and if 30 graduate, that's a great percentage. It's the most difficult military training in the world.

When he arrived, Tiger spoke to Class 259, there waiting for First Phase to begin, and told them something he'd never said in public: He wanted to be a SEAL when he was young. The class loved Tiger's advice about mental preparation and focus, while the instructors rolled their eyes when Tiger said he would have been one of them were it not for golf. They've seen Olympic medalists and Division I football players quit, unable to stand the pain. A top-ranked triathlete washed out.

The tour visited Special Boat Team–12 and SEAL Team 7. During one stop, a SEAL named Thom Shea helped conduct a weapons demonstration, with seven or eight guns spread out in front of him, from the Sig Sauer pistol through the entire sniper suite of weapons. Three years later, Shea would earn a Silver Star leading a team into battle in Afghanistan. Tiger stood on one side of the table, his arms crossed, a pair of Oakley sunglasses resting on the back of his knit cap. Shea says Tiger remained very quiet, taking in as much as he could, only turning on his famous smile when someone asked for a picture or an autograph. After the table show, Shea walked Tiger to another building for the next part of his tour. The two men talked on the way, and even a decade later, Shea remembers the conversation, because of everything that would happen later. Tiger wanted to know how SEALs kept their home life together despite the strain of constant travel and long separations. Shea told him that balance was the only thing that worked. He says Tiger asked how they kept this up, year after year of stress, the long slog always outlasting the romance of a job title. "It's a life," Shea remembers saying. "You just do it. You keep practicing."

The following Sunday, Tiger Woods won the Buick Invitational in a playoff.

Three months later, Earl died and everything started to fall apart.

II.

Twenty-five days after he buried his father and 15 before the 2006 U.S. Open, Tiger went back to visit the Navy SEALs, this time to a hidden mountain training facility east of San Diego. The place is known as La Posta, and it's located on a barren stretch of winding road near the Mexican border. Everything is a shade of muted tan and green, like Afghanistan, with boulders the size of cars along the highway.

This time, Tiger came to do more than watch.

He tried the SR-25 sniper rifle and the SEALs' pistol of choice, the Sig Sauer P226. One of the instructors was Petty Officer 1st Class John Brown, whose father also served as a Green Beret in Vietnam. Brown pulled Tiger aside. The sun was shining, a nice day, and the two men talked, standing on the northeast corner of a shooting facility.

"Why are you here?" Brown remembers asking.

"My dad," Tiger said, explaining that Earl had told him he'd either end up being a golfer or a special operations soldier. "My dad told me I had two paths to choose from."

Brown says Tiger seemed to genuinely want to know about their way of life. Tiger asked questions about Brown's family, and they figured out that Brown's wife and Tiger shared the same birthday. Tiger told him not to ever try to match Michael Jordan drink for drink. They talked about Earl, and Brown felt like Tiger wanted "safe harbor" from his grief, a way to purge some of it even, to prove something to himself, or maybe prove something to the spirit of Earl, whose special ops career never approached the daring of a SEAL team.

"I definitely think he was searching for something," Brown says. "Most people have to live with their regrets. But he got to experience a taste of what might have been."

The instructors gave Tiger camo pants and a brown T-shirt. He carried an M4 assault rifle and strapped a pistol to his right leg. On a strip of white tape above his right hip pocket, someone wrote "TIGER." SEAL Ben Marshall (his name has been changed for this story because he remains on active duty) took Tiger to the Kill House, the high-stress combat simulator where SEALs practice clearing rooms and rescuing hostages. Marshall is a veteran of many combat deployments and was with Tiger making sure he didn't get too hurt. The instructors ran the golfer through the house over and over, lighting him up with Simunition, high-powered paint rounds that leave big, painful bruises. "It was so much fun to hit him," Marshall says. "He looked like a deer in the headlights. I was spraying him up like it was nothing."

The instructors set up targets, some of terrorists holding weapons and others of innocent civilians. Under fire and stress, Tiger needed to decide who should die and who should live. During one

trip through the Kill House, the guys switched out a target of someone with a gun for one of a photographer, and when Tiger came
through the door, he killed the person with the camera, according to
two witnesses. The SEALs asked why he'd shot a civilian.

First Tiger apologized for his mistake.

Then he made a joke about hating photographers.

Eventually, Woods learned how to clear a room, working corners
and figuring out lanes of fire, doing something only a handful of civilians are ever allowed to do: run through mock gun battles with
actual Navy SEALs. "He can move through the house," says Ed
Hiner, a retired SEAL who helped oversee training during that time
and wrote a book called *First, Fast, Fearless.* "He's not freaking out.
You escalate it. You start shooting and then you start blowing shit
up. A lot of people freak out. It's too loud, it's too crazy. He did well."

At one point, Marshall put him through a combat stress shooting
course, making him carry a 30-pound ammunition box, do overhead
presses with it, do pushups, and run up a hill, with shooting mixed
in. Tiger struggled with slowing his heart rate down enough to hit
the targets, but he attacked the course.

"He went all out," Marshall said. "He just fucking went all out."

Marshall got his golf clubs at one point and asked Tiger to sign
his TaylorMade bag. Tiger refused, sheepishly, saying he couldn't
sign a competing brand. So Marshall challenged him to a driving
contest for the signature. Both Marshall and Brown confirmed what
happened next: Tiger grinned and agreed. Some other guys gathered around a raised area overlooking the shooting range. Marshall
went first and hit a solid drive, around 260 or 270 yards. Tiger
looked at him and teed up a ball, gripping the TaylorMade driver.

Then he got down on his knees.

He swung the club like a baseball bat and crushed one out past
Marshall's drive. Tiger started laughing, and then all the SEALs
started laughing, and eventually Marshall was laughing too.

"Well, I can just shoot you now and you can die," Marshall joked,
"or you can run and die tired."

The military men and their bravado sent Tiger back in time to the Navy golf course with Earl and those salty retired soldiers and sailors. He missed his dad, of course, but he also missed the idea of Earl, which was as important as the man himself. Sometimes his dad traveled to tournaments and never visited the course, staying put at a hotel or rented house in case Tiger needed him. They could talk about anything, from the big questions of life, like Tiger's completely earnest belief in ghosts, to simple things a man should know, like how to order spacers of water between beers to keep from getting so drunk. (That last bit came about after a bad night at a Stanford fraternity party.) Without Earl, Tiger felt adrift and lonely. He threw himself back into his circus of a life, moving from place to place. And in the months after the funeral, the extramarital affairs either began or intensified. That summer of 2006, he met at least two of the mistresses who'd eventually hit the tabloids.

To be clear, he'd always talked a good game about women, long before he married Elin Nordegren in 2004. In 1999, in the quiet Oregon woods near the Deschutes River with Mark O'Meara and one of the best steelhead guides in the world, Tiger held court about the perks of being a professional athlete. "I'm walking down the trail with him and he's bragging about his sexual conquests," says guide Amy Hazel. "And this is when everybody thought he was the golden boy."

He told just filthy stories that Hazel wouldn't repeat, but even with the boasts and dirty jokes, she saw him as more of a big kid than a playboy. "Nerdy and socially awkward" are her words, and he seemed happiest standing in the river riffing lines from the Dalai Lama scene in *Caddyshack*.

The sexual bravado hid his awkwardness around women. One night he went to a club in New York with Derek Jeter and Michael Jordan. Jeter and Jordan circulated, talking with ease to one beautiful woman after another. (Both declined to comment about the episode.) At one point, Tiger walked up to them and asked the question that lives in the heart of every junior high boy and nearly every grown man too.

"What do you do to talk to girls?"

Jeter and Jordan looked at each other, then back at Tiger, sort of stunned.

Go tell 'em you're Tiger Woods, they said.

If Tiger was looking for something, it was seemingly lots of different things, finding pieces in a rotating cast of people. He and Rachel Uchitel bonded over their mutual grief. His fresh wounds from losing Earl helped him understand her scars from her father's cocaine overdose when she was 15, and her fiancé's death in the World Trade Center on September 11. The broken parts of themselves fit together, according to her best friend, Tim Bitici. Sometimes Rachel stayed with Tiger for days, Bitici says. Nobody ever seemed to ask Tiger where he was or what he was doing. Bitici went with Rachel down to Orlando to visit Tiger, who put them up in a condo near his house. When he came over, he walked in and closed all the blinds. Then he sat between Tim and Rachel on the couch and they all watched *Chelsea Lately*.

"This makes me so happy," Tiger said, according to Bitici.

Many of these relationships had that odd domestic quality, which got mostly ignored in favor of the tabloid splash of threesomes. Tiger once met Jaimee Grubbs in a hotel room, she told a magazine, and instead of getting right down to business, they watched a Tom Hanks movie and cuddled. Cori Rist remembered breakfast in bed. "It was very normal and traditional in a sense," she says. "He was trying to push that whole image and lifestyle away just to have something real. Even if it's just for a night."

Many times, he couldn't sleep.

Insomnia plagued him, and he'd end up awake for days. Bitici says that Tiger asked Rachel to meet him when he'd gone too long without sleep. Only after she arrived could he nod off. Bitici thinks Tiger just wanted a witness to his life. Not the famous life people saw from outside but the real one, where he kept the few things that belonged only to him. This wasn't a series of one-night stands but something more complex and strange. He called women constantly, war-dialing until they picked up, sometimes just to narrate simple everyday activities. When they didn't answer, he called their friends. Sometimes he talked to them about Earl and his childhood.

We never see the past coming up behind because shaping the future takes so much effort. That's one of those lessons everyone must learn for themselves, including Tiger Woods. He juggled a harem of women at once, looking for something he couldn't find, while he made more and more time for his obsession with the military, and he either ignored or did not notice the repeating patterns from Earl's life. "Mirror, mirror on the wall, we grow up like our daddy after all," says Paul Fregia, the first director of the Tiger Woods Foundation. "In some respects, he became what he loathed about his father."

The military trips continued through 2006 into 2007, kept almost completely a secret. At home, Tiger read books on SEALs and watched the documentary about BUD/S Class 234 over and over. He played Call of Duty for hours straight, so into the fantasy that his friends joked that after Tiger got shot in the game they might find him dead on the couch. When he could, he spent time with real-life operators. Tiger shot guns, learned combat tactics, and did free-fall skydiving with active-duty SEALs. During one trip to La Posta, he remembered things they'd told him about their families, asking about wives, things he didn't do in the golf world; Mark O'Meara said Tiger never asks about his kids.

"If Tiger was around other professional athletes, storytelling would always have a nature of one-upmanship," a friend says. "If Tiger was around some sort of active or retired military personnel, he was all ears. He was genuinely interested in what they had to say. Any time he told a military-related story that he had heard or talked about a tactic he had learned, he had a smile on his face. I can't say that about anything else."

One evening, Brown and two other guys put Tiger in the back seat of a king-cab pickup truck and drove him an hour and a half out into the desert to a training base named Niland, where a SEAL team was doing its final pre-deployment workup, staging a raid on a mock Afghan village that had been built down in a valley. They stood on a hill looking into the darkness. The SEAL platoon charged toward the position. Flares popped off, trailing into the darkness, and the valley rocked with the deep boom of artillery simulation and the chatter of small-arms fire. In the glow, Tiger looked transfixed. "It was fucking awesome," Brown says, laughing. "I don't know if we just got a glimpse of him in a different light, but he just seemed incredibly humble, grateful."

His golfing team, particularly swing coach Hank Haney, understood the risk, sending a long email scolding Tiger for putting his career at risk: *You need to get that whole SEALs thing out of your system.* Haney does a lot of benefit work, including some for the special operations community, so stories would later trickle back to him about injuries suffered during training. Caddie Steve Williams thought the 2006 U.S. Open, where Tiger missed his first major cut as a pro, was the first time he'd ever seen Woods not mentally prepared. Tiger talked openly about the grief and loss he felt when he practiced, since that activity was so closely wound together with his memories of his dad.

The moments with the military added some joy to what he has repeatedly called the worst year of his life, and he chose to spend December 30, 2006—his 31st birthday—in San Diego skydiving with SEALs. This was his second skydiving trip; a month earlier, in the middle of a seven-tournament win streak, he'd gotten his free-fall USPA A license, now able to jump without a tandem. Across the country, in Florida, his reps put a news release on his website, revealing for the first time that Elin was pregnant. Tiger Woods was going to be a father.

Elin came with him to San Diego on his birthday, and they rode south and east of the city, near a land preserve a few miles from Mexico, halfway between Chula Vista and Tecate. The road curved at banked angles, and up ahead a small airport came into view. Nichol's Field is a collection of maybe two dozen buildings. To the east of the property, a cluster of metal huts sat behind red stop signs: warning, restricted area. This was Tactical Air Operations, one of the places where the SEALs practice jumps. The main building felt like an inner sanctum: a SEAL flag on the wall and parachute riggings hung from the ceiling. They wore blue-and-white jumpsuits, Tiger and the three or four SEALs. He learned advanced air maneuvers. After each jump, the guys would tell Tiger what to do differently and he'd go off by himself for a bit to visualize the next jump and then go back up in the plane and dive into the air, doing everything they'd said. "The dude's amazing," says Billy Helmers, a SEAL who jumped with him that day. "He can literally think himself through the skydives."

The SEALs put a birthday cake on a table in one of the Tac Air buildings. It had a skydiver decorated on it in icing and read "Happy Birthday, Tiger!" The team guys and their families gathered around and sang "Happy Birthday," and then Tiger leaned in and blew out his candles. Everyone took pictures, and in them Tiger is smiling, and it's not the grin that people know from commercials and news conferences. He looks unwatched and calm.

While he made friends with some of the SEALs, many of their fellow operators didn't know why Tiger wanted to play soldier. It rubbed them the wrong way. Guys saw him doing the fun stuff, shooting guns and jumping out of airplanes, but never the brutal, awful parts of being a SEAL, soaking for hours in hypothermic waters, so covered in sand and grit that the skin simply grinds away. One year during hell week, a BUD/S candidate collapsed, his body temperature below 90 degrees; the man, a former wrestler, would rather have frozen to death than quit.

Was Tiger willing to do that?

"Tiger Woods never got wet and sandy," says former SEAL and current Montana congressman Ryan Zinke, who ran the training facility during the years Tiger came around. The BUD/S instructors didn't like the way Tiger talked about how he'd have been a SEAL if he didn't choose golf. "I just reached out to the guys I know who jumped with him and interacted with him," says a retired SEAL. "Not a single one wants to have any involvement, or have their name mentioned in the press anywhere near his. His interactions with the guys were not always the most stellar, and most were very under-whelmed with him as a man."

Then there's the story of the lunch, which spread throughout the Naval Special Warfare community. Guys still tell it, almost a decade later. Tiger and a group of five or six went to a diner in La Posta. The waitress brought the check and the table went silent, according to two people there that day. Nobody said anything, and neither did Tiger, and the other guys sort of looked at one another.

Finally one of the SEALs said, "Separate checks, please."

The waitress walked away.

"We are all baffled," says one SEAL, a veteran of numerous com-bat deployments. "We are sitting there with Tiger fucking Woods, who probably makes more than all of us combined in a day. He's shooting our ammo, taking our time. He's a weird fucking guy. That's weird shit. Something's wrong with you."

They're not wrong, not exactly, but the SEALs are also viewing Tiger through their own preexisting idea of how a superstar should act, so his behavior processes as arrogant and selfish. That reaction has colored Tiger's relationships his entire life: People who meet him for 30 seconds love him, and people who spend several hours with him think he's aloof and weird, while people who hang around long enough to know him end up both loving him and being oddly protective. His truest self is shy, awkward, and basically well-intentioned, as unsuited for life in public as he is suited for hitting a ball.

"Frankly, the real Tiger Woods isn't that marketable," a friend says. "There isn't a lot of money to be made off a guy who just wants to be left alone to read a book. Or left alone to play fetch with his dog. Or left alone to play with his kids. Or left alone to lift weights. Or left alone to play a video game. Do you see a trend? Tiger was a natural introvert, and the financial interest for him to be extroverted really drove a wedge in his personality. Being a celebrity changed him, and he struggled with that—and he struggled with the fact that he struggled with that."

Tiger uses well-rehearsed set pieces as standard icebreakers—things that get trotted out again and again. Famously, in front of a *GQ* reporter in 1997, he told a joke that ended on a punch line about a black guy taking off a condom. He told the same joke in 2006 to a SEAL at a Navy shooting range and to a woman at Butter, a New York nightclub. Talk to enough people who've met him, and it starts to seem like he's doing an impersonation of what he thinks a superstar athlete is supposed to be. Once he bought a Porsche Carrera GT, similar to the one driven by many celebrities, but one of the first times he got behind the wheel, the powerful car got away from him, spinning off into the grass near his house. He took it back to the dealership.

Tiger bought a pair of combat boots. They were black, made by the tactical outfitter Blackhawk, popular with ex–special ops guys who become contractors and mercenaries. The boots were inevitable, in hindsight. You can't insert something as intense as the SEAL culture into the mind of someone like Tiger Woods and not have him chase it down a deep, dark hole. He started doing the timed 4-mile run in combat boots, required by everyone who wants to graduate from BUD/S. A friend named Corey Carroll, who refused to comment and whose parents lived near Tiger, did the workouts with him. They'd leave from Carroll's parents' home, heading north, out onto the golf course. The rare sighting was almost too strange to process: Tiger Woods in combat boots, wearing Nike workout pants or long combat-style trousers, depending on the weather, pounding out 8½-minute miles, within striking distance of the time needed for BUD/S.

Tiger knew the SEAL physical requirements by heart, easily knocking out the push-ups, pull-ups, and sit-ups. When he couldn't sleep, he'd end up at a nearby Gold's Gym at 3 a.m., grinding. One of his favorite workouts was the ladder, or PT pyramid, a popular Navy SEAL exercise: one pull-up, two push-ups, three sit-ups, then two, four, six, up to 10, 20, 30 and back down again.

Soon, the training at La Posta didn't cut it. He found something more intense with Duane Dieter, a man allowed by the navy to train SEALs in a specialized form of martial arts that he invented. Dieter is a divisive figure in the special operations world, working out of his own training compound on the Maryland shore. His method is called Close Quarters Defense, or CQD, and some students look at him as an almost spiritual guide, like a modern samurai. Others think he's overrated. For Dieter, few things were more important than ancient warrior principles like light and dark energy.

Tiger got introduced by the navy and learned CQD in Coronado. Hooked, he wanted to go further and ended up making trips to Dieter's compound in Maryland. He'd fly in and either stay at the facility or at the nearby fancy resort, Inn at Perry Cabin by Belmond, according to a source who saw Tiger with Dieter. He'd park outside a nearby Target, sending someone else inside for cheap throwaway clothes that they could ruin with the Simunition. The practice rounds left huge bruises. He did all sorts of weapons training and fighting there, including this drill invented by Dieter: He would stand in a room, hands by his side, wearing a helmet with a protective face shield. A hood would be lowered over the helmet, and loud white noise would play. It sounded like an approaching train, the speakers turning on and off at random intervals, lasting 30 seconds, or maybe just five. Then the hood would fly up and there would be a scenario. Maybe two people were talking. Or maybe one was a hostile and the other a hostage. If the people posed no threat, the correct response was to check corners and not draw your weapon. Then the hood would go back down, and there'd be more music, and when it came up, the scenario had changed. Sometimes a guy threw punches, to the body and head, and Tiger would need to free himself and draw his weapon. At first, the instructors went easy, not hitting him as hard as they'd hit a SEAL. Tiger put a stop to that, and soon they jumped him as aggressively as everyone else. When the drill finally ended, the room smelled like gunpowder.

An idea began to take hold, a dream, really, one that could destroy the disconnect Tiger felt in his life, completely killing off the character he played in public. Maybe he could just disappear into the shadow world of special operations. He mentioned his plans to people around him, one by one. He pulled over a car at a tournament once and told Steve Williams he wanted to join the navy. He told Haney he thought it would be cool to go through training. Once, Carroll had to talk him down via text message, according to someone present for the exchange, because Tiger wanted to quit golf and join the navy. There's only one reason to run 4 miles in pants and combat boots. This wasn't some proto-training to develop a new gear of mental toughness. "The goal was to make it through BUD/S," says a former friend who knew about the training. "It had nothing to do with golf."

To many people inside Tiger's circle, Jack Nicklaus's record of 18 majors wasn't as important to Tiger as it was to the golfing media and fans. He never mentioned it. Multiple people who've spent significant amounts of time with him say that. When Tiger did talk about it, someone else usually brought it up and he merely responded. The record instead became something to break so he could chase something that truly mattered. He loved the anonymity of

wearing a uniform and being part of a team. "It was very, very serious," the friend says. "If he had had a hot two years and broken the
record, he would have hung up his clubs and enlisted. No doubt."

Tiger talked about some of these military trips with his friends,
including describing skydiving to Michael Jordan, who saw a pattern
repeating from his own past. Years before, he'd lost his father, and in
his grief, he sought solace doing something his dad loved, quitting
the Bulls and riding minor league buses for the Birmingham Barons.
"It could be his way of playing baseball," Jordan would say years
later. "Soothing his father's interest."

Jordan looked sad as he said this, perhaps feeling the heaviness
of it all or even the luck involved. He somehow got through his grief
and reclaimed his greatness, while Tiger has tried and failed over
and over again.

"Ah, boy," Jordan sighed.

The point of no return came on July 31, 2007, a date that means
nothing to the millions of fans who follow Tiger Woods but was the
last real shot he had to avoid the coming storm. From the outside, he
was closing in, inevitably, on Nicklaus. But inside his world, a year
after his dad died, things were falling apart.

On June 18, Tiger became a father. In July, he flew a porn star
to Washington, D.C., according to a tabloid, to meet him during his
tournament, the AT&T National. He'd already met many of the mistresses who would come forward two years later. According to *The
Wall Street Journal*, the summer of 2007 is when the *National En-
quirer* contacted his camp to say it had caught him in an affair with
a Perkins waitress. Negotiations allegedly began that would kill the
tabloid story if Tiger agreed to sit for an interview and cover shoot
with *Men's Fitness*, owned by the same parent company as the *En-
quirer*. He did. The magazine hit newsstands on June 29.

On July 22, he finished tied for 12th at the Open Championship,
and then came home. In the weeks afterward, he'd announce that

he'd ruptured his left ACL while jogging in Isleworth. His news release did not mention whether he'd been running in sneakers or
combat boots. At the time, he chose to skip surgery and keep playing. Tiger's account might be true, as might the scenario laid out in
Haney's book: that he tore the ACL in the Kill House with SEALs.
Most likely, they're both right. The knee suffered repeated stresses
and injuries, from military drills and elite-level sports training and
high-weight, low-rep lifting. A man who saw him doing CQD training says, "It's kind of funny, when you have an injury it almost
seems like a magnet for trauma. He almost never had something hit
his right knee. It was always his left knee that got kicked, or hit, or
shot, or landed on. Always the left knee."

Whatever happened, he didn't take a break. Two days before the
tournament in Akron, he was in Ohio. That night, July 31, his agent,
Mark Steinberg, had people over to his home near Cleveland, including Tiger. According to both Haney's and Williams's books, Steinberg said the time had come for an intervention over Tiger's military
adventures. While Steinberg has a reputation as a bully in the golf
world, he cares a great deal about his client and friend. This all
must have seemed insane to someone who just wanted to manage a
great athlete: secret trips to military facilities, running around a
golf course in combat boots, shooting guns, taking punches.

That night after dinner, Steinberg took Tiger into his downstairs
office, a room in his finished basement. What they talked about remains private. But this was the moment when Tiger could have connected the dots and seen how out of control things had become.
Everyone felt good about the talk. Afterward, Haney wrote, Tiger
was different and the military trips became less of a distraction.

That's what they thought.

Consider Tiger Woods once more, tabloids snapping grainy long-
distance photos, his marriage suddenly in danger and with it the
normalcy he lacked everywhere else, his body taking a terrible beating from SEAL training and aggressive weight lifting, a year after
losing his father, adrift and yet *still* dominating all the other golfers

in the world. They never were his greatest opponent, which was and always will be a combination of himself and all those expectations he never could control. Tiger won Akron, then won his 13th career major the following week at the PGA Championship in Tulsa, and then, 15 hours after getting home from the tournament, he packed up and flew off again to do CQD training with Dieter. Steinberg's warning was just 13 days old.

Everything else might as well have been chiseled in stone on the day he was born. The two knee surgeries in Park City, Utah, a year later. The three back surgeries. The Thanksgiving night he took an Ambien and forgot to erase his text messages and how that enormous storm started small, with Elin calling numbers in his phone, confronting the people on the other end, including Uchitel's friend Tim Bitici, who was in Vermont with his family when his phone rang. The horrors big and small that followed. The butcher paper taped up over the windows to block the paparazzi. The sheet his crew hung over the name of his yacht. The Internet comments he read while driving to Augusta National before the 2010 Masters, obsessed over what people thought. The questions from his kids about why Mommy and Daddy don't live together, and the things he won't be able to protect them from when their classmates discover the Internet. The tournament where he shot a 42 on the front nine and withdrew, blaming knee and Achilles injuries.

That day, Steve Williams saw a friend in the parking lot.

"What happened?" his friend asked, incredulous.

"I think he's got the yips, mate," Williams replied.

In the 1,303 days between his father's death and the fire hydrant, Tiger set in motion all those things, and when he can finally go back and make a full accounting of his life, he'll realize that winning the 2008 U.S. Open a year before the scandal, with a broken leg and torn ACL, was the closest he ever got to BUD/S. He could barely walk, and he still beat everyone in the world. He won and has never been the same. The loneliness and pain tore apart his family, and the injuries destroyed his chance to beat Nicklaus and to leave fame behind and join the navy. He lost his dad, and then his focus, and then his way, and everything else came falling down too.

But first, he got one final major.

"I'm winning this tournament," he told his team.

"Is it really worth it, Tiger?" Steve Williams asked.

"Fuck you," Tiger said.

III.

He's been stuck ever since, in limbo, somewhere between a professional golfer and a retired celebrity. Right now, in early December, he hangs out on the edge of a putting green in the Bahamas, unable to play but still handling his duties as host. That means posing with a motorcycle and the CEO of the company that made it. While the camera crews get ready, Tiger walks onto the green. Zach Johnson and Justin Rose, both friends, knock around some balls and shoot the breeze. The guys talk about putters, about finishes and how that impacts the roll. Tiger knows the questions to ask, having developed a deep reservoir of knowledge that serves no purpose to someone whose body won't cooperate.

As he starts to pose with the motorcycle, Tiger glances back at his friends.

On his wrist, he wears a thin red string, a Buddhist reminder to show compassion and to mind the tongue. Like many things, Tiger keeps his faith to himself—though he has said he was raised a Buddhist—so it's hard to know how much he practices or if he ever goes to temple. It's interesting to consider. Buddhists don't believe in heaven or hell, or at least not in the same way as Christians. According to *Essential Buddhism*, by Diane Morgan, either place can exist on earth, and there are 11 ways for believers to feel pain: lust, hatred, illusion, sickness, decay, death, worry, lamentation, physical and mental anguish, melancholy, and grief. Since losing his father, Woods has burned with every single one of these, and in the years since he rammed his car into a fire hydrant, he's suffered nearly all of them all the time. He says he'll be back, and if he is lying to himself, maybe he can be forgiven that delusion, because according to the basic tenets of his religion, he has literally been living through hell.

While the media take photographs of the motorcycle, someone asks him about a golf course in California where Tiger played a tournament many years ago.

"First trophy," Tiger says.

"How old were you?"

"Four."

He talks a lot about the past now, which is new for someone who moved so fast through his first 40 years that he left people and places behind once they'd served their purpose in his life. Earl often spoke with friends about the strangeness and suddenness of Tiger's exit from their lives and how when Tiger left Teakwood Street for college, he abandoned his computer and Nintendo, his toys and posters on the wall, and even stray cash. This amazed Earl and made him strangely proud and also melancholy. Tiger had become something like a butterfly; Earl believed that his son had flown away unencumbered. When his tax lawyers advised Tiger to leave California after turning pro and set up his life near Orlando, he just vanished, not even stopping by the old Navy course to say goodbye. "He didn't tell me he was moving to Florida," says the pro, Joe Grohman, "and it broke my heart. I thought I was really close to the family. I didn't get to tell him goodbye. It was just over."

Tiger has cut off coaches and caddies and friends, rarely with a confrontation, just vanishing from their lives. It's not out of spite, really; he's focused on where he's supposed to be going. The Western High class of 1994 held its 20-year reunion and made sure Tiger got an invitation in the mail, but he didn't show. Grohman understands.

"He's still trying to be Tiger Woods," he says. "There's a time and place for things. There will be a day when he wants to come back to where it all began."

Even 10 years later, the loss of his father still exerts force and pull on his inner life. The anniversary of Earl's death is a time when he can't sleep, staying up all night with his memories. The wounds seem fresh. Tiger spent just 77 minutes on the ground in Kansas saying goodbye to Earl, before hurtling back into a destiny previously in progress. It's nearly certain he hasn't been back since. The sexton who runs the place says he's never seen Woods visit, and staff at the small airport nearby say they haven't seen him either. A book by a *People* magazine writer said Tiger visited once in 2007, around Mark Steinberg's military intervention, but that report could not be confirmed. Maybe he sneaked in and out, but if not, one day perhaps he'll walk across the field to the place where they left Earl's ashes, between Maude and Miles, in the shade of a bush and near a big red rock. He'll have to find the spot from memory because there is no headstone, even a decade after the funeral. Maybe he wants it private, or is simply unable to take such a final step, but whatever the reason, Tiger Woods never had one placed.

He buried his father in an unmarked grave.

The real work of his life—how to deal with having been Tiger Woods—will begin only once he accepts that his golfing career is finished. All driven people experience a reckoning at the end of their life's work, but when that work feels incomplete, or somehow tainted, the regrets can fester with time. This reckoning is coming for Tiger, which worries his friend Michael Jordan, who knows more about the next 10 years of Tiger's life than nearly anyone alive. It's jarring to be dominant and then have it suddenly end. "I don't know if he's happy about that or sad about that," Jordan says. "I think he's tired. I think he really wishes he could retire, but he doesn't know how to do it yet, and I don't think he wants to leave it where it is right now. If he could win a major and walk away, he would, I think."

A few months ago, sitting in his office in Charlotte, Jordan picked up his phone and dialed Tiger's number. It rang a few times and went to voicemail: *I'm sorry, but the person you called has a voice-mail box that has not been set up yet.* He tried twice more, the phone rang five or six times, and then he smiled.

"Playing video games," he said.

They texted in November, the day after a big group went out to dinner at Tiger's restaurant. Tiger got drunk, and they all laughed and told stories, and Michael thought Tiger seemed relaxed, which made him hopeful. Tiger talked about his injuries a lot but not much about the future. "The thing is," Jordan says, "I love him so much that I can't tell him, 'You're not gonna be great again.'"

The day after that, Tiger wrote him, and both men sounded like the stay-at-home dads they've become.

> TW: Thank you and your beautiful wife for coming. Need to do that more often. Thank the good lord for ice packs. I'm in heaven now. Bring babies next time.

> MJ: Haha. Any time my brother. Get some rest. We'll bring the kids next time.

> TW: I'm in. After school next week one day when the kids don't have soccer practice.

Jordan talks carefully, with no bravado or swagger, trying to say something important and true and empathetic—maybe hoping his friend will read it?—without crowding Tiger or saying too much. Jordan struggled and flailed in the years after he quit basketball, feeling like he'd hard-wired himself with all of these urges that now worked against any hope of future happiness. For years, he just tried to pretend like he wasn't lost. Time stretched out in front of him endlessly, and this same emptiness awaits Tiger.

"What does he do every day?" Jordan asks.

He's quiet and serious.

"I don't know," he says, answering his own question. "I haven't the slightest idea. I do not know."

He worries that Tiger is so haunted by his public shaming that he obsesses over it, perhaps sitting up in the middle of the night reading all the things people write and say about him.

"Rabbit Ears," Michael calls him sometimes.

He hears everything. For Tiger, this dwelling on old mistakes is a path to madness. Nothing can take him back to 2006 and give him a second chance. "That bothers him more than anything," Jordan says. "It looms. It's in his mind. It's a ship he can't right, and he's never going to. What can you do? The thing is about T-Dub, he cannot erase. That's what he really wants. He wants to erase the things that happened."

Slowly, year by year, Tiger's name will not be spoken in the same way and with the same frequency. Without a new passion, Tiger just might sit down there in his enormous, empty mansion and slowly go insane. Jordan's post-retirement salvation came because he and his longtime girlfriend, Yvette Prieto, got married. Now they have twins, and he's created a life for himself, something to occupy his time and his thoughts. They are happy together, and more than once Jordan has told Tiger he needs to allow someone new into his circle, to build a new life with a new person and, along the way, find some new perspective about the journey that brought him here.

"He has . . . ," Jordan says, and he pauses, searching for the right word, ". . . no companion. He has to find that happiness within his life, that's the thing that worries me. I don't know if he can find that type of happiness. He's gonna have to trust somebody."

Tiger is not totally alone, kept company by memories of the life he once knew and those moments when he is happiest: the time he spends with his daughter, Sam, 8, and his son, Charlie, 7. The best of Earl lives in the actions of his son; in fatherhood, Tiger has equaled and even surpassed his own dad. He is utterly devoted to his children. Every single person interviewed for this story says so. Sam and Charlie never met their grandfather, and they don't remember Tiger as a dominant golfer, but they will grow up knowing that their father cares more about them than anything he does on the course.

In the Bahamas, *USA Today* golf writer Steve DiMeglio saw them riding in a golf cart with Tiger and asked if they'd rather be their dad or soccer star Leo Messi.

"Messi!" Sam said without missing a beat.

"He's playing," Charlie explained.

Tiger laughed and dramatically dropped his head.

Then he joked, "Well, he's right."

He and Elin have a better relationship now, and Tiger wishes he'd have worked to create this bond while they were still together. His friends talk of how much he regrets losing his marriage, especially in those moments when he and Elin are with the kids and he glimpses little flashes of the life he threw away. Now he shares custody, and when the children go back to their mom's place and his big house falls quiet, he's surrounded by people who work for him and trophies he won as a younger, more powerful man.

There's a clear view out the windows past the two swimming pools and hot tub, toward the four greens he had built, a practice facility for a game he's almost finished playing. He's got endless stretches of time now to stare and think. His old house near Orlando, the last place they all lived, stood in a cluster of trees across from the Isleworth driving range. He loved sunsets there, all of them together, his golf having finally created the family he craved as a boy. Elin and Charlie would sit in a cart and watch. Yogi, a labradoodle, would roll in the grass, sniffing around. Sam would hand him golf balls, and he'd hit punch shots for his border collie, Taz, to chase.

The sun would set and they'd all walk together in the shadows toward home.

In Chicago, the Final Wait for a Cubs Win Mixes Joy and Sorrow

A city has waited 108 years.
Now it must wait one day more.

CHICAGO, ILL.—Cubs fans awoke Wednesday to one last wait, with little to do before Game 7 but think, about themselves and their families, about the people who've come and gone during these 108 years of failure. Hundreds found themselves drawn to Wrigley Field, where workers were already breaking down the concessions and cleaning out the freezers. Some people said they didn't even mean to come. They started off on a trip to the store and ended up standing in front of the stadium's long brick wall facing Waveland Avenue. Many wrote chalk notes to the dead. Some dedicated messages. *This one's for you, Dad.* Others wrote names. Dan Bird. Ben Bird. Eugene Hendershott. A man with a bright smile but melancholy eyes wrote the name of his late wife, Andrea Monhollen. They met four blocks from here, on Racine. She's been gone six years.

"Cancer," John Motiejunas said.

He looked around at the names, each one as special to some stranger as his wife's name is to him. All these chalk ghosts longed to see a day like this one. Each name represented an unfulfilled dream. The big bright murals made the wall seem fun and festive from afar, but a closer look revealed life stripped of romanticism. "A lot of people waited their whole lives," Motiejunas said. He took a picture of the wall and then left, walking through the light rain that had begun to fall.

A little boy named Conley, not yet 3 years old, carried two big pieces of chalk while his grandmother, Maggie O'Connor, worked to keep him out of the street. The kid drew wherever he wanted, bouncing around. His grandma looked at him, without the baggage of the past century, and she laughed.

"He'll get used to them winning," she said. Conley wrote "Go Cubs Go," in the uncertain script of a toddler, then stopped strangers on the sidewalk to tell them about it. He asked one of them to draw with him, and after some squiggles, he stood back to admire his work.

"A seahorse!" he said.

I didn't know exactly what to do while waiting on the final game of the World Series, so I woke up early on Wednesday and went to church. The priest at the cavernous, ornate Holy Name Cathedral didn't mention the Cubs during the homily, but his talk about suffering and faith resonated with those who came to celebrate All Souls' Day. Yes, Game 7 was played on the same day as the annual Catholic holiday to remember and celebrate the dead and pray for their safe passage from purgatory into heaven. You can't make this stuff up.

The hyperfocus of camera lenses will make the last 24 hours in Chicago seem like one big explosion of joy, but that's not really true. The whole exercise has produced its own extremes. On one hand, people have been going wild, with Eddie Vedder and Bill Murray closing down one of those 5 a.m. dive bars on Division Street—closing it down together—and fans lighting off cherry bombs near Wrigley. Yet there's also this palpable sadness. Nobody could really be sure how they'd feel when it all ended, whether they'd be full of joy, or grief, or both.

The question felt personal to me. My wife's grandfather, a decorated World War II veteran, who survived being named Bob Weinberg in a German prisoner of war camp, died in May. He grew up in

Chicago and loved the Cubs, and as the season went on, my wife and I talked about how cruel it seemed for a man to live for 94 years, survive his bomber being shot down and being held captive, only to die five months before the World Series he longed to see. With him in mind, I reached out to a half-dozen area hospitals and to the team itself, looking for fans who were hanging on, hoping to find someone who might beat Bob's odds. The Cubs connected me with a woman named Ginny Iversen. She listened to the games on the radio religiously, even at 93, and loved to tell people she shared a birthday with Andre Dawson.

She never really grew up, wearing a tiara and feather boa to her 90th birthday and trying to do one of those college girl no-hands shots on her 92nd birthday—her kids loved to pull out photos of her with an entire shot glass in her mouth. Somewhat recently, an equally old male suitor gave her a diamond ring, which he then forgot about, which of course led to him buying her a second ring. She seemed hilarious to me, but her family didn't think she was up for a stranger to visit. I disengaged and didn't think about her much until yesterday.

At the Wrigley Field memorial wall, I saw a woman writing on the metal gates to the bleachers themselves, across the street from Murphy's. Mary Beth Talhami (I'd learn her name later) finished her message and stood back to admire it: "Mom, thank you for teaching us to believe in ourselves, love, and the Cubs! Enjoy your view from the ultimate skybox!"

I took a picture of her, close enough to overhear her conversation with another stranger to her left. Mary Beth talked about her mom and how ESPN had contacted the family. The dots connected in my head. The hair stood up on my arm.

"That was me," I said.

She told me her mother was Ginny Iversen and then, starting to shake and cry, she told me the news. Her mom died between Games 2 and 3.

Twenty miles northwest, cars parked in groups along the wind-

ing paths of the All Saints Cemetery. An hour remained until the
5 p.m. closing time. It's a Catholic burial ground, out in the middle-
class suburbs, and there are dozens, maybe hundreds, of Cubs flags
and hats and license plates and signs. It's one of many places around
Chicago this past week where the conflicting ideas of joy and pain
leave the realm of the psychological and become attached to action.
People come here for many reasons, to say a little prayer, or talk to
someone, to themselves, or to believe that their loved one knows
what is happening tonight. Last Friday, an old man in a Cubs jacket
stood over a grave and left a pennant and a Cubs pumpkin. Yesterday, a middle-aged woman named Maureen stood for the longest
time at a grave not far away. A sign read BELIEVE. Maureen touched
her hand to the Cubs logo on her chest and smiled, looking back at
the ground.

"My son," she said.

Then she pointed across the rolling hill to the most famous grave
in the cemetery, which is where she was headed next, to pay respects
to Harry Caray before going to watch the game. His stone has green
apples on top, an inside joke referencing a quote about the Cubs one
day making it to a World Series just as surely as God made green
apples.

A man stood at the grave, unloading five more crates of apples,
arranging them in a half-moon. One of the cemetery custodians,
named Don, helped him. Some women, there to visit other graves in
the area, did too. I walked up, and Don grinned at me and introduced his friend, Coley Newell, who happened to be Harry Caray's
son-in-law. They had some times. The night the Bulls first won a
title, he and Harry watched the game at Gibsons Steakhouse. Harry
pulled him down to Division Street, lined with bars, and the crowd
went berserk and mobbed them. Cops had to pull Harry up on horseback to ride him to safety. "He was the best father-in-law ever," Newell said. "He got me in more friggin' trouble."

Newell pointed at a spot he'd cleared among the apples.

"This is where the radio is going."

One of the women did a double-take.

"You're gonna broadcast the game?" she asked.

Newell nodded. He pulled out and switched on the radio—tuned to the local broadcast so Harry "wouldn't have to listen to Joe Buck"— and covered it with a plastic carton. He snaked the antennae through a hole he'd cut, then covered it with duct tape to keep out the rain.

"There's the real mojo," Don said.

"Yes, it is," Newell said.

He's done this before every World Series game, turned on the radio and let it play once the place closed. With the pregame show already started, he listened to the announcers debate Corey Kluber and the Cubs' ability to hit him.

Newell kneeled down and said a prayer.

Then he drove back toward the city to watch the game. The custodians locked the fence by the road, and near the back of the cemetery, a radio at the foot of Harry Caray's grave played the national anthem and the lineups and the first pitch.

Nobody but the dead were around to hear.

Mary Beth Talhami got to her local bar just as the game began. They love her at a place called Wildwood Tavern, in the suburb of Niles, and the owners saved a barstool for her. Her friends hugged her and told her that her mother was up there helping the Cubs tonight. It's been six days since Ginny Iversen died, taking her last breath wrapped in a Cubs blanket she loved. The baseball has kept Mary Beth distracted; she hasn't even bought a dress for the funeral. People from the neighborhood filled the bar, which served steaks and cold beers, and when the Cubs got their first out of the game, Mary Beth grinned.

"Twenty-six to go," she said.

The Cubs looked dominant, a repeat of the Game 6 performance, and for the first time, she allowed herself to feel confident and to consider a life after this season. When the Cubs took a 4–1 lead, her lip began to quiver. A friend hugged her, and she started to cry, sitting in this bar, wearing her mom's Cubs jacket, waving a plastic Cubs flag that had been in her mom's room, drying her eyes with a Cubs rally towel someone brought her mom the week before she died. Mary Beth stood up and walked outside. A friend named Sarah watched her leave, concerned. Some of Mary Beth's friends worry that a reckoning is coming soon and that the end of this season, win or lose, might knock her off course.

"It's happening," Sarah said.

Mary Beth returned and still struggled to keep away the tears.

"It's real," she said. "I think her dying is finally setting in."

Mostly, she wanted to see some sign that her mother's presence wasn't gone forever. Two hours after Ginny died last week, Mary Beth sent out a text message to the select people who needed to know: "The bad news is my mom passed away. The good news is there is another angel in the outfield." When she met me randomly, that was a sign, too, and after we left the chalk wall at Wrigley, she sat in her car and sobbed, then ran into Murphy's Bleachers to do a shot of Jameson for her mom. She and her friends all carry these desires; the owner of the place, Ellie, had started finding dimes everywhere after her dad died. Each of those dimes is a message. Today, Mary Beth saw a rainbow and said out loud to her mom, "Can't you leave me alone already?" So the Cubs' performance had become tightly wound together with all sorts of deeper and more personal questions, which raised the stakes for her.

The score stood at 6–3 in the eighth inning.

"Four outs," she said, holding her mom's towel to her face, which was too new to be laced with the light orange scent of Ginny's favorite perfume, Emeraude. She looked down to make eye contact with the bartender, so he could pour victory shots.

"Get ready," she said.

"Now?" he asked.

"No!" she said. "No bad mojo."

The Indians scored, and then hit a two-run homer, tying the

game. She pulled the towel up over her eyes and said, over and over, "Oh my fucking God."

Her niece texted her.

"I'm shaking."

"Keep the faith, baby," Mary Beth responded.

"I wish I was with you," Elly wrote.

"You are, sweetie."

The game went into the rain delay, then the 10th inning, and she stood up and leaned toward the screen. She wondered if her mom was pulling a prank on her.

Then it happened.

The Cubs scored two runs, then got the final three outs, and the bar around Mary Beth got loud. People jumped up, and the young people to her right hugged and danced and high-fived. Others pounded on the bar, and the stereo blared "Go Cubs Go!" Mary Beth remained quiet, holding her victory shot. She raised her glass and tipped it toward the ceiling, toasted her mom, but then the sobs hit so hard, her shoulders shaking violently, that she couldn't drink. Until faced with it, she'd never known how she'd react to the Cubs winning a World Series. Turns out, she thought about her mom. The glass stayed in her hand for 30 seconds or more, until she finally steadied herself and knocked it back. Then she put her head in her hands and began to cry. That night, she fell asleep wrapped in her mom's Cubs blanket, the one Ginny wore the night she died.

The town went nuts. Cars sped down the freeway, waving flags out of windows, weaving through traffic. Huge crowds gathered on Michigan Avenue, and every horn seemed to honk at once. Cops blocked the exits near the stadium. Wrigleyville turned into a loony bin, with one person collapsing to their knees to weep, while others set off fireworks. Near downtown, the *Chicago Sun-Times* and the *Chicago Tribune* rolled off the presses, packed into bundles and fork-lifted into waiting trucks. The truck drivers hung out in their ready room for assignments. Many wore Cubs gear, and they all talked about the game.

Truck 376 rumbled out of the loading bay, Al Mocchi behind the wheel. A big guy, a union guy, he looked both friendly and like he could handle himself, in that typical Chicago way. He's driven a newspaper truck for more than 30 years. His father did it for more than 30 too. It was about 2:45 a.m. Tonight at some spots, he said, they'd deliver about 25 times the number of *Tribune*s and maybe eight times the number of *Sun-Times*es, both papers going out together. At the first stop, a fan bought a copy, right off the truck, then held it up in the air like the Gospel, carrying it to his friends.

"It's gonna be one of those extraordinary evenings," Mocchi said.

He and his two-person team stocked convenience stores and honor boxes. Along the river, a couple walked home, the man carrying a box.

"This guy's got a pizza and a girlfriend!" Mocchi said. "What else do you need?"

A man in a white van cut them off to buy two copies of each paper right from the truck. Other people pointed when they drove by, some people understanding that the passing newspaper delivery meant that the next day had in fact arrived, and the sun would be coming up in a few hours, and that the headlines proved none of it had been a dream. The no-curse world had begun. Mocchi made a loop through the quiet city, except for the random stray stumbling Cubs fan. At one stop, Mocchi checked Facebook. All the posts were about the Cubs or Harry Caray, whose grave still had a radio playing at it 20 miles to the northwest.

"If he could be here to see this," said Shawn Brown, riding shotgun.

"You never know," Mocchi said. "He might be."

He left the truck idling outside a 7-Eleven, while he and his team lugged in bundles. A couple at the counter was paying for Gatorade and Bagel Bites when the woman saw the papers.

"Wait!" Grace Kingston said. "I WANT ALL OF THOSE!"

She settled on five copies of the *Tribune*—the A1 headline read

"AT LAST"—and carried her proof home with the electrolytes and carbs, the three most essential food groups of a post-curse hangover. An hour later, a little after 4 a.m., the drivers dropped me off at my hotel, 20 hours after the previous morning's Mass. After saying goodbye, I sat down to read the paper, first the celebratory front-page story about the Cubs, then working my way through the rest. At the back of the business section, I found 39 death notices, people who almost made it. One was for Mary Beth's mom, Virginia Iversen, page six, column two. At the bottom it read: *Memorial contributions may be made to Chicago Cubs Charities.*

The address listed is for Wrigley Field.

NOVEMBER 2016

Pat Riley's Final Test

This was the NBA legend's most difficult season in 50 years. So why, after nine championships, doesn't he just walk away? If only it were that easy.

The digital clock above the door in Pat Riley's presidential suite counts down the minutes to tip-off. The room is in a back hallway underneath the arena, a few feet from the secret path beneath the bleachers that he takes to his seat. I sit on the couch and read a laminated prayer card the team made for the game. Nobody else is here; his wife, Chris, is out blessing different parts of the arena. Tip-off is 29 minutes away, the last game of the season. The Heat need to win and see one of two other teams lose in order to make the playoffs. Still no sign of Riley. For the past two months, he and I have spoken nearly every day, which continues to shock his wife, who knows how private he can be. But earlier today, someone with the Heat suggested I tread lightly. The boss is in a mood. A peak state of Rileyness.

Then my phone buzzes.

"R u here?" Riley texts.

He sends his assistant, Karen, down to get me.

"It's tense," she says as we climb the stairs and approach the glass walls of his office, where he sits in an easy chair near the sofa, alone. It's quiet and dark, the blinds half-drawn, blocking out the view of the water. A three- or four-day growth on his face makes him look gaunt and tired. Around him, he's got the talismans that might bring him luck: a strange statue of Buddha reimagined as a Heat fan, and a Bob Dylan lyric taped to his bookshelf: "When you got nothing, you got nothing to lose."

Karen hands him a coffee, in one of those thin green Gatorade cups.

He sighs, and shifts his weight, and sips.

These past months have been an emotional time to be around him; the public highs and lows have been mirrored by the most difficult private challenge he's ever faced. Not long ago he said the scariest thing in the world was "extinction," or the emptiness that might swallow him if he ever managed to leave basketball behind, which he's considering. Waiting out the start of the game, we circle a familiar subject: There are changes he'd like to make in his life, if he could ever escape the seductive rhythms of the NBA calendar. The prayer cards being passed out downstairs have a quote on the back, part of which asks: *Will I lie down or will I fight?* For the past 50 years, and especially this season, that question has been central to Riley's daily life, a man perpetually seeking out opportunities to prove himself worthy of his reputation. The problem is that every time he proves himself, he puts off his future by another day.

A horn sounds somewhere below, breaking the stillness of his office.

"Watch the time," Karen says.

"What time is it?" he asks.

"Three minutes to 8," she says.

Riley slips on his jacket, and we walk past the empty offices. His feet don't make any sound on the soft red-and-black carpet in the back stairway down to the court. The noise of the arena gets louder the closer he gets, thumping bass at first, then the high-pitched whine of a packed house. He loves these gladiatorial walks, a feeling few people ever know, the pounding adrenaline and the roaring, unseen crowd. Minutes from tip-off, he passes the empty locker room. His team is on the floor. There's a mural there in the hall, a blown-up photograph of Ray Allen's famous 2013 3-pointer in the Finals, and he stops to stare for a moment. He looks at the fans in the background of the photo, studying the desperation in their faces, he says, like he's looking in a mirror at himself.

———

This season has challenged Riley as much as any in the past 50 years. The troubles began swirling three years ago, in the summer of 2014. Behind the Big Three—LeBron James, Dwyane Wade, and Chris Bosh—the Heat had been to four straight Finals, winning two titles, and Riley felt as if he had built something greater than his Showtime Lakers, something to rival even the Bill Russell–led Celtics. But James was a free agent that summer, and Riley and his guys flew out to Las Vegas to make their case for him to stay in Miami.

Riley told his lieutenant, Andy Elisburg, to get the two championship trophies LeBron had won and pack them in their hard-shell carrying cases. Elisburg also brought charts and an easel for a presentation about the free agents the Heat would pursue. The day of the meeting, a hotel bellhop followed them with a luggage cart carrying the presentation and the two trophies. Riley brought wine from a Napa vineyard named Promise. It was the same label Maverick Carter had presented Riley with when they did the deal four years earlier. Riley respects Carter, and when he walked into the suite and saw James with agent Rich Paul and friend Randy Mims but no Maverick, part of him knew the meeting wasn't sincere. He told Elisburg to keep the trophies and easel in the hall. James and his associates were watching a World Cup game, which they kept glancing at during the presentation. At one point, Riley asked if they'd mute the TV.

Riley flew home worried and got a text telling him to be ready for a call. About 15 minutes later, his phone rang and Paul was on the other end. The agent handed the phone to LeBron, who started by saying, "I want to thank you for four years . . ."

"I was silent," Riley says. "I didn't say anything. My mind began to just go. And it was over. I was very angry when LeBron left. It was personal for me. It just was. I had a very good friend who talked me off the ledge and kept me from going out there and saying something like Dan Gilbert. I'm glad I didn't do it."

The next year, the Heat missed the playoffs, and Riley was consumed with self-doubt, his own mind whispering that he'd stayed too long. Then last season Miami lost Bosh to blood clots, but the team still fought to the playoffs, falling to the Raptors in seven in the Eastern Conference semifinals. On the flight back from Toronto, Riley and his staff drank wine and debated the free agents they'd get to join Wade for another deep playoff run.

The beginning of July, all that fell apart.

Wade decided to leave Miami, his bond with Riley fractured. They'd been like family once, with Wade visiting Riley at home and Riley a guest at Wade's wedding. But with Bosh's return in grave doubt, Wade saw an uncertain future in Miami—and just like that, the Big Three had disintegrated. Hurt and wounded, Riley and his wife booked a last-minute trip to Paris, leaving three days later for a reprieve and a few Bruce Springsteen shows. During the first one, Springsteen played Riley's favorite song: "Land of Hope and Dreams." It's an anthem for Riley, because he spends a lot of time imagining the future he might have, when all his battles have been fought and won. He dreams of a different life, and not in an abstract way. He *sees* it, down to the taste of the dinner he'll eat and the music he'll play.

That night, standing close to the stage, he sang along. The people who recognized him in the general-admission pit saw the exterior: good-looking, tanned, and well-dressed. Most can't see past that image, which is perhaps its point. His inside is as messy and complex as his outside is manicured and defined. Chris Riley has always viewed any issue, including the pain over losing Wade, through her intimate knowledge of her husband's hidden motivations and scars: It'd been 60 years since he scored 19 points as a sixth-grader, and the same nun who locked him in the church basement, forgetting him there with the rats and cobwebs, gave him a standing ovation after the buzzer, setting into motion all the urges that sent him running to Paris.

Back home, his friends wondered how he might be handling such a public failure. Two pals from various yacht trips over the years, Dick Butera and Peter Guber, ran into each other during the off-season, their conversation recounted by Butera.

"Have you seen Pat?" Dick asked. "Is he gonna stay?"

"Pat will always be Pat," Peter said.

"You mean the contest is still on?" Dick asked.

"The game is never gonna be over," Peter said.

His friends know him well. Eight days after returning from Paris, Riley went to Erik Spoelstra's wedding, at an old mansion and gardens on the water in Miami. Randy Pfund, who left his job as Heat GM after Riley stopped coaching in 2008, walked over to his table to say hello. Riley didn't open with tales of Paris or gushing praise for the flowers or the bride. Almost immediately, he started giving his side of the Wade departure.

"Within 15 seconds," Pfund says.

Even as he obsesses over the Heat, in this or any other year, part of Riley's mind is never far from his estate on the Pacific in Malibu. Sometimes he checks the live security cameras just to feel close to the place. He and Chris spend about a month there at the end of every off-season, surrounded by their oldest friends. She calls it their "heart home."

Last year he took the most concrete action he's ever taken to make that dreamed future a reality. He signed a new five-year contract, with the understanding that he can work anywhere, including his perch overlooking the Pacific. His friends have been wondering for years when he'd head west, all of them following the internal conflict they've come to know as Miami vs. Malibu. "I love the schism because that's all he talks about," says his friend, the actor Michael Douglas. "That's all he talks about, getting back to Malibu to that house."

When Douglas discusses Riley's life in Florida, and the one he might live in California, he's not talking about geography. Each place serves as an easy code to describe the competing sides of Riley's personality. Miami represents the man living 6 inches in front of his face, Douglas says. One of many examples: Near the end of his last season with the Lakers, in 1990, he screamed at the players in a hotel ballroom and punched a mirror, shattering it and cutting his hand so deeply that bright red blood covered the sleeve of his crisp white shirt. He has punched mirrors and walls, wept and raged and trashed locker rooms. He has carried and nursed grudges. "Is Pat a dick?" Pfund says, repeating a question. "I know hundreds and hundreds of people who would say worse than that."

The other Riley loves emojis—texting hearts, smiley faces and sunsets, praying hands, cute baby heads, and palm trees. He has written six unproduced screenplays. Enamored of his 5-year-old grandson, he's teaching him about old cars and buying him toys that play the Motown classic "My Girl." There's a contagious joy in his eyes. At bar mitzvahs, he's been the only adult on the dance floor of kids, leaving when the music stops and he's covered in sweat. He shows up for people who matter to him; when his college teammate Tommy Kron died, the family walked into the church that morning to find two people: the priest and a grieving Riley. He's been all over the world with friends on boats; he's often the one with binoculars scanning coasts for little bars where they can surrender for an afternoon and night. "They drink and they sing and they play music," says actress Lynda Carter, a longtime friend best known for playing Wonder Woman. "And he loves Springsteen and Motown and doo-wop. He and my daughter, Jess, were singing these duets, 'Red Dirt Road,' by Brooks & Dunn. They are crooning together and playing air guitar."

The flexibility in his contract about Malibu, then, isn't about distance. It's a vow he's making—about the kind of person he can still be, even as a 72-year-old man. The entire estate, from the porches with the million-dollar views to the bocce ball court near the beach, is full of little promises.

He's got a guitar collection out there, because one day he swears he will learn to play "My Girl" for Chris. He dreams of strumming her that song, and she dreams of planting a garden, and they both dream of hammocks on the beach. He's planning to move half his antique cars—he's got nearly a dozen—out to Malibu. Five minutes from the estate, he found a storage facility to keep them all. He rented every available bay, so they're all sitting there empty, waiting. The owner called him not long ago, worried that one person had all his space and wasn't using it, wanting a long-term tenant and not some fickle rich guy who might up and leave.

"What is your plan?" the man asked.

"These are going to be filled one day," Riley said.

He owns three houses in a row, purchased one at a time starting in the Showtime days when his kids were young. One of his many dreams is for the family to have a compound, for Pat and Chris to have a house, and for James and Elisabeth to each have one too. That vision got him through many long seasons and those lonely nights in hotel bars—the belief that he wasn't giving up a life, just postponing it a bit. For 30 years, he's told himself a story about the man he will be, about the family he will have, once he reaches his destination. But now his kids are grown, 32 and 28, with lives of their own and no time for a compound. They're busy.

He waited too long.

Pat Riley began his NBA playing career in 1967. In October, when the 2016–17 campaign began, it marked the 50th year he's lived by the code of Riley: When the team sucks, *he* sucks. And the Heat suck. They suck in ways big and small. The team blows a 19-point lead in the home opener. Wade beats the Heat in his return to Miami, off an infuriating and iffy foul call. On December 12, they are third-to-last in the conference, 7–17, when the Riley family gets news that makes all that losing cease to matter.

Lis, their 28-year-old daughter who'd gotten married the year before and moved to Denver, notices she has massively swollen lymph nodes. Pat and Chris rush to Denver, where a doctor tells them what they'd feared the most: It looks like cancer, lymphoma, and they should schedule a procedure and then wait for confirmation.

The Heat lose four of five, but Pat's mind is elsewhere. For all his children's lives, he has felt as if he could solve any problem they encountered. When his son, James, went to boarding school, Pat flew up early to make sure the young man's room was arranged perfectly, likely in search of a grand gesture to ease his guilt for all he'd missed. The morning James was scheduled to report, Pat found the dorm locked around 5 a.m., so he climbed in the window and went over everything again, down to the space between shirts in the closet. On the day of Elisabeth's wedding, he raised hell with the planners, making them redo the draping and piping on a table minutes before rushing to change clothes and walk her down the aisle.

But illness he cannot fix.

"A father's worst feeling," Riley says, "is the feeling of helplessness when his little girl is exactly that: helpless."

On Christmas Eve, Pat and Chris fly to Denver to see Lis and her husband, Paul. The four of them pile into a hotel suite. Pat opens a few bottles of Screaming Eagle, a cabernet they love. Lis gives them matching red-and-black-checked pajamas, so Pat and Chris put them on and all four curl up to watch movies, like they did when the kids were young. Outside, the snow comes down. Chris holds Lis on the couch, while Pat and his son-in-law sit on sofas on either side, all eight feet on the same ottoman. In the hotel suite, Pat thinks about game days when the kids were growing up. It's funny what comes back when you're scared. Chris would keep the children occupied so he could nap, and then he'd get up and come down to the big center landing and whistle. He can really whistle—once he randomly saw Magic Johnson walking down a beach in the Bahamas and hid behind a dune and let out a loud one, watching the star jump and swivel—and when he whistled for his kids, he'd yell, "Triple kisses!" They'd come running and give him a kiss good luck. Sitting on a couch, wondering if his daughter might have lymphoma, he remembers triple kisses.

———————

The memories come: Lis in her wedding dress, the day they brought James home, stopping first at the Pacific Ocean so the baby boy could see the wonder and the power Pat and Chris loved so much. Sliding back, his own wedding, the yellow 1967 Corvette he drove when he met Chris, the last time he spoke to his father, his benchwarming in the pros, everybody's All-American at Kentucky, back to the streets of Schenectady, New York. He can smell the high school gymnasium.

Maybe it was his senior year. He drove the lane and thought he'd been fouled. When the referee called a charge, he turned and headed the other way. The gym got murmuring and tense, and Riley didn't see his father running drunk onto the court—exactly like the scene in *Hoosiers*, he'd tell people years later, on the rare occasion when he'd share the story—and going after the ref. Lee Riley had been a baseball player and often blamed people for his unrealized dreams, including this particular official, who'd umpired the minor league games he managed. Pat didn't even know his dad was at the game, Lee having hidden beneath the bleachers, and Pat saw his beloved high school coach, Walt Przybylo, take charge and escort Lee off the court so the game could resume.

Riley adored Walt, later hiring one of his sons as a scout for the Heat. The night before Kentucky's NCAA final against Texas Western in 1966, stress caused Pat's feet to break out in painful sores. While Pat tried to sleep, Walt sat up all night gently soaking his feet, an act almost biblical in its devotion.

Lee and Mary Riley did not come to the game. They never saw him play a single time in college or the NBA. They never explained why.

Lee played for 17 minor league teams in 16 seasons and quit in 1943 to work in a factory during the war. A year later, the Phillies offered him a major league contract, and for four glorious games, he was delivered this miracle of a second chance. He got one hit in

12 at-bats, on April 30, 1944. The next day the organization bought
a minor league team in upstate New York and sent Lee to play for it.
Pat was born 10 months later. In 1952, when Lee was managing a
minor league club, he got suspended 90 days for stalling during a
game. He quit professional baseball. When he got home, he burned
all his gear and memorabilia and rarely spoke of those lost years. In
1970, he died, leaving many things unsaid. "I can't remember my
father ever telling me he loved me," Pat says. "Not much from my
mother either."

In his mind, Pat finds himself pulled toward 58 Spruce Street.

He remembers it as a dark place, loud with unspoken words. The
Rileys didn't talk about anything. Pat had a sister die in infancy 10
years before he was born, according to a book about World War II
baseball, which dedicated a section to Lee Riley. Until I brought this
to his attention, Pat had never heard the story of his infant sister. It's
possible the book is wrong, he says, or that his parents kept the secret
to themselves. His mom rarely left the house, and he'd come home to
find her sitting downstairs, on top of the only heat register, trying to
stay warm. Another family lives in the house now, but there remains
a worn spot on the floor and wall in the shape of Mary Riley.

He remembers his trips back home through the years and how
every single time, he would find himself driving past all these
places, his house, Walt's house, the bar where his dad drank away a
decade, the high school gymnasium. Once he accidentally set off the
alarm in the gym, which is now named after him. He remembers his
greatest games and the time his dad ran onto the court to defend
him. That's how he decided to eventually tell that story, cleaning up
his father whenever he could, even to himself. Riley talked about
Lee to his players, to schoolkids and corporate executives. Over
time, he rewrote his own father, punching up stories and inventing
others, a mixture of Lee and Walt and the books Pat read for inspi-
ration. Imagination and willpower were always Pat's two most important gifts, and along the way he used both to create the man he
thought Lee Riley deserved to be. Before one speech in 1997, at the

ceremony naming the high school gym in Riley's honor, a friend's video camera catches Pat and his mom talking.

"Make sure you don't tell anybody when I'm not telling the truth," he said.

His mom and older sister burst out laughing, and he went onstage.

He told that auditorium of students about his dad coming into his room at night to give him wisdom, telling him he was made of special stuff. Chris Riley, a trained therapist, saw through him then and sees through him now. Over the years, she's watched her husband construct the dad he wanted. There were no fatherly bedside chats on Spruce Street.

"Are you kidding me?" she says. "It was so much bleaker than that."

Out in Denver, in the dark of the hotel suite, they watch movies, a Christmas special, then *The Accountant* and *Deepwater Horizon*. Everybody sleeps in the next morning. Nothing matters but the wait, not the losses piling up, not anything, until January 11, when the doctors deliver surprising news.

No cancer.

A month later, a perfect Sunday, Pat Riley cranks his black 1971 Chevelle, wanting to escape the busy streets of Miami Beach, aiming toward the vast nothingness to the southwest. He downshifts, the 502-horsepower Chevelle bucking and roaring under the yoke of the lower gear. The sound blasts off the art deco facades. Since his daughter's news, the Heat have, improbably, gone on a winning streak. The team won at home and on the road, knocking off the Warriors with a last-second shot, fighting out of an 18-point fourth-quarter hole to beat the Nets. They've run off 13 straight victories, transforming themselves from a team that was better off tanking to a playoff contender.

Now on the road, Riley is exhaling.

The stereo plays "Listen to the Music," then "Born to Run," and he turns up the volume. He laughs and talks to people a lane over in traffic when he accidentally grinds the gears. A circle of sweat spreads on the back of his shirt. He seems light and happy, and he says he's been reborn.

His arm hangs out the window. "I owe everybody a lot," he says. "A lot. I owe them all a lot, but . . ."

He pauses, considering how many times he's climbed a mountain only to get knocked down and start climbing again. "I don't owe them anything anymore," he says forcefully, as if conviction will make the words true. He's trying, still deeply invested in the positive parts of building and running a team but saying he's free at last from the negative motivations he's never been able to control. In two days, he and Chris are flying to the Bahamas to sail around on a boat with their oldest and best friends, a break after the stress and joy of the past two months. He would have never done that 10 years ago, he says.

His slicked-back hair is white now and a little fluffy on the sides. The outskirts of Miami pass in a blur of car dealerships, no-cover strip clubs, and canals. He shifts gears and accelerates, hurtling away from the city where he's worked these past 22 years.

"I don't have to get pulled back into this one more time," he says.

He almost got away. That's the thing. Four years ago, he missed his chance. Now, of course, he sees the lost moment so clearly. He remembers the night, August 10, 2013, his 50th high school reunion, a party decades in the making, part of the Schenectady he's carried with him: intense loyalty for the people who held him up, and a loneliness Chris could sense when they met. He longed to go back—to the time and the place—and two months after the 2013 Finals, flush with back-to-back titles, he did.

He served as social chair for the event, booking the Four Tops *and* the Temptations. No detail escaped his attention; he even stopped at a local production studio to review the short video that would play during the event. His close friends Paul Heiner and Warren DeSantis oversaw logistics. Riley demanded to pay for all of it, a bill that eventually topped $160,000.

"This fucking ridiculous reunion of yours," Heiner came to lovingly call it.

Stage lights bathed the gymnasium in purple. The music started, one familiar hit after another. Pat and Chris danced right up in front. If it's possible for an entire life to lead to a single moment, this was it: back-to-back titles for the second time in Riley's career, listening to the music he and his wife loved, in the place where his journey began. He couldn't remember a happier time, and somewhere in the revelry, he realized he should walk away from basketball. "I thought this is what life should be," he says. "Friends, family, and fun. A lot of thought about enough is enough. A time to leave with all debts paid to the game and nothing to suck me back in."

The Four Tops came out for a duet with the Temps and called Pat up onstage.

The band kicked into "My Girl."

A yellow spotlight pointed down on him when the last verse came around. "I don't need no money, fortune, or fame . . . ," he sang, a little shaky. "I got all the riches, baby, one man can claim."

He pointed at Chris in the front row, and for just a little while, it seemed as if he might get out, a legend by any definition, with nine rings as a player, assistant coach, head coach, and president, his marriage and family intact, nothing to prove.

He stayed.

It's mid-February, and even as the Heat push toward the eighth and final spot in the playoffs, the rise and fall of the Big Three shadows the season. The week before the All-Star break, Dwyane Wade appears on Yahoo's popular basketball podcast. For the first time, he says a driving reason for his departure from Miami was hurt feelings over Riley never calling him. Wade says Riley didn't reach out, and Dwyane felt he deserved respect after helping deliver three titles. Heat PR man and longtime consigliere Tim Donovan doesn't alert Riley to the interview, but Pat has clearly heard about it because he shows up late for a lunch and immediately wants to tell his side.

When the conversation naturally drifts toward other topics, he steers it back.

Riley says that Wade's agent asked to deal directly with the owners instead of with Pat, so he merely honored that request. Mostly, he just wishes the whole thing had gone differently. "I know he feels I didn't fight hard enough for him," he says. "I was very, very sad when Dwyane said no. I wish I could have been there and told him why I didn't really fight for him at the end. . . . I fought for the team. The one thing I wanted to do for him, and maybe this is what obscured my vision, but I wanted to get him another player so he could end his career competitive."

When he describes his reaction to Wade's leaving, it's always in terms of how sad it makes him feel, and while his emotions toward James's return to Cleveland were primal in the months, and even years, afterward, now he understands why LeBron had to leave.

"He went home because he had to go home," he says. "It was time. It was really time for him to go home, in his prime. If he's ever gonna do anything in Akron again, this was the time to do it. Otherwise, he'd have had a scarlet letter on his back the rest of his whole life."

But of course, Riley says, almost immediately after LeBron left, Bosh's camp wanted to reopen a deal they'd just finished, knowing the Heat had money and felt vulnerable. Bosh threatened to sign with the Rockets. In the end, Riley gave Bosh what he wanted. Now he wishes he'd said no to Bosh's max deal and given all that money to Wade. (James and Bosh declined to comment for this story. Wade issued a statement thanking Riley for their years together.)

"You never think it's gonna end," Riley says. "Then it always ends."

The Heat's climb into playoff contention hits a spot in Riley's brain nothing else can hit. *You've still got it, Riley. One more time.* It starts as a whisper, which these days he says he chooses not to hear. With the team clawing toward that eighth and final seed in the East, he says, "I've let go of all the stuff that used to hold me to the grind." He and Chris sit at a back table at a South Beach steakhouse, looking out at the water. A staff member calls him Coach.

"Am I different?" Pat asks.

"He's on his way," Chris says.

"I'm on my way," he says, smiling.

"I can't say the craziness isn't still there," she says.

"I wanna win, honey," he says. "We both wanna win."

Reaching into her purse, Chris hands him a small ziplock bag of pills, a cocktail of homeopathic medicine and vitamins they take to ward off the kudzu creep of time. Both preach the effectiveness of Eastern medicine. Although Pat went to a therapist only once—five minutes into the session, he burst into tears, stood up, and never returned—Chris says he's done a lot of soul-searching about many things, mainly his father, the taproot of his drive and his inability to stop driving.

She stops and starts, trying to articulate her thoughts.

She exhales.

"He's good," she says finally. "He's much better. He's clearly forgiven his father. That's the peace he's made. Now, whether he comes to peace with himself with that is another thing."

She hears what he says about not owing anyone anything anymore.

"He's talking about it," she says. "Do I trust it?"

She's right to be skeptical. Sitting on his desk at the arena, he's got a monitor with a live video feed from the practice court. On a random Tuesday during the second half of the season, around 4:30 in the afternoon, he works at his desk. With the team on the road and no players to watch, he leans over a piece of paper, grinding on a task he should probably delegate, drawing up the seating charts for a charity dinner.

"He's putting in 12 to 14 hours," she says.

He insists he's different, and while Chris Riley believes he's sincere in his desire, she understands his personal code, perhaps even better than he does: The better the Heat play, the louder the siren song of more becomes.

"How do you change what got you everything you've got?" she says.

"It's embedded," he says.

When she looks at him, she sees a man with an incredible tolerance for pain and work, but she also sees a sixth-grader getting a standing ovation from the nuns.

"You perform to get your goodies," Chris says. "You can psychologically know your issues, but the key is: Can you change the habits?"

The stretch run is a test. With just 20 games left in the season, Riley has done the math. The Heat need to go 13–7 to beat out the Pacers and Bulls for the eighth seed. Tonight, in March, Cleveland is in the building, photographers hanging in the private underground concourses, trying to snap a photo of LeBron. Watching the digital clock in his suite, Riley leans back on a red chair with his arms crossed. He's holding court with one of his oldest friends, Peter Guber, who sits on a low-slung couch to his left. The playoffs are within reach.

"You've crept up from the bottom," Guber says. "You're right on the cusp."

"Are we really the 11–30 team or the 17–4 team?" Riley says.

LeBron doesn't play, resting, and the Heat blow out the Cavs. There's almost a fight at the end of the game, and after it, Miami flies to Cleveland for an immediate rematch. Already, Riley is thinking about setting the table one last time, not necessarily winning a title but putting the pieces in place. He isn't going to Cleveland, he says when asked, because that time in his life has passed. In 1985, for Game 6 of the Finals, he wanted to wear a white tuxedo and a shamrock bow tie in Boston—"a lot more hubris then," he says—but now that belongs to Spoelstra and the players.

"I will go work in the garden and pick some fresh vegetables and play with my grandson while they battle," he says. "We will have a great meal as we watch the game on TV."

"You have a garden?"

"A major plan," he replies. "Right now all imagery, but I see it."

He sees the vegetables, with Chris in those thick gloves with a shovel, yet he also sees one more title run. The competing visions leave him conflicted. "I NEED ONE MORE," he writes in a text message immediately after talking about the garden. "AND I KNOW THIS WILL BE THE TOUGHEST TO GET."

The team wins that night in Cleveland and keeps winning, muscling past Chicago and Detroit. On the second full day of the NCAA tournament, the Heat finally make it to eighth place alone.

Riley flies west to scout games.

That first night, he stops over in Malibu before a flight to Sacramento in the morning. He lounges on the deck. The clock on his phone reads 4:48 p.m. It's the "golden hour," as he calls it, which usually means he turns on the "R&B 2" playlist, watching the sun set to a soundtrack of the Chi-Lites and Frankie Beverly. But today, he listens to just a few songs on repeat, by singer-songwriter Jason Isbell, "Something More Than Free" and "Traveling Alone."

They're about loneliness and labor and the emptiness of being made to travel a road not of your choosing. *I've grown tired of traveling alone.* The ocean is close enough that the waves drone white noise instead of rising and falling swells. His two lives flash through his mind, the one he keeps dreaming about and the one he's actually living. The songs repeat again. He calls Chris to talk about what he feels. Three decades ago, they planned a life here, in their heart home, with this view every day. He wants more Malibu and less Miami, feeling his "tipping point" close at hand, as he puts it, but there's another flight to catch in the morning. He stares out at the sunset.

"Instead of this," he says, "I go to work!"

The memories come again, punching walls in Miami after losing a playoff series, unable to face the team; headlines in New York when he left—"PAT THE RAT"—back to 1985, a cramped, un-air-conditioned locker room beneath the Boston Garden. The Lakers screamed and poured champagne. They'd finally beaten the Celtics—and in Boston—avoiding three straight Finals losses and the likely end of Riley's career. No more newspaper stories about the "LA Fakers." Pat had wanted only to find Chris. *Where was she?* Then he saw her, leaning against the wall by the training room. "I was across the room by the shower entrance," he says years later, "but noticed she was watching and waiting for me all the time to free myself of the others. When we finally locked eyes and moved toward each other, that path opened like the Red Sea. The tears just flowed before we could embrace. Tears just flowing with happiness, joy, and relief at the sight of each other and this big moment. We embraced hard, and I lifted her up. My Girl Chris, man. She said we earned this. She said this is ours forever."

These things come to him on a barstool on the next-to-last day of the 2016–17 season.

He orders a double martini.

The story doesn't end with the embrace, he says.

He stirs his drink with a spear of olives.

Twenty-one years later, in 2006, he mistakenly threw away the ring he won that night, along with all his Lakers rings, the real ones mixed together with dozens of worthless samples for the Heat championship ring he was designing. The company gave him exact replicas, but they felt too shiny, with not enough dents and scratches, so he put them in a bag and beat them against a wall. Instead of adding scars and patina, he just knocked loose a bunch of diamonds. When he got them fixed, he locked the replicas in a safe at home. With Pat Riley, there's no self-curated shrine to his own former glories. The past can't possibly compete with the season he's living and breathing today, waiting out the next-to-last afternoon with a martini in a South Beach bar.

It's April 11, five days since the Heat slipped out of that eighth playoff spot they'd worked so hard to earn. He feels tired and depressed. The losses and the shrinking math have pushed Riley into a hole, drowning in the darkness. He hates how a loss, even after all these years, crushes the joy he'd felt hours earlier playing with his grandson. One game remains, tomorrow night. Miami needs to win, then hope for Chicago or Indiana to lose. Inside, he already knows the truth. In about 18 hours, they will come up one victory short of the playoffs—all these months culminating in exactly nothing, just a guy coming home and staring at a quote on his mirror: Warriors don't live in the past; the past is dead; life is now and the future is waiting.

Over drinks, the day before that 82nd and final game, next season comes into focus. They're not good enough to beat the Warriors with the current lineup. *He's* not good enough. The team needs at least one star, and probably two, to compete.

The sun makes the waterfront room feel light and easy.

A bartender talks with a singsong Dublin lilt.

Sitting on his stool, Riley tells stories about the Native American chief Tecumseh, and about an old Thoroughbred horse who broke his leg in the homestretch and got a bullet to the head instead of a garland of roses. Finished with his martini, Riley orders one more before heading home to dinner, planning his goodbye speech to this team he's grown to love. The simplicity of tomorrow clarifies him. He smiles. In the late-afternoon happy hour glow, he sees himself clearly, not as he wants to be but as he is. No roses for him, just a long stretch of track and a bullet with his name on it, one day, when he can't run anymore.

"You know the greatest lie in the world?" he says, starting to laugh. "Pat's retiring to Malibu."

APRIL 2017

Holy Ground

Walter Wright Thompson died before he could fulfill
his dream of walking Augusta National during the Masters.
His son took that walk for him.

AUGUSTA, GA.—Most everything makes me think about my daddy, and this morning, of all the stupid reasons to fight back tears in public, it's chipped beef on toast. I'm sitting at the corner table on the clubhouse veranda, waiting for Arnold Palmer to hit the ceremonial first shot of the Masters. Man, my father loved watching Arnie. To do it from the veranda with a plate of chipped beef? Hotty Toddy, brother. Only, the excitement of incredible moments like this is muted for me now. I've learned in the past three years that I did many things solely to tell Daddy about them later.

The crowd stands on Washington Road, waiting for the gates to open. For a moment, the course is quiet. Birds chirp. Mowers drone. Soon, another lucky diner asks if he can join me. His food arrives first. As we talk a bit, bundled against the chill, he looks at the empty space in front of me.

"What did you order?" he asks.

"Chipped beef on toast," I say. He laughs. "Breakfast of champions," he says.

"It was my dad's favorite meal," I explain.

"Did you ever bring him here?" he asks.

There is a silence. "No," I say, turning away.

Daddy watched the Masters every year. He dreamed of attending just one, and he's always on my mind when I come here for my job. Indeed, for all of us lucky enough to actually walk through these gates, we cannot leave without having thoughts of our daddies, for

Augusta National is a place for fathers and sons. Davis Love III navigates the same fairways as Davis Love Jr. New fathers carefully hold toddlers' hands. "Can you see?" you'll hear them say. Strong arms tenderly steer stooped backs. "Look out, Dad," you'll hear them say softly. That is Augusta.

When Jack Nicklaus finished his final round ever at the Masters, his eyes welled on the green. He glanced at his son, who was caddying for him, and repeated his own father's last words, "Don't think it ain't been charming." As Jack ended his relationship with this special place, he looked at his son and thought of his father. That is Augusta.

When Tiger Woods won for the first time, his eyes searched the gallery near the scoring shed for Earl Woods. They hugged, Tiger's head cradled on his father's shoulder. And when he walked off the green almost a decade later, and Earl Woods was no longer there, Tiger remembered that shoulder and he mourned. That is Augusta.

This, too, is Augusta: me, needing a daddy more than ever, finishing the chipped beef on toast, walking the grounds in search of fatherly wisdom. Me, a 30-year-old man, who failed in my promise to bring Daddy to this place he longed to visit, unable to control my emotions when I see a father and son standing by the first fairway. The boy is a half-head taller and growing. Both wear blue Penn State gear. I see myself in that boy, standing with his father, both thinking they have all the time in the world.

THE FIRST TEE

We were a father and son in my dad's imagination before my parents even knew I was a boy. On the day I was born, he sat down and wrote a letter to himself, cataloging his thoughts as his first child came into the world. He called me his son, with daughter written each time in parentheses, just in case. When I arrived, before my mother even cleared her head, he had already filled out the birth certificate. There was never even a discussion of what I would be called. "Walter Wright Thompson Jr.," he wrote.

Walter Wright Thompson Sr. had grown up in the Mississippi sticks with three brothers. Many of the traits my friends would recognize in me came from him. He loved to be the loudest guy in the room, and he loved telling stories, and hearing them too. He loved his favorite places to eat beyond any normalcy and the sound of the ocean and the hum of late-night conversation. He loved working hard.

His own dad was a tough man with unfulfilled boyhood dreams. Nothing was good enough. When my daddy, a star quarterback, would run for three touchdowns and throw for two more, Big Frazier would be waiting after to ask why he'd missed that tackle early in the third quarter. Daddy decided that when he had a son of his own, he'd do it differently. He'd give his whole heart, shower all the love and attention and approval he could muster. He would be a good daddy. A sweet daddy.

I remember tailgating before Ole Miss football games, him throwing passes just far enough away that I'd have to dive. I remember Destin, Florida, when I dropped my favorite stuffed animal, Sweetie, and didn't tell him until we got back to the condo. He spent hours looking for that rabbit, and he found it too. I keep it around, but I don't ever tell anyone why. When I look at it, I can feel how much he loved me. I remember skipping school to go fishing, and I remember promising not to tell Mama. I remember him always reminding me that "you catch more flies with honey than with vinegar" and "if it feels wrong, it is." I remember him taking me to see *Superman* the night it opened, even though I was in trouble; I remember watching *The Guns of Navarone* a thousand times with him. And I remember, as clear as if it happened yesterday, that April day in 1986 when Jack Nicklaus charged toward his sixth green jacket.

I was playing in the other room, probably with that G.I. Joe aircraft carrier, when he called my name. I didn't want to go. He called again. So I went into their bedroom. He was lying on his stomach.

"Jack Nicklaus is going to win the Masters, son, and you've got to watch this. You will remember this for the rest of your life."

So we lay there, my feet only coming to his knees, watching. I was 9. He was 40, six years younger than Jack, and he cried when the final putt went in. I can't remember now if I'd ever seen him cry before.

The years slipped away, but every April, we lay down on our stomachs—tumbuckets, he called 'em—and oohed over the azaleas and aahed over Amen Corner. Each time, he'd smile and mention that, one day, he'd sure like to see what such a place must look like in person. He grew older. I went to college and, as a freshman, called him to ask if he was watching this kid named Tiger Woods. He was. I sat in the Phi Delta Theta house three states away. I could picture him lying on his stomach.

Home didn't feel so far away.

THE FRONT NINE

It has been 10 years. I no longer watch the Masters on television, and I pinch myself each time I get the credential, though I try to hide it. Sportswriters are supposed to act jaded, right? I'm sitting right now with colleagues in the press center interview room. Tiger Woods is at the dais, no longer the kid he was a decade ago either. Normally, he's full of boring blather, using a lot of words but carefully saying nothing. Only now he's talking about fathers and sons, about losing one and gaining another. I lean in a bit. He talks about regret and the things he wishes he'd done. He talks about what kind of parent he'd like to be.

"Here I am, 31 years old," he says, "and my father is getting smarter every year. It's just amazing. But hopefully, my child, down the road a little bit, will say the same thing."

That, to me, is the definition of growing up. There comes a time when every son starts the slow transition to father. Mine began four years ago. My dad felt pain and went to the doctor. A scan revealed cancer. He was 57 years old, with marriages to attend and grandkids to spoil. Instead? He was in a fight for his life. He pulled into a parking lot on the way home and read the report. It said something about the pancreas. He understood he was in trouble. Up a creek without a paddle in a screen-bottomed boat, he'd say.

But the man had never backed down. Once, in college, he knocked out an All-SEC football player for messing with his brother. He attacked this disease just as viciously. After the first chemo session, he stopped at a greasy fast-food chain to get a sack of sliders, an f-you to the poison. To walk through a hospital with him was to understand his gift for life. All the nurses and doctors and patients—especially the patients who sat through the treatments alone—called him by name. For each, he had a kind word and a smile. He raised the energy level of every room he entered.

We took a fishing trip he'd always wanted to take. I knew there wasn't any time to waste. We spent a glorious few days on a river in Arkansas, filling our cooler with trout, talking late into the night. "I'm not afraid," he told me. Before leaving the fishing camp, I made a reservation for a year later. This, he said, we had to do again. "We'll be here," he said, almost whispering. "I guarantee it."

Back home, he spent hours alone, at his spot behind the house. There was a canebrake out there, and a brick wall, and tall oak trees and a creek. He'd sit there, long past sunset, and he'd think about his life. It's where he prepared to die. Once, my mom pointed out toward his silhouette, tears filling her eyes and running down her cheeks, and said, "It just breaks my heart. I think he's scared."

Still, he read the right books, by preachers and by Lance Armstrong, and he'd make damn clear he didn't want to know the odds. So we didn't tell. But we knew. And they weren't good. I wept the first time I Googled pancreatic cancer. What would I do without a daddy?

Only, sometimes, it does happen like in the movies. He responded to the chemo. The doctors saw the tumors shrinking and, finally, a scan revealed he was cancer free. We couldn't believe it. He didn't act surprised.

Of course, I was at the Masters when we got the news.

Daddy and I made immediate plans for a vacation. We'd go back to Destin, where he'd found my stuffed animal. I bought the tickets and, the day after the tournament, I drove to Atlanta, met him at the airport, and, together, we flew south. In the air, I gave him my Masters media credential. He collected them, kept them hanging by his bathroom mirror to remind himself that his son had gone places. He treasured the parking passes, too, and faithfully affixed them to his truck after I left Augusta.

In Florida, we sat in lounge chairs by the ocean. We ate quail and grits, and Daddy talked the place into giving us the recipe. We drove in a Mustang convertible with the top rolled back, and we made plans. His reprieve made him realize that he needed to stop practicing law 16 hours a day and do those things he'd always dreamed of doing. He wanted to visit China, stand above those gorges. He wanted to see Tuscany, rent a villa.

Mostly, he wanted to go with me to the Masters.

"It's a done deal," I told him. "Done deal."

We celebrated his birthday. I picked up dinner, the first and only time I ever did that. We laughed, and I gave him a present: a black Masters windbreaker. He held it up before him, glanced at me, words failing. He slipped it on and went outside to read. I shuffled off to bed. With the cancer gone, time was no longer precious; we had all the time in the world. But something made me take one last look, seeing him sitting on the balcony, thin and pale, the waves crashing somewhere out in the blackness, a thin ribbon of smoke rising from an ashtray.

THE TURN

Three months later, I got the call. I was in Pittsburgh for a Chelsea–AS Roma soccer game. Mama was crying. They'd run some tests, and the results were in.

"It's cancer," she sobbed.

Two months later, he felt bad and went to the hospital. The doctors weren't too worried. Mama and Daddy asked, "Do we need to call the boys?" Love is a strange thing—you go from a fraternity dance to the altar of a church to a cold hospital room, asking: Is one of us about to die? The doctors said no.

They were wrong.

As I sat in Kansas City, watching the movie *Miracle*, my father passed away. It was only a few days away from our return fishing trip. My mom didn't want to tell me until I got back to Mississippi, so she made what had to be the toughest phone call of her life. After watching her husband of 34 years take his final breath, she called me and said it didn't look good and that I needed to bring a suit. I refused to pack funeral clothes, holding out hope.

The next morning, I landed in Memphis and took the escalator down to the baggage claim. I saw my brother, William, at the bottom. I smiled and waved. He just shook his head. At that moment, my mother stepped out from behind a sign. I knew.

"Your sweet daddy died," she said.

I dropped my suitcase and cell phone. Someone got them, I guess. The next moments are fragments. A parking garage, a silent car, relatives, pats, looks away, driving, buildings, thirst, I'm really thirsty, could someone please get me some damn water, traffic, interstate on-ramp, off-ramp, driving. I could only get out one question.

"Was he scared?" I asked.

Mama shook her head no.

The funeral week was a blur. When we picked out his favorite Zegna sport coat, I went into his bathroom, holding those Masters credentials in my hands. I took them out, slipping them into the jacket pocket. If there was an Augusta National in heaven, I wanted him to get in.

"I'm sorry, Daddy," I said to the air. "You didn't get to go."

Seven months later, I was back at Augusta. It was a hard week. I wore a pair of his shoes around the course, trying to walk it for him. I wrote a column about it for my newspaper and, as I'm doing now, tried to find some closure. Then, I believed my grief ended with the catharsis of the last paragraph. I was naive, as I found when I returned to Augusta in the coming years, finding my pain stronger each time.

Exactly a year after he died, my family gathered at home. We had a baby tree, grown from an acorn that came from the sturdy oaks in Ole Miss's legendary Grove, where Daddy spent so many happy afternoons. We gathered at the spot where he'd sat, where he'd made his peace, and we dug a small hole, filling it in with the roots of the sapling and potting soil. I carefully patted down the earth around the stalk. Then it was done.

That night, I couldn't sleep. Outside, rain poured down, soaking the tender roots. It rained an inch, then two, then more. The creek rose. I worried about my daddy's tree, so I went to stand guard. Soaked, cold, shivering, I stood by the tree, protecting it as I'd been unable to protect him.

I stared out past the canebrake and the brick wall and the creek. The sky was black. I wondered if Daddy was looking down on me, watching me, seeing my successes and failures. I wondered if he was proud of me. I wondered if there was a way I could still ask questions and he could still give me answers. I'd always counted on him for the answers.

"Daddy," I said aloud, "are you out there?"

I waited, but I heard no answer, just the shattering windows of water falling from the sky.

AMEN CORNER

Maybe I'll find those answers out here, at this place he loved so much. Is that crazy? Nothing seems crazy to me anymore. The grass shines like polished green mirrors. The flowers explode with a rainbow of shrapnel: pinks, purples, whites, yellows. Mostly, though, I see the fathers and sons, like the Livelys from Charleston, West Virginia, sitting in front of me, watching the par-3 tournament. For 15 years, he'd entered the lottery for practice-round tickets. This year, he won, and he took his two sons out of school for a day. I wanted that to be us.

Down by Ike's Pond, television reporter Jim Gray interviews players as they leave the course. He asks what I'm working on, and when I tell him, he nods, pointing to a white-haired man sitting in the sun by the water. It's Jerry Gray, his father, and for 16 years, he's come with his famous son to Augusta. "It's the only week we spend together all year," Jim tells me, and, again, I'm jealous. It doesn't seem fair. Sometimes, a boy needs a daddy.

I just got married about a year ago, and I knew he'd have loved to stand up at the front of that church. In a way, he was: In the pocket of my tuxedo, I carried his yellow LIVESTRONG bracelet and, as Sonia started down the aisle, I rubbed it once, just to let him know, if he was watching, that he might be gone but he wasn't forgotten.

I just bought my first house, and I knew he'd know whether I wanted a 15-year balloon. What's a good interest rate? How do I pick a neighborhood? What is PMI?

I'm thinking of starting a family of my own someday, and I want to know how to be a good daddy. What should I let my son do? What should I tell him about crossing the street? About sex? How do you remove a splinter without making him cry? How to make him love you more than life itself? I know he'd know the answers, especially to the last one.

So I've been looking. I try to find messages, things he might have left behind to lead me down the right path. I know he thought like that. For months after his death, my mother found flashlights in every room of the house. Big ones, small ones, medium-sized ones, all with fresh batteries. Then she realized: He'd put them there for when he was gone, in case she got scared in the dark, all alone.

Every now and then, I'll discover something prescient. I have the note he left me when I visited him for what turned out to be the last time. There is a quote: "To influence people, appeal to their dreams and aspirations, not just their needs." He wrote in blue ink: *WWT, Jr, We are so glad to have you home for a few days. Love, Daddy.*

Or the prayer he read at his last Thanksgiving, when we all still believed. Maybe he knew differently, for he wrote, to himself at the bottom: "What a great prayer for all of us this Thanksgiving day, and for all the tomorrows none of us can take for granted."

But those small whispers and nudges are rare, so I try to find bits of wisdom and the comfort of his presence in the places he loved. I eat at the Mayflower Café in Jackson, Mississippi, I stay at the Hay-Adams Hotel in Washington, D.C., and now, I've come here, to this wonderful, ageless cathedral, walking up and down the perfectly manicured fairways, hoping to find a father. I walk up No. 10, crossing 15 near the grandstand, working back and forth through the pines, making my way toward Amen Corner. He first told me about it. The most amazing place in golf, he'd say reverently. Maybe he'll be here. Maybe he knows his son is lost.

I climb the bleachers, find a spot to sit alone. As I did standing on that rainy night by the small tree, I try to talk to him. There are things I need to ask. How do you be a father? Are you proud of me?

"Daddy," I whisper, "are you out there?"

Something amazing happens. Understand that I don't believe in stuff like this and am certain it is a coincidence . . . but, as the words are leaving my mouth, from across the course, a roar rises from the gallery, breaking the silence, the voices collecting into throaty applause, moving through the pines until it fades away, silence returning to Amen Corner.

THE 18TH GREEN

Golfers come and go. As the sun warms my face, Jim and Jerry Gray climb the bleachers. They watch a few groups move through and, as they walk away, Jim carefully holds the rope up so his father can slip beneath it. It's a touching moment, something a good son should do for his dad.

Watching this, I realize something. Although I relate to Jim, I also hope that someday, my boy will do the same for me. It's the way with fathers and sons. The hole in your chest after losing your daddy never gets filled. You don't get a new father. You become one yourself, and my transition from son to father is nearing completion.

I walk back. As the clubhouse gets bigger on the horizon, I see a dad and his boy standing near the 10th fairway. Both are wearing golf clothes. I see myself in that father, hoping he can mold his boy as his own daddy molded him.

It occurs to me that all my questions have already been answered. I've been shown how to be a daddy. I just need to throw passes a little long so he'll have to dive. I need to make sure he doesn't lose his stuffed animal, and I need to take him fishing, and I need to make him promise not to tell Mama. I need to make sure he knows that you catch more flies with honey than with vinegar and that if it feels wrong, it is. I need to watch *The Guns of Navarone* with him. And I need him to lie next to me, on our tumbuckets, as I explain about a golf tournament in April in Georgia, about Amen Corner and Jack Nicklaus and I need to tell little Walter Wright Thompson III that his grandfather was a great, great man.

The clubhouse is in front of me now, and I have one final task. Once I bought my daddy shirts and windbreakers. On this afternoon, I have something different in mind. I hurry into the cavernous golf shop, past the framed posters and women's clothes to the back of the store. This is unfamiliar territory. I search the wall for the things I want, and I ask the clerk to take them down.

I buy a tiny green Masters onesie; then I pick out a small knit golf shirt, for a toddler. I have one just like it, so, someday in the next few years, when I finally become a father myself and continue this timeless cycle, my son (daughter) can have a connection to this place that's meant so much to me.

At the counter, the woman takes off the tags. When she sees the cute little clothes, she coos. Her words make me hopeful.

"Oh," she gushes, "good daddy!"

APRIL 2007

Acknowledgments

Although all these stories have my byline on them, none of them are individual efforts. There is the essential work of editors—Jay Lovinger, Paul Kix, and Rachel Ullrich edited the specific stories included in this book, but there have been so many others—and of fact-checkers and other writers who helped talk me through my thoughts and the story arc. The Michael Jordan story that appears in this book is the product of an ESPN process, to be sure, but also of the night that a bunch of friends who are *Washington Post* reporters gathered at the Tune Inn on Capitol Hill after I'd finished my reporting but before I went home to write. That night I talked through the story arc with them, and because they're all pros, the questions they asked and even the looks on their faces helped me understand what I needed to do when I got home. My favorite recent memory is a big lunch at Smith & Wollensky in New York with a table of writers. Those are the moments that recharge the batteries, refill the tank, whatever metaphor you want to use. I leave those gatherings feeling almost reborn. It's funny. A writing life can be lonely, but to me it has been dominated by deep friendships and rivalries. I've been pushed to get better because I didn't want to be left behind, or because there were people getting praise who I felt I was better than, or because I wanted to hold up my end of the chain in a talented, world-beating staff. There are many reasons people try to be great in this business. Every story stands alone when published, but it doesn't stand alone from the writer's perspective. There are an endless list of influences and motivations that mix and blur into something like a philosophy, and I'm not sure how to properly thank something so personal and hard to explain. This book doesn't exist, and my career doesn't exist, without friends and enemies and brothers and sisters and mentors and the endless stories that I admired and feared and longed to equal and maybe even best. I thank all of you. You know who you are.

That said . . .

None of this happens without Mama and Daddy. They raised me with curiosity, confidence, and empathy, the three most important traits in my line of work, and their belief carried me when I wanted to try to be the very best at something. I've written about my father a lot, but I want to say something about my mama here. She is the most selfless, kind person I have ever met. The way she handled losing my father—focusing on her two boys, who had lost a father, even while she had lost the rock and anchor of her own life—is remarkable only when viewed by people who don't know her. She does everything with the people she loves first and foremost in her mind, lessons she learned from her own parents, who were both truly good people. Mama can hang with Hollywood directors and rock stars just as easily as she can sit with her Sunday lunch crew at Abe's. She is truly the best person I know, and in many ways, I feel as though I succeed because she prays for me, and she's got a lot of points built up with the Big Man. (God, not Clarence Clemons.)

None of this happens without Willie being such a devoted brother and for being such a good Japan running partner. You are the smartest person I know, and so quick to master a skill, whether video game designing or cooking or blacksmithing. Seeing the world through your eyes always makes me laugh, smile, and, in the end, feel smarter.

None of this happens without Sonia, who believes in my dreams and has made them her own, who is my first and best editor and sounding board, who is fun and funny, who is smart and kind, who is beautiful and can hang at my family Thanksgiving or in the second row at a Dead show, who is just as weird as I am but hides it better, who I am confident will be the last face I ever see in this world, which is a morbid, strange, and yet comforting thought.

None of this happens without Wallace, who has allowed me to see through the matrix and understand what matters and what doesn't. I feel as though I will always strive to be, and fall short of being, the person she sees when she smiles at me. I am actually sad for her to realize I'm just as flawed and confused as everyone else. Right now, she sees the absolute best in me, and that makes me want to truly live up to that ideal.

None of this happens without Seth Wickersham. I don't know where to begin. We met on the Mizzou football beat and have remained friends and brothers ever since. You help me keep the promises we made all those years ago—these drums and these guitars, you know—and the best part of my journey has been watching you take yours. I love the end of a night when there's a Maker's Mark and a Black Label on ice in crystal glasses and there is an unspoken, silent toast that sums up worlds of ambition and striving and work and relief and joy. I love those toasts. Thank you. For everything.

None of this happens without Jay Lovinger, my first editor at ESPN, who took a newspaper reporter and turned him into someone who, at the very least, passes for literary enough that some book editors decided to publish a collection. He saw a me that I didn't see, and he helped shape me in the image of so many other great writers he edited through the years. Several years ago, when I switched to the incredible Paul Kix, I never really told Jay how much he'd meant to me or my career or my life. He came into my life around the time my father died, and he filled that void for me. I love you, Jay (and Gay and Wendy and Woo).

None of this happens without Scott Moyers, book editing ninja, adopted Ole Miss Rebels fan. For real, it doesn't happen at all without his faith. Thank you, Scott.

And . . . David Black David Black David Black. The best agent in the world and a dear friend and fellow warrior.

Index

ABOUT THE AUTHOR

Wright Thompson is a senior writer for *ESPN The Magazine*. He lives in Oxford, Mississippi, with his wife, Sonia, and their daughter, Wallace.